LIVING TO
100

LIVING TO
100

LESSONS IN LIVING
TO YOUR
MAXIMUM POTENTIAL
AT ANY AGE

Thomas T. Perls, M.D., M.P.H., and
Margery Hutter Silver, Ed.D.

Harvard Medical School and
Beth Israel Deaconess Medical Center

with John F. Lauerman

BASIC
B
BOOKS

A Member of the Perseus Books Group

Copyright © 1999 by Thomas T. Perls.

Published by Basic Books,
A Member of the Perseus Books Group

Designed by Elliott Beard

FIRST EDITION

A CIP catalog record for this book is available from the Library of Congress.

ISBN 0-465-04142-6

99 00 01 02 / RRD 10 9 8 7 6 5 4 3 2 1

To Leslie, my reason for living to 100. — TTP

To Bob, Althea, Julie, and Alec, for their patience and invaluable support. To my mother, for being a wonderful model for aging. And to my grandson Casey, who will live to 100. — MHS

To the source of all my best genetic information, my parents, David and Kathleen. Thanks for teaching me what it means to love. — JFL

For age is opportunity no less
Than youth itself, tho' in another dress
And as the evening twilight fades away
The sky is filled with stars, invisible by day.
—HENRY WADSWORTH LONGFELLOW,
"Morituri Salutamus"

CONTENTS

LIST OF
ILLUSTRATIONS

PREFACE

I N THE FALL OF 1998, Tom was picking up his daughter at school when one of her teenaged friends asked what our book was about. Tom replied that it explores how people live to extreme old age, and explains how more of us can follow in their footsteps. But as he answered, Tom wondered how this 16-year-old would react to a story about people at the opposite end of the age spectrum. The response was unexpected.

"Great!" cried the young man, "I want to buy the first copy!"

Everyone, young and old, is intrigued by the mysteries of long life. Who lives to 100? How do they do it? Are centenarians different from the rest of us? Is living that long worthwhile? These are the questions that led to our launching the New England Centenarian Study (NECS), the first comprehensive investigation of the world's oldest people. Since 1992, we have been systematically analyzing the mental, physical, and emotional health of all the centenarians within a defined geographic area. The goal is to use our discoveries about this specific group to expand our understanding of the aging process in the larger population.

Although we had suspected when we started our study that, contrary to popular perception, very old people were generally a hardy group, our results nevertheless far exceeded our expectations. What emerged is a portrait of men and women who appear to be the world's ultimate survivors. Indeed, many of the centenarians in our study have lived through traumatic and life-altering experiences, and their histories testify to great personal strength and stamina. Yet they have not washed up at their hundredth birthdays like shipwrecked castaways, having barely survived life's journey; rather, they have arrived in full sail, bearing their most precious possession—their health.

Millions of people are finding themselves on the voyage to old age, and perhaps extreme old age. Each year, the average age of the world's population increases. Life expectancy is climbing in most countries; in industrialized nations it has grown from 46 in 1900 to 77 in 1998. Older people are losing their minority status; in fact, they are becoming an increasingly important force in politics, business, and culture. In a phenomenon known as "rectangularization," the U.S. population has transformed from a bottom-heavy triangle, in which the majority of people were younger than 20, into one in which almost all age groups from 0 to 80+ are roughly the same size. By the year 2020, one out of six Americans will be over the age of 65— equaling the number of people under the age of 20. Similar trends are taking place worldwide. Today, one in ten people on Earth is 60 or older; by the year 2050, it will be one in three. Developing nations are catching up with industrialized populations quickly. For example, it took 115 years for the 65-and-over population in France to rise from 7 percent of the total populace to 14 percent. In Tunisia, the same transformation will take 15 years. To paraphrase Pogo, "We have met the aging, and they is us."

Despite this demographic shift, society continues to hold a distorted view of older people. Aging is disparaged as a desperate fate one accepts with forced bravado; satisfied older people are considered exceptions who defy imposing, inescapable odds. Older people are cordoned off as "the aging," "the elderly," and "seniors," as if they inhabited another planet. Many people would sooner take a walk on the dark side of the moon without a space suit than land on the cratered surface of 100 and beyond.

The NECS challenges these powerful fears and prejudices. It promises to help radically reshape society's perceptions of old age. As scientists, we have looked carefully at the minds, bodies, and day-to-day lives of extremely old people and found them to be in much better condition than anyone—even many of our fellow researchers—expected them to be. The NECS provides scientific results that confirm what gerontologists have suspected for years: Growing older does not necessarily mean growing sicker. In fact, the principal reason society is becoming older is that it is so much healthier, and those health gains extend well into the later years of life. The key to preserving health and vitality, it appears, lies not in learning how people stay young, but in understanding how they age well.

Aging research itself has been recognized as an important medical specialty, and has certainly played a role in allowing people to become centenarians. Grant-making organizations like the New York–based American Federation for Aging Research (AFAR) and Washington D.C.'s AARP Andrus Foundation afford young scientists the opportunity to study these issues as they begin their careers. The important work of these and other organizations has led, for example, to a better understanding of the aging process and to improvements in the health of all Americans as they age.

Not long ago, a friend told us about a conversation she had with her six-year-old granddaughter.

"How old are you, Grandma Ann?" asked the child.

"Ninety-eight," replied our friend.

"Are you going to live to be 100?" the little girl asked, wide-eyed.

"I haven't made up my mind about that yet," our friend said. "I'm going to have to think about it."

Today, each of us is faced with similar questions: Is living to old age something we want? And how much are we willing to do to make our later years healthy? For those who are prepared to make crucial choices that will affect their long-term health and longevity, the NECS offers more than a motivational boost. It provides hard facts about the mental, physical, and emotional health of the world's oldest people, information that no one of any age can afford to ignore. Centenarians paint a stunning picture of aging's potential. They demonstrate that long life can mean a healthy, enjoyable life, a life with friends and loved ones close by, a life of satisfaction.

As nearly 74 million baby boomers—the largest generation in history—move into middle age and beyond, we suggest that, rather than vainly attempting to preserve fading youth, they face the real possibility of living to a very old age. The NECS has revealed the delights of the later years; the indefatigable men and women we have met have shown us that the landscape of old age can be less like a desert and more like a wild prairie waiting to be transformed into an orchard. With the new information contained in this book, baby boomers have a chance to set new standards for health and longevity. We hope that *Living to 100* sparks this kind of enthusiasm in our readers, and shows them how much all of us can learn about aging, not only from books such as this one, but from the dignity, intelligence, and wisdom of older people themselves.

ACKNOWLEDGMENTS

J UST AS NO ONE LIVES to 100 without the help and support of friends and family members, we could never have written *Living to 100* without the assistance of colleagues, collaborators, and confidants. First, we thank the centenarians and their families who have participated in the New England Centenarian Study and the Centenarian Sibling Pair Study. Although we have focused on the stories of relatively few, all these remarkable people were critically important to the accuracy and credibility of the study. We hope that our readers will join us in acknowledging these pioneers for the insight they offer into what it means to live into extreme old age.

The growth and maturation of the studies that led to *Living to 100* were cultivated by several organizations that had the foresight to assist young investigators and support novel ideas: the John A. Hartford Foundation and the Commonwealth Fund, the Alliance for Aging Research, and the American Federation for Aging Research, all of which support the Paul Beeson Physician Faculty Scholars in Aging Research Program; the Alzheimer's Association, which provided crucial support; the Andrus Foundation; the National Institute on Aging; the Neuroscience and Education Foundation; and Dr. Robert Moellering of the Department of Medicine at New England Deaconess Hospital and now Chief of Medicine at Beth Israel Deaconess Medical Center, who secured funding when the project was in its infancy. Mike Grossman and Herb Lee also provided financial support and encouragement.

Several people gave us crucial assistance at important points in the writing of *Living to 100*. Kristen Wainwright of the Boston Literary Group alerted us to the fact that we had a story to tell. Jo Ann Miller, Executive Editor at Basic Books, was both persistent and patient in providing astute editorial guidance through the long process of writing and editing. Richard Fumosa, Senior Project Editor, was especially diligent in reviewing the manuscript and preparing it for publication. Virginia LaPlante's help was critical in organizing our thoughts into a narrative. Elizabeth Fried Ellen researched several sidebars, and provided assistance in writing chapters 7 and 8. Anne Perls, Marianne Perls, and David Lauerman gave valuable commentary on the text at several stages.

There are also many colleagues whose insights, criticisms, commentary, and hard work fill us with admiration and gratitude. We thank our collaborators at the Massachusetts General Hospital Alzheimer's Disease Research Center, Drs. John Growdon, Bradley Hyman, E. Tessa Hedley-Whyte, and Kathy Newell, for their work on the centenarian brain autopsies. Dr. Ruth Fretts of Beth Israel Deaconess Medical Center was an imaginative and committed collaborator on the maternal age study and continues to help us study the evolution of longevity. Several colleagues provided us with crucial consultation: Dr. Cheryl Weinstein, also of Beth Israel Deaconess, sharpened our understanding of the aging brain; Drs. Louis Kunkel, Alli Puca, Leonid Kruglyak, Jan Vijg, and Eric Lander helped clarify the genetic implications of our findings; and Dr. Marilyn Albert of Massachusetts General Hospital guided us with the initial selection of neuropsychological tests. Numerous investigators in the aging field stimulated our thoughts and imaginations, especially Drs. Claudio Franceschi, Bertrand DeJardines, Giovanella Baggio, Richard Suzman, Bernard Jeune, Jean-Marie Robine, Michel Allard, Kenneth Rockwood, Nir Barzilai, David Curb, and James Vaupel. We also extend our thanks to our research staff, past and present: Maureen Shea, Jennifer Bowen, Rachel Hitt, Dellara Farmanfarmaian, Stephen Brent Ridge, Ellen Bubrick, Laura Alpert, Kathreen Bochen, Melissa Freeman, and Michael Young.

Finally, we must give thanks to our mentors, whose teaching and perspective were indispensable to our work. The late Lillian Blacker was a great teacher to John. Dr. T. Franklin Williams, Professor Emeritus of Medicine at the University of Rochester School of Medicine and Dentistry, masterfully demonstrated for Tom the art and science of medicine and continues to be his most valued advisor. Liebe Kravitz, social worker at the Beth Israel Deaconess showed Tom the power of empathy and listening. Drs. Lewis Lipsitz and John Morris, codirectors of the Hebrew Rehabilitation Center for Aged Research and Training Institute, and Brown University's Dr. Vincent Mor helped steer him on the road to the study of centenarians. Dr. John Miner encouraged Margery's postdoctoral training in neuropsychology and gave her the opportunity to take still another path in her career. To all these people, and to our long-suffering, loving families, we give our thanks.

TTP
MHS
JFL

THE SECRET OF
CELIA BLOOM

Searching for a Centenarian

CREDIT: ANNE PERLS

Coauthor Tom Perls sits in the lap of his great-grandmother and first centenarian Julia Grunewald, age 102.

CELIA BLOOM was a new resident at the Hebrew Rehabilitation Center for Aged—and she was nowhere to be found. Mrs. Bloom was never in her room, and that posed a problem. Because she was a resident at this academic long-term care facility, she needed to be seen by her care providers on a regular basis. But in this resident, we met an unusual obstacle: In order to track Mrs. Bloom's health status, it was first necessary to track down Mrs. Bloom herself, and that was becoming a challenge. Each time we went to see her, Mrs. Bloom was out.

The explanation for Mrs. Bloom's continued absence was simple: She had a busy schedule. She was an accomplished pianist who gave daily concerts throughout the 750-bed facility. She played Mozart and Chopin, or led sing-alongs of the popular songs that she and many other residents grew up with. Her volunteer work occupied her all day long. It took a signed medical order to the nursing home staff to guarantee that Mrs. Bloom would stay in one place long enough to get the physical examination she required.

When we finally caught up with Mrs. Bloom, we found a short, sturdy woman with lively eyes and a good sense of humor. She appeared to be in her late seventies, and confessed that before her recent move to the long-term care facility she had not formally seen a doctor in six years. And why would she have? She couldn't recall having been sick in years, not even a cold. Both her hearing and eyesight were excellent, she had all her own teeth, and she got around entirely on her own—no cane or walker. Mrs. Bloom was not in the least depressed and appeared to have no physical or mental problems of any kind. In fact, the main reason that Mrs. Bloom had come to the nursing home was to socialize with people her own age, or close to it. Mrs. Bloom was 103 years old.

MRS. BLOOM VERSUS THE PREVAILING WISDOM

Mrs. Bloom's vigor and creativity were a mystery to the professionals who observed her. She bluntly contradicted everything we had been taught in gerontology. We had all learned the prevailing wisdom: Aging brings on a cascade of ills and health problems leading to deterioration of the physical, mental, emotional, and social dimensions of life and, eventually, to death. All the available data indicated that the centenarian population should be racked with dementia. "Age-associated" declines in personality, mental abilities, and physique were studied as though they could be predicted by years alone. The prevailing wisdom was clear: Aging diminishes memory, creative thinking, learning ability, and other forms of cognition. It was accepted dogma that older people lose bone and muscle mass—forever. Aging invariably brings on diabetes, cancer, heart disease, stroke, Parkinson's disease, and a host of other ills. The high proportion of older people who were supposedly depressed—greater than 20 percent by some estimates—was understandable, given the way their lives were conventionally perceived.

Lasting images in literature have contributed further to the stereotype of old age as a period of unrelenting decay. No picture of the extreme old is quite as ghastly as the Struldbrugs, the creaky, wrinkled creatures that populate one of the many lands in Jonathan Swift's *Gulliver's Travels*.

In talking they forget the common appellation of things, and the names of persons, even of those who are their nearest friends and relations. For the same reason, they never can amuse themselves with reading, because their memory will not serve to carry them from the beginning of a sentence to the end; and by this defect they are deprived of the only entertainment where they might be otherwise capable.

They were the most mortifying sight I had ever beheld, and the women more horrible than the men. Besides the usual deformities in extreme old age, they acquired an additional ghastliness in proportion to their number of years, which is not to be described . . .

Swift portrayed the Struldbrugs as selfishly and unwisely refusing to relinquish life, although their ability to enjoy and benefit from living had long passed. This image of older people has hardly changed in the centuries since Swift wrote. In 1968, Robert Butler, the first director of the National Institute on Aging, coined the term "ageism," to describe the "systematic stereotyping of and discrimination against people because they are old."

Ageism is prevalent even in popular books about medicine. Samuel Shem's 1978 satire, *The House of God*, tells the story of a medical student learning the pain, frustration, and anger that come from caring for patients who don't get better. The book's narrator reserves special vehemence for the oldest, most frail people, or "GOMERs," which is short for Get Out of My Emergency Room! Each time a medical student reads this popular book, the stereotype of older people as inevitably and unsalvageably sick is further reinforced.

In our careers working with older people, both of us have often seen them written off as powerless, inconsequential, and unworthy of attention. Our work in nursing homes in the 1970s had awakened us to how negative attitudes about aging can affect the care of older persons. In one nursing home, for example, residents on each floor, most of them aged 80 and older, were lined up on either side of the hallway at 8 A.M. Some spoke slowly and incoherently, others appeared unkempt and uncared for, and most stared off into space, their mouths agape. There was nothing anyone would call conversation among the 30 or so people strapped into their wheelchairs—just the sound of breathing, sighing, sometimes crying.

As the residents waited, the nursing home staff proceeded down the hall, giving each resident a medicine cup. Accompanying the tranquilizers and other drugs was an unspoken assumption: These people have nothing to live for. Their bodies are no longer beautiful, their minds have lost their creativity, their spirits have departed. The best and most humane thing we can do is to help them forget their misery and uselessness.

Around that time, the image of aging in America grew more negative and distorted, and the lives and experiences of older people became more devalued. Even some of the strongest voices in praise of older people focused on the accomplishments of their youth and middle age, as though their productive years had vanished. Their capacity to function independently and grow in their old age was dismissed, as though at some point they had lost all their inner strength and resources. In his 1970 novel *Mr. Sammler's Planet,* Saul Bellow shows how old age is equated with foolishness and irrelevancy when 70-year-old Artur Sammler, a one-time acquaintance of H. G. Wells, agrees to lecture to college students on "The British Scene in the Thirties." Just as Sammler is warming to his subject, recalling a quote from George Orwell, a heckler shouts out:

'Old Man! Orwell was a fink. He was a sick counterrevolutionary. It's good he died when he did. And what you are saying is shit.' Turning to the audience, extending violet arms and raising his palms like a Greek dancer, he said, 'Why do you listen to this effete old shit? What has he got to tell you? His balls are dry. He's dead. He can't come.'

The heckler makes simultaneous assumptions about Mr. Sammler's intellect, health, and sexual potency based on age alone. The tendency to demean and trivialize the abilities, lives, thoughts, and histories of people because of their age still haunts us today. While advances in public health and medicine have given us the gift of longer life, pessimists deem the aging population a Trojan horse bursting with modern-day Struldbrugs, each with expensive needs and nothing to offer society in return. These doomsayers have attracted a national audience: In 1984, Colorado Governor and presidential candidate-to-be Richard Lamm proclaimed that the terminally ill elderly have a "duty to die and get out of the way."

Myths about aging further contribute to the disparagement and neglect of older people. It is accepted as fact that most older people require aggressive, costly care at the end of life; but according to Gene Cohen, director of George Washington University's Center on Aging, Health, and Humanities, only a small fraction of people over 65 receive bold, lifesaving treatment measures in their last few days. Actually, says

Cohen, the older people are at death, the less likely they are to have received high-cost, high-tech care. The notion that health care costs are grossly inflated due to the provision of unnecessary, futile care for older people is also disputable. According to Cohen, even the most draconian limits on acute care would save only a fraction of 1 percent of the total health care budget. Spending on older people is not the driving force behind rising health care costs, nor will it bankrupt the nation.

Despite researchers like Butler, Cohen, and others whose work exposes the flaws in popular perceptions of aging, major gaps in knowledge persist, particularly with regard to the extreme old. For instance, the relationship between aging and cognitive ability was highly debated among gerontologists and neurologists. A recent prominent study of East Boston residents attempted to determine the rate of Alzheimer's disease among older people. In a result that surprised most observers, the rate of Alzheimer's disease increased inexorably in people over age 65. Of those 65 to 74 years old, 3 percent were reported to have probable Alzheimer's disease, compared with 18.7 percent of those 75 to 84 years old, and 47.2 percent of those over 85 years. Other studies portended an exponential increase in the rate of Alzheimer's disease that would culminate in everyone aged 100 and over—inside nursing homes and out—having some level of dementia.

When we met Mrs. Bloom at the elder-care facility, her mental clarity made us wonder whether she was an anomaly, or rather somehow representative of centenarians. We were particularly struck by Mrs. Bloom's uncannily sound mental health. Such high functioning in a 103-year-old did not synchronize with current views of aging and the brain. We decided to investigate further with more centenarians.

At the time, we found that there were 11 centenarians at the Center for Aged besides Celia Bloom. In our informal survey, using well-accepted but basic measures of cognitive function, 3 of the 12, or one-quarter, were cognitively intact. That quick calculation gave an early indication that a small yet significant proportion of the centenarian population was unaffected by dementia. The idea piqued our attention: No one had previously been able to identify a population that was "immune" or even relatively resistant to dementia. As several studies had hinted, even a person who was mentally intact until relatively late in life still stood a very high chance of developing dementia later. Many neurologists believed at the time that anyone who lived long enough would inevitably develop Alzheimer's disease as a natural consequence of aging.

Yet the lively centenarians in our study were already at the far reaches of the human life span. The surprising nursing home data seemed to indicate that anyone who had escaped Alzheimer's disease for 100 years or more had a fair chance of avoiding the disease completely, and that good mental function among the extreme old was far from being a rarity.

Although the observation was intriguing, it was still too early to begin thinking about a large-scale study of centenarians. Mrs. Bloom seemed relatively healthy compared to many people even 20 years younger, but that could just have been exceptional good luck. Perhaps the Center for Aged was unusual in having some of the best mentally preserved centenarians in the world. There was no way of telling without out more data.

Fortunately, the Hebrew Rehabilitation Center for Aged's Research and Education Institute kept detailed medical records on 5,000 older patients: 2,500 living in nursing homes and 2,500 in the community. A computer program scored each subject's cognitive and functional status on a scale of 1 to 5. Ability to carry out mental activities—like planning a day, knowing how to get from one place to another, being able to anticipate appointments—and to do household and self-caring tasks— cooking, eating, and dressing—were all included in the score. If accepted concepts about aging held true, the overall scores should have dropped for subjects in the later decades of life.

At first glance, analysis of the data bore out the conventional wisdom. Overall functional status declined gradually from the seventies to the eighties to the nineties. However, when the groups were divided into males and females, a strange trend appeared. The overall cognitive function of men in their nineties was actually better than that of men in their eighties. There was not enough data to indicate whether women would show a similar rise, but the suggestion was there: Men who lived into their nineties were healthier than men just a few years younger. They had less dementia. They were better able to take care of themselves.

After only a month's study of the subject, a wide discrepancy had already appeared between what the scientific literature predicted about the oldest old and what we were actually observing in the dining rooms and activity areas of the nursing homes where we worked. While our ingrained biases told us "Older equals sicker," our eyes told us that the oldest old were sometimes among our healthiest patients. We began to suspect that a previously undetected process may have been taking place. Perhaps rather than having *survived* disease, centenarians were more likely to have altogether *avoided* the chronic and acute diseases associated with aging in order to live to 100. What emerged from this sudden intuitive realization was the hypothesis that has become the study's guiding light ever since: One must stay healthy the vast majority of one's life in order to live to 100.

THE CENTENARIAN PHENOMENON

Before we began our study, there was no understanding of how people come to their station as centenarians, nor how they even "get on the train." The proliferation of centenarians is a fairly new phenomenon. Twentieth-century public health measures, such as the widespread availability of clean drinking water, nationwide vaccination efforts, and the systematic prevention of maternal and childhood mortality, have allowed many more people to survive to much older ages. Treatment of heart disease, pneumonia, diabetes, cancer, and other avoidable causes of death has also made a notable impact on Western life expectancy. As a result, people are now living significantly longer than they were at the turn of the century. In the United States, average life expectancy at birth for men and women combined has risen from just under 50, at the turn of the century, to an average of 77 years.

Centenarians were once as rare and remarkable as we now consider septuplets to be. Some researchers believe that in countries with relatively small populations, such as Denmark, there may have been no centenarians before the nineteenth century. Others have speculated that, before 1900, the worldwide incidence of centenarians may have been as small as one per century.

Still, there is some evidence, most of it from paintings and important documents, that nonagenarians and centenarians have existed throughout much of recorded history. Biblical supercentenarians, such as Methusaleh (said to have lived to 969), his son Lamech (777), and his father Enoch (365), may have lived to be very old, but there is no reason to believe they were actually centenarians. But the Greek poet Sophocles lived to at least age 90. Athanasius, Patriarch of Alexandria, reported that St. Anthony, an Egyptian monk and ascetic, died in A.D. 356 at the age of 105. Leonardo da Vinci, in his sixteenth-century *Corpus of Anatomical Studies* notes the autopsy of a 100-year-old man. Genoa's Andrea Doria (1466–1560), the most important admiral of his day, was fighting naval battles up to age 89 and died at 94. Before he died in 1576, Titian claimed to have lived 100 years. Although he likely exaggerated his age by as much as ten years, this would have still made him about 90 at his death. According to Vasari's *Vite*, Michelangelo lived to age 89.

Modern times have been more hospitable to the extreme old. In 1900, only one in 100,000 Americans was a centenarian. Today, centenarians are at least ten times as common—one in 8,000–10,000. In industrialized countries the number of centenarians is increasing at the exceptionally rapid rate of about 8 percent each year—compared to a 1 percent growth in the general population—and the centenarian boom is expected to gather strength (see figure on p. 11). In 1953 less than 200 centenarians were living in France; today there are 3,000. Queen Elizabeth sent birthday greetings to about 300 centenarian British subjects in 1955; by 1987 she was signing 3,300 cards. Today there are about 50,000 centenarians in the United States. James Vaupel of the Max

Planck Institute for Demographic Research in Germany estimates that 100,000 centenarians worldwide will welcome the year 2000, and by the year 2050 there may be nearly 1 million in the United States alone!

At the Center for Aged, Rabbi Samuel Seicol announces to his congregation the name of a new centenarian two or three times each month. Royda Crose remarked in *Why Women Live Longer Than Men* that if Willard Scott of the *Today* show were to announce all the names of people turning 100 each week, he would take up an entire program. Even Hallmark Cards is getting into the act, with birthday cards designed especially for centenarians.

Living to 100 has become a new social phenomenon, not unlike the four-minute mile. Before Roger Bannister ran one mile in 3:59.4 in May, 1954, academics and fellow athletes predicted failure. The four-minute barrier was cast in the role of a sacred, preordained limit to man's speed and endurance. Once Bannister performed his feat, the aura disappeared. One didn't have to be a superbeing to run a mile in under four minutes. Today, even high-school and college students run four-minute miles and better. More people than ever before can run the mile in five minutes,

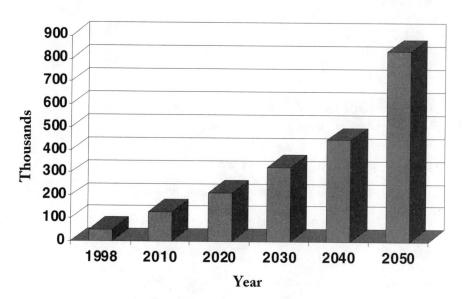

Current and Projected Numbers of U.S. Centenarians

(SOURCE: DATA FROM THE U.S. CENSUS BUREAU AND THE NEW ENGLAND CENTENARIAN STUDY.)

too. Like a rising tide that raises all boats, Bannister's four-minute mile permitted people all over the world to run faster than they thought possible. These faster running times have come about not because of a fundamental change in human physiology, but because of a transformed understanding of what is possible. A similar transformation in attitude has been inspired by centenarians. George Bernard Shaw half-humorously predicted this surge in longevity in *Back to Methusaleh:*

> Among other matters apparently changeable at will is the duration of individual life. If on opportunist grounds Man now fixes the term of his life at three score and ten years; he can equally fix it at three hundred, or three thousand or even at the genuine Circumstantial Selection limit, which would be until a sooner-or-later-inevitable fatal accident makes an end of the individual.

Many people want the cachet, the respect, and the reputation for wisdom of centenarians . . . without having to take the time to live to 100. Centenarianism gives legitimacy to a lifestyle, and aura to a region. "Hot spots" where centenarians are supposedly commonplace provide

In the Cards

Birthday cards for centenarians were once as rare as the folks receiving them. Now, the Hallmark company has found it profitable to sell cards for people celebrating their hundredth birthdays—a sign of an important new market! Here's a sample:

Your one hundredth birthday must surely hold for you

So many precious memories and many dreams come true

May the memories of happy times the years have brought your way

Add to your deep contentment on this very special day.

Hallmark says that by the end of the decade, they expect to sell more than 70,000 centenarian birthday cards each year.

fodder for medical journals, television specials, and yogurt advertisements. One village in the Ukraine was believed to be such a centenarian breeding ground, and a Russian stamp was printed featuring the face of a Ukrainian man reportedly 148 years old. Later, when birth records were examined closely, these claims were shown to have been false. The villagers had altered their birth records years before to escape conscription into the Russian Army. What started out as draft-dodging earlier in the century turned into an international hoax by the 1980s. Similarly, when a surprisingly large number of Ecuadorian highlanders passed themselves off as centenarians, a group of Japanese investors bought into the concept, purchasing land to establish a spa near the purported "fountain of youth." That too proved to be a hoax, after careful examination of vital records. Since initiating our study, we have also heard implausible claims of extreme age. One man wrote from Iran that a woman in his village recently turned 160. Luckily, he noted, she has twin 123-year-old sons to take care of her!

Despite the most genuine efforts, the inescapable fact is that not everyone is fated, or able, to be a centenarian. Some people are predisposed to acute or chronic diseases; others meet with accidents or make personal lifestyle decisions like smoking that leave them vulnerable to fatal illness. One in ten Americans over age 65 has diabetes; the same proportion suffers from Alzheimer's disease; and at least one in three is affected by high cholesterol levels and/or high blood pressure.

Centenarians are the navigators who have successfully completed a long, perilous voyage. Somehow, this one relatively small group of people has nimbly negotiated the vast maze of maladies, mishaps, and military conflicts that commonly lead to death. Not only do they escape death, but by and large they escape ill health for most of their lives. And, as we have found, their experience has much to tell us about how to live, too.

A NEW APPROACH

The elusive Mrs. Bloom raised interesting questions for us. Why had she been so healthy for so long? What enabled her to age so well, while others aged so poorly? Was it because of a more fortunate genetic endowment, as has been so long believed? Had she simply done a better job of taking care of herself than the rest of us? Did she possess some secret key to the fountain of youth? Or was she just lucky? How had she survived from year to year, enjoying life as she appeared to? How had she overcome the emotional upsets that had surely beset her along the way? And what can others do to be more like her?

Earlier studies of centenarians had attempted to answer these questions. The Georgia Centenarian Study, published in 1992, aimed to identify factors required for successful aging. That study enrolled cognitively intact centenarians who were still living in the community. The ongoing French Centenarian Study found its subjects to be extraordinarily vigorous and mobile: In one year, 2 percent had visited a foreign country, 17 percent had traveled to another part of France, and 6 percent had used public transportation. Subjects in this study were restricted to centenarians referred by their physicians. Thus, the people receiving regular medical care were enrollees whose physicians were confident in their ability to enter the study.

In 1994, we began to imagine a broader and more comprehensive study that would include individuals from all walks of life, at all levels of income, social status, and health. This, we believed, was the most reliable, scientifically valid way to find out anything substantive about how people live to 100.

Many colleagues warned us that it would be difficult, if not impossible, to carry out a population-based study of centenarians. Such a study would require identification of all centenarians within a given geographical area, and that plan, they said, was doomed to fail. Sam Preston, a University of Pennsylvania demographer, cautioned about flaws in the U.S. Census data. Most centenarians live no more than a few years past their hundredth birthdays, and since the Census collects data in ten-year flights, many centenarians fall through the cracks. Preston also pointed out that, although the annual death rate among centenarians is about 50 percent, the U.S. Census bases its assumptions about centenarian mortality on death rates in younger age groups, and consequently overestimates centenarian numbers. We had to do better.

Before going ahead with a population-based study of centenarians, we had to prove its feasibility. Fortunately, we are based in the Commonwealth of Massachusetts, which has the oldest and one of the most complete systems of record-keeping for vital statistics in the United States. Many Massachusetts towns have their own censuses, and the raw data are available to the public. These local censuses can be painstakingly accurate. In some Massachusetts towns, residents must register with the census in order to vote. While many local censuses fail to count nursing home residents, Massachusetts nursing homes are frequently required to submit lists of residents. In the most meticulous communities, failure to respond may be followed up by a visit from the police. We eventually settled on eight communities around Boston: Quincy, Belmont, Cambridge, Somerville, Waltham, Framingham, Lexington, and Dedham. These towns had very accurate local censuses and appeared, in combination, to represent all of New England's socioeconomic levels.

We also perused local newspapers, looking for news of centenarians who might have moved into the area between census-takings. We scanned obituaries for centenarians who might have recently died, and we looked up accounts of centenarian birthday celebrations. Because New England in general has a more stable population than demographically younger parts of the country, our centenarian subjects and their families were less likely to move during the study period.

We were also aware that some previous studies had not verified centenarians' birth dates. We checked the ages of all our subjects against birth certificates. The fact that about half of our centenarians were foreign-born could have complicated verification of their birth dates, but most came from British commonwealth countries—Ireland, England, and Canada—where vital records are good. To prevent any noncentenarians from mistakenly enrolling, we also used "family reconstitution," a process in which we painstakingly gather all the available data about a person's major life events—marriages, childbearing, and deaths among relatives—to ensure that they fit into a reasonable chronology. If a woman who claimed to be 100 had had a documented child in 1960, we would examine her records more skeptically, since she would have to have been at least 60 when her child was born. Thus far, we have encountered only one potential subject who was incorrect about her age, and this was probably unintentional on her part.

The reliability of Massachusetts's local censuses gave an enormous boost to our study. Once we had shown that our data collection methods were sound, the Alzheimer's Association became very interested in our approach and in 1995, with funding from the Alzheimer's Association and New England Deaconess Hospital (now Beth Israel Deaconess Medical Center), we began the New England Centenarian Study (NECS), which is now based at Harvard Medical School's Division on Aging and Beth Israel Deaconess Medical Center in Boston.

Enthusiasm for the study runs high, and we have enrolled approximately 85 percent of the centenarians in the targeted towns. (Normally, the best-enrolled studies of older people attract about 40 to 45 percent of the eligible population.) Perhaps our high enrollment rate has something to do with the respect and reverence families feel about their centenarian relatives. Family members agree with us that there is something special about these matriarchs and patriarchs, and they are just as curious as we are to discover what it is.

We have met with 169 centenarians, administered neuropsychological testing to 74, performed personality testing on 60 centenarians, and autopsied 13 centenarian brains. We continue to gather blood samples and information about family trees from them and their siblings to explore the genetic basis of longevity.

A surprise feature of centenarians turns out to be not their sameness, but their heterogeneity and unpredictability. Their incomes in our study range from extreme poverty to vast wealth. They come from all ethnic and racial backgrounds; about half are foreign-born, while close to half are Massachusetts natives. Their level of education ranges widely, from second grade to the doctoral level. Their physical status at age 100 also varies considerably.

We were astonished to discover how many centenarians were healthy and living in the community. Fifteen percent of our centenarians were still living independently at home, which means that about 7,500 centenarians nationwide may still live at home, cooking their own meals, balancing their own checkbooks, reading their favorite novels, getting together with their families and friends, some even working! About 35 percent of our centenarians lived with their families, while the remainder lived in nursing homes. About three-quarters of them suffered from some level of dementia, but the remaining 25 percent were completely free of significant cognitive disorders. The oldest subject in the study so far is 112 years old, and is still reading the *New York Times* at breakfast each morning.

Four out of five men who made it to 100 were in extremely good mental and physical health; on the other hand, women's mental and physical status spanned the spectrum from the incredible independence and vigor we saw in Celia Bloom, to others who were completely dependent and uncommunicative. This surprising gender difference was just one of many puzzles we were to confront and solve as we probed the mysteries of aging.

The first centenarian we interviewed for the study was Mae Vogel. When her husband became disabled, Mrs. Vogel went to work at the age of 40, cleaning homes and offices to support her daughter and two sons. She moved to the Boston area in her mid-nineties to be closer to her daughter, Frances, but continued to keep her own apartment and cook her own meals. Not long before we spoke with her, Mrs. Vogel had suffered a fall and had been admitted to a nursing home. Although she appeared to have lost much of her vigor, she responded to our questions without complaint, listening through a pair of amplifying earphones that made communication easier.

After spending a few hours testing Mrs. Vogel and getting to know about her life, we realized that the commonly accepted profile of successful aging, which assumes that the person will be well-educated, employed in a profession, and financially secure, is dangerously flawed. This was another of many myths of aging that the study exploded. Determination and energy to overcome obstacles appear to be much more important to longevity than traveling an easy road in life.

THE OLDER YOU GET, THE HEALTHIER YOU'VE BEEN

As more centenarians entered the study, patterns in their health histories emerged. For example, centenarians do not suffer long, gradual declines in health. About 95 percent of our centenarians are physically healthy and cognitively independent into their nineties, with low rates of mental illness and depression. They are not the Struldbrugs that Governor Lamm insisted should step aside.

Centenarians are far more likely to have a near lifetime of excellent health, followed by a quick decline before death. At the time of their recruitment, about half of our centenarians were at the end of the long, healthy portion of their lives. By their own account and those of their relatives, they had already begun suffering from age-related illnesses such as dementia, heart disease, and other chronic diseases. These subjects were unlikely to live much more than another year. But the more striking fact is that they had lived such a large part of their lives in excellent health, only to spend a minor portion in sickness at the end.

Another 35 percent were still in very good health at age 100, perhaps living at home, and looking forward to another four or five years of life at the least. Then there were the very exceptional centenarians, those who looked about 30 years younger, who were still playing golf (and winning), who were active professionally or even working full time. Centenarians at this level of health would frequently reach ages greater than 105. Some of these hardy centenarians underwent hip surgery past the age of 100, yet they required only minimal time to recover. They were shockingly healthy and resilient.

We began to see that attaining old age is not a process of declining health, but of avoiding disease. This finding is in complete opposition to everything thought about aging in the past. Rather than "the older you get the sicker you get," we came to an alternative conclusion: The older you get, the healthier you've been. This paradigm shift was a whole new way of thinking about how people attain extreme old age.

Among the first centenarians we enrolled in the study was Edward Fisher, a retired tailor who spent most of his days mending clothes for other residents at the Center for Aged. At the age of 102 he was able to run a sewing machine, hem skirts, and cuff pants; he could even thread a needle, no mean feat for a centenarian. He had a female friend with whom he spent hours each day, talking, playing cards, and taking walks. When we tested his cognitive abilities, Mr. Fisher had only mild deficits in abstract thinking, which in no way diminished his poker winnings. Yet according to the common misconceptions of the time, Mr. Fisher should have been completely demented.

When we expressed our surprise at his good mental health, Mr. Fisher agreed to allow us to autopsy his brain after his death. The only way to confirm that someone suffers from Alzheimer's disease is to actually count the number of neuritic plaques and neurofibrillary tangles—the telltale lesions that define the disease—that have invaded the brain tissue. Our careful inspection of Mr. Fisher's 102-year-old brain yielded evidence of another very unusual trait among centenarians. Pathologists generally expect such an old brain to be full of plaques and tangles "consistent with age." But Mr. Fisher's brain was relatively free of the physical signs of Alzheimer's disease; it was consistent with his behavior, not his age. This was physical evidence that plaques and tangles, the markers of Alzheimer's disease, do not progress with age itself. Rather, aging and Alzheimer's disease are two separate processes. It is possible, we saw, to live one's entire life, even to age 102, without Alzheimer's disease. Perhaps other diseases once thought to be inevitably linked with aging—cancer, stroke, heart disease—may prove avoidable as well.

Mrs. Bloom, Mrs. Vogel, and Mr. Fisher revealed to us the possibility of a completely new pattern of aging that had never before been recognized. Centenarians live in very good health and functional status for the vast majority of their lives. Somehow they manage to escape or markedly delay the diseases that most people fall prey to between their fifties and nineties. In a visible way, these centenarians represent the difference between aging and disease; they demonstrate that becoming old and becoming ill are not the same thing.

Because we actually took the time to talk to the oldest people in the world, we realized that our core assumptions about aging had to be questioned. Far from appearing weak, depressed, and confused, extremely old people often live surprisingly productive lives, learning new forms of artistic expression, and waking up each day with eager anticipation. Some are just as able to recall yesterday's appointment with a lawyer as to remember pivotal life events from 70 years ago. Even those who have lost these abilities in their hundreds are reported to have been robust as late as their nineties. Just as impressive as their ages are their attitudes. They have a fighting spirit. They take extraordinary measures to maintain their physical strength and thinking ability. They refuse to see age as a limitation on their enjoyment of life.

Meeting these centenarians in their homes is often like having an audience with a potentate from a small nation. There may be a table neatly set with snacks and teacups. The family often gathers around, embellishing the conversation with their stories and observations. In the center of it all sits our centenarian subject like a philosopher king or queen, beneficent, wise, and clearly in possession of some ineffable secret.

Many centenarians are willing to volunteer homemade recipes for longevity. James Hanlon, a 106-year-old who still lives at home with his 101-year-old wife, Florence, attributes his vigor to the leg lifts he performs each morning in bed, followed by a couple of cups of weak coffee and a breakfast concoction that includes oatmeal, apples, raisins, and olive oil. Mrs. Hanlon adds parenthetically that the reason they've been married for almost 80 years is much simpler: "Don't make a federal case out of everything." Marie Knowles, a 100-year-old woman living at home, believes in eating sparsely, wasting nothing, and staying positive: "I try to make each day—at least a part of it—a joyful day and not a day of finding fault."

Most of our sessions with centenarians are filled with informative and lighthearted conversations, but we are aware that our time with these energetic and entertaining friends is limited. Each completed testing and interview session may be our last opportunity to get to know that person, so we race back continually for one more visit, before anything happens. Learning to accept that even our strongest centenarians live but a limited number of years past 100 has only reinforced our determination to communicate their secrets of life and health to others.

In the near future, older people will become the norm rather than the exception. More than half of today's 74 million baby boomers will live past age 85, but unless they take the proper steps, many of them will bear a heavy burden of chronic disease along the way. Enjoying the longer life afforded to us by new public health measures and technology means maintaining a high standard of health and independence for many more years than most people ever anticipated. Centenarians, who represent the gold standard for aging well, should be society's role models. They are our "resident experts," who can help shape the way we live. People who are serious about remaining productive, enjoying life, and managing health care costs must learn to follow their admittedly long paces.

Willa Cather wrote in her 1913 novel *O Pioneers!* that "Of all the bewildering things about a new country, the absence of human landmarks is one of the most depressing and disheartening." Centenarians like Celia Bloom are our own landmarks, staking out the territory of a healthy old age. They are exemplary, not only in their ability to stave off death, but in the way they embrace life and health. Centenarians have brought a windfall of new discoveries about aging, and may lead to a far greater understanding of the aging process. Through the New England Centenarian Study, we have seen the golden fruits of health and longevity, and discovered secrets that may help us combat some of the most feared scourges of ill health and old age. With their help and example, old age becomes a much more inviting, desirable destination. Centenarians have given us a gift. They have opened the door to a whole new region of life, and shown us that within, rather than a ruined summer garden, there can be a bountiful winter crop. In the following pages, we will discuss their revelations, and how they contribute to the quest for a long, healthy life.

2

BEAUTIFUL
BRAINS

Disease-free Aging

*Centenarian Anna Morgan's lifelong charisma, vitality, and
intelligence shone through at age 101.*

NEW MEDICAL DISCOVERIES often arise from a surprising clinical observation, a chance sighting of an unusual disease condition or novel behavior. Diabetes was identified when ancient Greek physicians noticed that the urine of some of their patients attracted flies and bees, and was sweet to the taste. Centuries passed before the cause of the disease came to light. AIDS came to national attention when a startling number of young gay men appeared at clinics with strange, rarely seen cancers and infections; it took several years to trace their symptoms to HIV, the causative virus. The inquiring eye of the physician fully engaged in his or her work has always served as the gateway to relevant new medical knowledge.

In 1993, Celia Bloom and Edward Fisher, two cognitively intact centenarians living in the Hebrew Rehabilitation Center for Aged (HRCA), provided just such an opportunity. This time, though, it was not abnormal disease symptoms or behavior that caught our eye, but rather good health. Older was supposed to mean sicker, yet two of the oldest people in a facility designed to care for older, frail people were healthier than men and women 20 and 30 years younger. Why, we wondered, didn't more of these people have Alzheimer's disease, as would have been predicted by numerous epidemiological efforts? And what could centenarians tell us about the possibility of avoiding diseases of aging, particularly Alzheimer's disease?

THE "INEVITABILITY" OF ALZHEIMER'S DISEASE

Only 30 years ago, mental decline was considered an inevitable consequence of old age. In fact, the common term for dementia was "senility," a word deriving from the Latin word for "old." When that catchall term lost credibility, it was replaced by a new label: "organic brain syndrome." Still, when older patients complained about memory loss, their doctors often replied, "What do you expect at your age?" Both doctors and patients were resigned to the idea that, with or without disease, the brain would disintegrate as time went on.

This fatalistic attitude was not limited to the aging brain. During the same period it was widely believed that the heart also became damaged and balky as a result of age and age alone. Not until the 1960s did high blood pressure, rich diets, smoking, and sedentary lifestyles gain notoriety as risk factors for heart disease. Then, as epidemiological information began to mount about who suffered from heart disease, and what they ate, drank, and smoked, the picture was clarified. Heart disease, it was discovered, was neither natural nor inevitable. In fact, over the past few decades people have learned to avoid most forms of heart disease just by eating less fat, detecting and adequately treating high blood pressure, exercising more, and avoiding tobacco.

Our knowledge of dementia's underlying causes has grown more slowly. In 1906, German neurologist Alois Alzheimer examined the brain of Auguste D., a 56-year-old woman who died after several years of mental degeneration. Alzheimer found that the nerve cells, or neurons, in her brain were visibly diseased. The brain's gray matter was larded with deposits of an unknown protein that Alzheimer called "senile plaque." Cellular structures within the brain neurons were knotted into neurofibrillary tangles that looked like the raveled roots of a pot-bound plant. A few years later, when psychiatrist Emil Kraepelin found the same lesions in several other demented patients, he suggested the name "Alzheimer's disease" for the strange disorder.

For many years, Alzheimer's disease (AD) was thought to be extremely rare. Most cases of dementia, or "organic brain syndrome," were attributed to "hardening of the arteries," another catchall explanation implying that blood flow to the brain had become insufficient. In the early 1980s, however, awareness of dementia began to rise. When former screen actress Rita Hayworth was diagnosed with Alzheimer's disease in the mid-1980s, the news made headlines. Her daughter, Yasmin Khan, made a sizable contribution to the Alzheimer's Association, enabling more education and research in the field.

The only negative side to the attention Alzheimer's disease received was that it replaced "senility" and "organic brain syndrome" as the de facto wastebasket that held all cases of cognitive decline in the aged. But research began to show that there were other, equally threatening forms of dementia in old age: vascular dementia, caused by insufficient blood flow to multiple regions of the brain, usually as a result of small strokes; normal pressure hydrocephalus, an excess of fluid in the brain that can cause gait disorders and confusion; Pick's disease and other incurable forms of brain degeneration; depression, which often causes symptoms similar to those of Alzheimer's disease; infectious brain diseases, such as some forms of meningitis; dementia related to long-term alcohol use; prescription-drug side effects; and systemic infections that sometimes cause dementialike symptoms in older people.

Neurologists recognized that it was increasingly important to differentiate between these forms of dementia and dementia-like diseases. Some of them, like depression and infections, could be treated and dispensed with, while others, like vascular dementia, although not reversible, could be slowed or even halted with proper treatment. But Alzheimer's disease merited continued research to determine its specific causes and to develop prevention and therapies.

Consequently, in the early 1990s, determining the true rate of Alzheimer's disease in the general population became an important goal for researchers. The 1994 Canadian Study of Health and Aging, for example, suggested that dementia was a virtual certainty in anyone over age 100. Their findings were consistent with the conventional wisdom that the prevalence of Alzheimer's disease doubles every five years between the ages of 65 and 85. But just a quick look at our analysis of the functional scores of 5,000 nursing home and community residents revealed a direct contradiction with these projections.

How could this have occurred? There was no cure for Alzheimer's disease, nor for arthritis, osteoporosis, many dementias, or any of the chronic diseases that typically erode older people's physical and mental functioning, so the relative good health of the extreme old owed nothing to drugs or surgery. The only logical way to improve the overall functional scores of the extremely old population would be to eliminate a large number of sick people from it, leaving a healthy cohort.

This phenomenon, which is common in the natural world, is called "demographic selection." It is similar to the concept of natural selection, the evolutionary mechanism by which fitter organisms live to reproduce and pass on their genes, while species without the ability or advantages to compete for resources tend to die out. But while natural selection may take thousands of years to cause the extinction of an unfit species or to create a new organism, demographic selection takes place in a single generation. Certain people were being selected to live into extreme old age for very specific reasons.

The agents of demographic selection may vary widely in different populations. In developing countries, childhood afflictions, such as infectious diseases, malaria, malnutrition, and other factors, kill many children. Consequently, any child with access to basic preventive care will have a considerably higher chance of surviving to an older age. The study of 5,000 older subjects revealed a similar phenomenon. Men with poor cognitive function had a very high mortality rate, and were dropping out of the population, leaving behind a group with good cognitive function. Most of the people who had lived to extreme old age had somehow escaped or significantly delayed Alzheimer's disease; the demographic selection process had yielded a group of people who, relative to the rest of the population, were Alzheimer's-resistant.

A DISEASE-RESISTANT GROUP

The counterintuitive results of the HRCA study generated tremendous interest among scientists. Dementia researchers had been looking for a break just like this. One of the main obstacles to studying Alzheimer's disease has been the inability to determine whether it is a consequence of normal aging, or a disease that some people succumb to and others escape. Answering this question is crucial to developing

Alzheimer's disease prevention and treatment. If Alzheimer's disease is just one manifestation of normal aging, then the best we can hope for is to delay it as long as possible. On the other hand, to be able to identify people who never contracted the disease would offer the possibility of developing prevention approaches so the disease could be completely eradicated.

But the very nature of Alzheimer's disease has made it extremely difficult to study. The disease occurs so gradually and in so many older people that it is almost impossible to identify conclusively which people will *never* develop the disease. In some cases, neurologists can rule out most other causes of dementia with testing, leaving Alzheimer's disease as the probable cause. Certain forms of genetic testing may help approximate an individual's likelihood of developing the disease later in life. But these tests cannot be conclusive without a direct look at the brain, and that view is inaccessible in living, breathing patients. Scientists have been in desperate need of subjects who they can comfortably predict will never develop Alzheimer's disease.

Centenarians had the potential to fill this need beautifully. If we could prove them to be relatively resistant to Alzheimer's disease, we would finally have a living population in which we could gain concrete information about prevention, perhaps treatment as well. Looking at the extreme old for behavioral, genetic, and social commonalities would provide not only the chance to learn how they have avoided so many of the diseases that disable and kill such a large proportion of the population, but also the opportunity to harvest new knowledge from the courage, wisdom, and strength they invested in living such long lives.

No one knew why these cognitively intact extreme old had escaped or delayed Alzheimer's disease for so long. Would their brains contain plaques and tangles? It was certainly possible. People with heart disease don't always manifest symptoms; their cardiovascular systems compensate for blockages or damage by promoting the growth of alternative blood vessels. Perhaps the brains of centenarians were using an analogous form of compensation.

Indeed, the ability of the brain to continue performing in the face of disease and damage is renowned. The billions of neurons the brain harbors give it a sizable reserve capacity. A large percentage of neurons in a crucial area must be destroyed before thinking ability changes substantially. For example, 80 percent of the dopamine-producing cells must die in the substantia nigra, the brain area affected by Parkinson's disease, before the characteristic symptoms of tremor and slowed movement appear. In the same way, all of us lose thousands of brain cells every day of our adult lives. Healthy centenarians may have lost hundreds of millions of neurons by the time they reach their hundredth birthdays.

One potential mechanism for overcoming brain damage is the growth of new dendrites. These branchlike extensions reach out toward neighboring neurons, where they allow the exchange of electric and chemical messages. Existing cells can grow new dendrites, sometimes replacing or replicating existing connections, sometimes creating new links to neurons. Such growth takes place throughout life and can compensate for cell loss.

New dendritic formation may be stimulated by learning new skills or taking up new activities. Studies had shown that people with higher levels of education tend to enjoy lower rates of dementia in old age. Would we find well-educated centenarians whose testing showed that they were high-functioning, yet whose brains were nonetheless full of plaques and tangles? Perhaps they were like well-trained tennis players who could continue to win despite a shoulder injury because their forehands, backhands, and volleys were keeping them in the game. In the same way, education and the resulting formation of additional dendrites may have created functional reserve, which allowed educated centenarians to compensate for the damage of Alzheimer's disease. If well-educated centenarians functioned better than the less educated with the same level of Alzheimer's pathology, it would indicate that "brain-training" should be part of the anti-Alzheimer's strategy. But there was only one way to determine whether centenarians had overcome Alzheimer's disease, or whether they had simply never developed it: We had to autopsy their brains.

TESTING CENTENARIAN THINKING

In the first phase of our study, we administered tests to living centenarians to determine whether they possessed normal cognitive function. This was the most important step in determining which patients had dementia, and among those, which had Alzheimer's disease. This also gave us a needed behavioral basis for comparison when we went on to the autopsy phase of the study. Autopsies of deceased centenarians' brains would allow us to see whether they had somehow overcome, compensated for, or escaped the brain changes of Alzheimer's disease. In this way, we would determine whether centenarians were a select population in whom Alzheimer's disease—seemingly so pervasive among older people—was somehow delayed or, in certain individuals, completely absent. We would also be able to determine the true rate of Alzheimer's disease in centenarians, and compare it with the ominous trends seen in the Canadian Study of Health and Aging and other research efforts. This exhaustive approach was to become an acknowledged first in the study of centenarians.

Studying the extreme old raises many issues. The physical and sensory limitations of people this age had to be considered, and we selected our study instruments accordingly. We chose shorter tests over longer ones, sacrificing as little as possible in accuracy. In case hearing loss prevented an older person from understanding questions, we used an amplifying system with headphones that could be placed right over the subject's ears, if necessary. And we used a copier to enlarge all the visual material from our tests so our interviewees would be sure to see them. Time was never a factor in the testing: If a centenarian appeared too tired to continue, complained of fatigue, or was simply having a bad day, we would end the session and return later. In some cases, several testing sessions were necessary to get all the data. Half the study subjects were foreign-born, and we always encouraged family members to help with translations and explanations, although they were discouraged from giving hints that would help their relatives "pass the test."

In September 1994, we conducted the first battery of the New England Centenarian Study neuropsychological tests with Mae Vogel, age 104. She had lived independently until recently, when a series of falls led to her admission to a nursing home, where she suffered not only loss of independence but was isolated by her profound hearing loss and inability to read because of her vision impairment. We posed our questions through earphones to compensate for her hearing problems.

Although Mrs. Vogel had demonstrable deficits in memory, language, and other cognitive functions, she did not seem to fit the Alzheimer's disease profile. Her sudden mental decline upon her nursing home admission was unlike the gradual onset and slow progression that is characteristic of Alzheimer's disease. It was likely to be related to depression because it had started with a major change in her life: entering the nursing home. Her hearing and vision loss also played a part. And Mrs. Vogel had suffered several small strokes, indicating that her moderate dementia might have been at least partially due to vascular problems. Thus, even in demented subjects, there was already some evidence that Alzheimer's disease was less than universal.

That same day, we met with Sister Mary Rose Sheehy, who lived in the Bethany Nursing Home for older nuns. At Bethany, Sister Mary Rose's life was not that much different from her earlier convent life. Everyone in the nursing home knew and loved her. She played the piano, and spent her time reading, drawing, praying, and talking with friends. Her cognitive test scores were just as poor as Mrs. Vogel's. But because she was functioning so well, she was classified as having only mild dementia. The comfortable, familiar environment and support of her living situation made her dementia much less debilitating. For Sister Mary Rose, the nursing home recreated her previous life; for Mrs. Vogel, the nursing home was the antithesis of her previous self-sufficient, independent life. The different reactions of these two patients demonstrate how allowing older people to remain in their own communities can minimize the impact of dementia.

We were anxious to compare these nursing home residents with centenarians living in the community. We got our wish within a few days when we traveled to the urban home of Maria Piazza, who had suffered a stroke earlier. Three generations of the family lived in the three-story home Mrs. Piazza's husband had bought many years earlier. As we conducted the testing, a son who lived in the apartment downstairs read the *Boston Herald* at the kitchen table, by Mrs. Piazza's side. Grandchildren wandered in and out of the room, occasionally talking and joking with Mrs. Piazza. Although she appeared to be presiding over her home as she probably had for years, Mrs. Piazza's test scores indicated mild dementia. Like Sister Mary Rose, she had been protected from the debilitating shock of a confusing new environment by the closeness and predictability of her family existence.

We soon encountered another community-dwelling centenarian: Edward Bernays, the father of the modern field of public relations. When we sat down in his spacious Brattle Street home in Cambridge, where he lived with a couple who kept house for him, he immediately began to instruct Margery in how psychologists could change their public image. For nearly an hour, he delivered a fascinating monologue on public relations.

Yet despite Mr. Bernays's obvious cognitive strengths, we soon saw that he was not completely mentally intact. He repeatedly asked us who we were and what we were doing in his home. Cognitive testing showed that, although his abstract reasoning, language abilities, and long-term memory were almost completely preserved, Mr. Bernays's short-term recall was severely damaged. He regaled us with stories of his work with Henry Ford on their early efforts to market the Model T. The chief obstacle to automobile sales, Mr. Bernays recalled, was that there were so few roads to drive them on. One of the few paved roads in the country was the highway from New York City to Albany. At Mr. Bernays's urging, Ford struck a deal that resulted in more paved roads being built, and at the same time established what was to become one of the nation's largest industries. Mr. Bernays's recall of the detail of this process, and his understanding of why it had taken place, was remarkable.

For older people in the early stages of Alzheimer's disease, preservation of long-term memory with poor short-term memory is common. But Mr. Bernays had a history of strokes, both large and small, that could have created the same pattern of mental function and deficits that we were observing. A diagnosis of Alzheimer's disease was far from clear. Still, throughout all these old memories, Mr. Bernays's charming personality and brilliant conversation shone through, even though he had little recall of recent events or conversations that had happened just minutes before.

Having a deficit in one area of brain function need not completely debilitate older people. While his short-term memory was gone, and he could not live independently, Mr. Bernays's social skills and personality remained intact. As he demonstrated in discussing the image problems of psychologists, he still had a deep understanding of the field of public relations, and was able to pass that understanding along to others. He showed how people with cognitive impairment can continue to contribute in areas that they know very well.

Thus far, although all four centenarians had some level of dementia, our data indicated that all the centenarians in our study were completely cognitively intact at least well into their midnineties. We could already see that their onset of dementia was considerably delayed compared to the rest of the population. In three of the four cases we had evidence that other possible explanations lay behind their dementia, so the diagnosis of probable Alzheimer's disease was not appropriate. Perhaps this indicated some added functional reserve or an unusual ability to adapt to cognitive insults. We would not know the answer until we were able to look directly at their brains. Until then, we held on to our suspicion that Alzheimer's disease was neither inevitable nor universal.

In addition, these first four subjects surprised us with their level of functioning. All had experienced some cognitive decline, yet each of them had clearly retained their personalities: their preferences, their idiosyncrasies, their style of communicating to others. We began to suspect that there was something special in centenarians' lifelong personal and emotional styles that might play a role in their superior functional abilities. (It was at that point that we decided to add personality testing to the study. We'll discuss this fully in the chapter 3.)

THE CENTENARIAN JACKPOT ✳

We were already somewhat convinced of the uniqueness of centenarians at that point, but we only needed to talk with Lola Blonder to be completely won over. Confined to a wheelchair within two rooms of her home in Lexington, Massachusetts, Mrs. Blonder still had a vigorous mental life at age 101. Each time we visited, she was holding long, animated conversations with her daughter. Mrs. Blonder had taken up painting in watercolors in her nineties, and a friend came to paint with her once a week. Her hearing and vision were both excellent, and she proved to be a captivating storyteller, recounting the tales of her experiences in Vienna and the fledgling state of Israel.

Mrs. Blonder passed each portion of the cognitive testing battery with flying colors. But more impressive than that were her dignity, energy, imagination, and magnetism. This was a centenarian who had sacrificed nothing to time. Although she was somewhat physically disabled, warmth and energy exuded effortlessly from her.

Mrs. Blonder was the first of several subjects whom we began to think of as the "centenarian jackpot." They were heretofore hidden treasures, a group of physically and mentally healthy people of 100 years or more. For a time, we felt as though we were living in another world. Here were people who had been born before the invention of the television and the telephone, before the atom bomb, before the automobile. They had lived through two world wars. They were people who seemed to have stepped out of time, and yet they lived on in our era.

Fred Flagg, a metallurgist and amateur musician, was at age 100 still completely mentally intact and always ready to engage in lively conversation. There was psychologist Lucy Boring, who, despite some memory loss, was still playing and winning at bridge at age 109. Alfred Benedetti was competing in the Senior Olympics past the age of 100, and had no mental deficits. Angelina Strandal, at age 101, continued to keep house for her children and to read and write poetry. And Dirk Struik, at the age of 100, was still publishing and occasionally lecturing in the field of ethnomathematics, and continues to do so at 104.

We had been careful to design the NECS as a population-based study, one that would fully represent centenarians and their capabilities. We had planned to avoid the kind of selection bias that would restrict our experience to only the healthiest, best mentally preserved subjects. In order to find out the true prevalence of cognitive disorders and health in centenarians, we had to be as thorough as possible in seeking out and enrolling all the centenarians in our target towns, without respect to their level of functioning. And yet these people who had drunk so deeply from the cup of age—a cup supposedly laced with Alzheimer's disease, heart attack, stroke, and depression—were still eagerly coming back each day for more. It seemed incredible that these phenomenally enduring people had been out in the public, living among us, and we had virtually ignored them as a group.

Many of the centenarians who suffered from cognitive deficits nonetheless demonstrated that they had retained important parts of their personalities. After her testing session, 110-year-old Etta Parker, who probably suffered from Alzheimer's disease, recited all of John Greenleaf Whittier's poem "Barbara Fritchie" to us in a loud, clear voice. At 101, Myrtle March was gracious, humorous, and sociable. And there were many others whose presence and individuality still stay with us.

In early 1995, we met a woman who would prove to be one of our most fascinating subjects: Anna Morgan. In accordance with the study design, we asked Mrs. Morgan if she would be willing to donate her brain so that we could look for the plaques and tangles that indicate Alzheimer's disease.

"But I'm still using it," replied Mrs. Morgan with a smile.

Indeed she was. From the time we met her at the age of 100 until she died almost two years later, Anna Morgan was one of our most remarkable and mentally vigorous centenarians. She was born on November 1, 1894, in Providence, Rhode Island, of German and Spanish ancestry. When she was eight, the family moved to a Rehoboth, Massachusetts, farm as a hedge against hard times. Her experience with life on a farm—where work went on every day, despite the weather or holidays—inspired her to support the efforts of workers all over the country in the years to come.

Young Anna thrived in school and, at a time when few women continued their education past the eighth grade, studied for two years at Pembroke, then the women's college at Brown University. Her first marriage was to a Cuban veterinarian, and she moved to her husband's homeland, where she saw the social and economic conditions that were later to spark her outrage and political activism.

During the Great Depression of the 1930s, Mrs. Morgan raised money to buy ambulances for the Royalists in the Spanish Civil War. She collected food for families of the unemployed in Columbus, Ohio, where she had moved with her second husband, an archaeologist.

She later ran a bookstore that sold political literature. In 1952, she was called before the Ohio State Committee on Un-American Activities. Her refusal to answer questions led to her being charged with contempt.

"They were right," she told us, "I had a very healthy contempt for the Committee."

Seven years later, in a decision with implications for many people who refused to recognize the authority of these committees, the United States Supreme Court overturned Mrs. Morgan's conviction on the basis of her First Amendment rights.

When we met Mrs. Morgan, she was still deeply aware of current events and politics. Despite cataracts, glaucoma, and macular degeneration, she read a newspaper each day with the aid of bright lights and a magnifying glass. She placed telephone calls and stuffed envelopes for local groups, such as Mobilization for Survival. During her nineties she wrote more than 1,200 pages of memoirs, a portion of which were published by the Rehoboth Historical Society. She also worked on an effort for a postage stamp to commemorate the black singer, actor, and political figure Paul Robeson.

Mrs. Morgan was always very practical, and never afraid of controversial topics. In the 1920s, when she returned to Rehoboth from Cuba with her first husband, she distributed condoms to local farm wives, which was illegal in the state at that time. Even on her hundredth birthday, when most of us would be content with being surrounded by family members, she was testifying at the Massachusetts State House on health care matters.

The Life of a Centenarian

Anna Morgan was born on November 1, 1894, in Providence, Rhode Island, the daughter of German and Spanish ancestry. At left, Anna Morgan, age 10 in 1904, with her brother, mother, and sister.

Anna at bat and her sister behind the plate on the family farm in Rehoboth, Massachusetts. Anna did well in school, and studied at Pembroke, then the women's college of Brown University. Here, Anna is in her late 20s.

Anna on a trip to Mexico, at age 43, Having grown up on a farm, she had great sympathy for the plight of migrant farm workers and worked on a Committee for the Protection of the Foreign Born. She and her husband frequently visited Mexico.

Anna at age 61, with her second husband, Richard Morgan.

At age 90, Anna accepting an award from Mobilization for Survival, an activist group based in Cambridge, Massachusetts. Anna was involved in such groups throughout her life, and spent hours making telephone calls and stuffing envelopes. In 1952, she was called before the Ohio State Committee on Un-American Activities. Her refusal to answer questions led to her being charged with contempt. Seven years later, in a decision with implications for many people who refused to recognize the authority of these committees, the United States Supreme Court overturned Mrs. Morgan's conviction.

Anna playing with a great-grandchild at age 101. She was energetic and cognitively intact until her final days, and wrote 1,200 pages of a biography in her 90s, a portion of which was published by the Rehoboth Historical Society.

By the time we saw Anna Morgan, her excellent mental and physical functioning was not so surprising as it might have otherwise been.
We had already met so many healthy centenarians that our threshold for
shock had risen considerably. But it was always interesting to see what
hidden deficits testing would reveal.

Finding subjects like Mrs. Morgan was an important reminder that
we weren't only studying dementia; we were more concerned with the
true effects of aging. Can mental deterioration be considered "normal"
at any advanced age? Even if we were to find that Alzheimer's disease
and aging were not linked, we might find that some other, perhaps more
subtle form of cognitive decline was caused by aging.

But if we were to find completely cognitively intact centenarians,
we would have to entertain the idea that aging itself could not be
blamed for dementia. This would have important implications for
diagnosis and treatment: Any time cognitive impairment was seen in
an older person, a cause would have to be sought and found. We would
have to intensify our efforts to look for dementias caused by reversible,
treatable disorders. No patient should again go to a doctor with symptoms of dementia and hear the words, "What do you expect at your
age?"

ASSUMPTIONS DEFIED

We look for impairment in more than one area of brain function
because dementia involves difficulties in not just memory, but other
mental abilities as well. The most comprehensive test we use measures five cognitive domains: attention, memory, construction, conceptualization, and initiation/preservation of ideas and behavior. To
this battery we added tests of language, executive functions, and
new learning that would help us find out which particular brain
areas were affected. Different patterns of deficits in these domains
can help us determine the kind of dementia a subject is suffering
from.

We test attention first. Deficits here would probably indicate some kind of problem in the brain's frontal lobe. Attention affects all facets of brain function, from memory to the ability to take note of what one is hearing and seeing. If a person cannot focus or sustain their attention, it may be all but impossible to complete the testing process.

Attention is often one of the last functions to be affected by Alzheimer's disease. Many of our centenarians still had sufficient attentional ability to repeat five numbers. Mrs. Morgan was easily able to repeat seven-digit strings of numbers, and to connect a long number sequence, an exercise that measured her ability to sustain attention. She was a shining example of why we think that normal aging should not mean loss of attention abilities.

We're naturally interested in several facets of how aging affects memory. Working memory is the ability to manipulate information while holding it in the mind, as you might do when calculating the price per ounce of a package of spaghetti. But we don't take centenarians to the supermarket, we just ask them to repeat strings of digits backwards, starting with two digits. Some centenarians had surprisingly good results with this difficult portion of the test. At the age of 101, Ruth

Anna Morgan's copy of a drawing of a diamond in a square demonstrates that at age 100 she retained her visual-spatial abilities. She was able to interpret and reproduce accurately what she saw, despite serious vision impairment.

(SOURCE: ADAPTED AND REPRODUCED BY SPECIAL PERMISSION OF THE PUBLISHER, PSYCHOLOGICAL ASSESSMENT RESOURCES, INC., 16102 NORTH FLORIDA AVE., LUTZ, FL 33549, FROM THE DEMENTIA RATING SCALE, BY DR. STEVE MATTIS, © 1973.)

McShane was able to repeat up to eight digits backwards, which is better than most younger people. The average number of digits that 70-year-olds can repeat backwards is five, and the typical 40-year-old can repeat only six digits backwards! Mrs. McShane's mental ability may have owed something to her previous work as a bookkeeper, which she pursued into her nineties. To us, it was another indication that acquired skills don't have to decline as we age.

Mrs. Morgan was able to recite up to five digits backwards and spell the word "world" backwards, which showed that her working memory was not impaired. "As long as you don't ask me to stand on my head," she said with a laugh. She was tireless throughout the testing.

We are interested in whether aging diminishes the ability to learn new information and recall it later, a function located partially in the frontal lobe, but primarily in the hippocampus, a part of the temporal lobe. We gave subjects six words—"evening," "plant," "open," "machine," "fire," "horse"—and asked them to repeat the set three times to ensure that they were committed to memory. (If subjects didn't learn the words after three repetitions, we repeated the list until they did.) Then for one minute we sat in silence, after which the subject was asked to repeat the words. This tests the ability to recall information without distractions. We then asked the subject to count backwards from 20 and to recite the alphabet rapidly. Testing memory of the six words at this point indicates how distraction affects recall. After three more minutes, we ask the subject to repeat the list once more, to determine whether he or she has a rapid rate of forgetting.

Surprisingly, there was a wide range of responses to this portion of the test. Mrs. Morgan remembered the six words with no difficulty. She also performed flawlessly when we read her a list containing the original six words mixed in with new words, which tested her ability to recognize memorized words. On the other hand, Lucy Boring could not remember the words on her own, but could pick all of them out of the list we provided. This raised the possibility that her dementia was not caused by Alzheimer's disease, which would have prevented her from storing the word list in memory. Based on the projections made by numerous studies of aging and Alzheimer's disease, we would have expected the vast majority of our subjects to perform poorly on all these memory measures. The fact that close to one-third did not was another strong hint to us that living to 100 does not necessarily mean living with Alzheimer's disease, and that other, perhaps more preventable, causes of dementia may lie at the root of cognitive deficits in many of the extreme old.

We also test visual-spatial capacity—how the brain makes sense of what it sees. This is the type of intelligence involved in map-reading and finding the way from one room to another. We test subjects' visual-spatial capability by asking them to copy various geometric figures.

Mrs. Morgan was able to draw even the more complicated figures very well, despite her poor vision. We then asked her to draw the face of a clock. We assessed her planning abilities by noting whether she placed the numbers accurately, and we could tell something about abstraction abilities by whether she could set the hands to indicate a time of 10 after 11. People with dementia usually set them at the numbers 10 and 11, but Mrs. Morgan set the hour hand at 11 and the minute hand at 2.

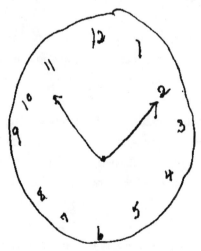

This freehand drawing of a clock by Anna Morgan shows that she retained adequate planning abilities to place the numbers, and the reasoning ability to convert the verbal instruction—"set the hands at ten after eleven"—to placing the hands at 11 and 2. A person with dementia would more likely set the hands at 10 and 11. With a predrawn circle, Anna Morgan's clock drawing was even more accurate.

We've found that many centenarians maintain their visual-spatial capabilities by taking up painting and other activities. Lola Blonder painted in watercolors, Alfred Benedetti was an accomplished draftsman, and Marion Macdonald created elaborate holiday cards for her friends. These people may have increased their functional reserve by pursuing these self-expressive visual activities.

The NECS investigates abstract reasoning, or conceptualization, by asking centenarians to find similarities between words. How are an apple and a banana alike? How are a table and a chair alike? How are a boat and a car alike? Answers such as "fruit, furniture, and transportation" get higher scores than "they both have peels," or "they both have four legs," because recognizing that individual items are part of a larger class requires a higher level of abstract thinking than simply finding a characteristic the two items have in common. Mrs. Morgan completed this task very successfully, providing the same answers we would have expected from a mentally intact person 30 to 40 years younger.

The integrity of the brain's "executive functions" determines whether subjects can initiate and stop mental processes appropriately. If people are unable to stop repeating an activity, this is called "perseveration." Executive functions also include the abilities to plan and organize, stay on track, control impulses, shift from one activity to another, and show good judgment. We tested centenarians' initiation ability by asking them to name as many supermarket items as possible in one minute. Mrs. Morgan named 14. To test for perseveration, we asked them to copy a drawing in which a design is repeated five times. If they continue with the activity past the prescribed number, we call it a perseveration problem. Getting off track, or perseverating, suggests impairment of executive functions, which are also primarily located in the frontal lobe. In the "trail-making test," centenarians are asked to draw a line from 1 to A to 2 to B to 3 to C, and so on. This tests their ability to shift their attention back and forth between two different sets of items. Mrs. Morgan did this slowly because of her vision impairment, but made no errors.

We also gave subjects four mathematics problems of one-digit addition, subtraction, multiplication, and division, and four more problems

using three or more digits each. Mrs. Morgan made only two minor calculation errors, again related to her vision problems: She had trouble
seeing numbers she had to carry. Dirk Struik, the former MIT professor, and Ruth McShane, the former bookkeeper, also did well on this
test. Another former bookkeeper with Alzheimer's disease, however,
performed poorly. The most difficult mathematical task to perform was
long division, a complex undertaking. Of the mathematical tests we
posed to centenarians, long division was probably the least frequently
performed in their earlier lives, and thus would not be as deeply
ingrained among most people.

In addition, we evaluate how people use language. Alzheimer's
disease often robs patients of the ability to name an object, a condition called "anomia." We showed Mrs. Morgan pictures of 15 objects,
including a bed, a house, a flower, a camel, and a pair of tongs. A person with Alzheimer's disease might have difficulty remembering the
word "tongs," instead saying "You pick things up with it." Anomia
happens to all of us once in a while. You may forget a close friend's
name, or the name of a familiar object, like "pajamas." For most of us,
it doesn't mean much. Concern about Alzheimer's disease should only
begin if the problem becomes consistent and begins to interfere with
work or conversation. Anomia, along with other associated language
problems, can be one of the most debilitating effects of Alzheimer's
disease. Although she would still have been considered in the normal
range had she missed even two of the 15 items, Mrs. Morgan scored
perfectly on this test. Her ability to name objects appeared as good as
that of anyone at any age.

The most impressive part of Anna Morgan's testing session was the
final section. In order to evaluate subjects' recall and new learning abilities we tell them a rather whimsical story about Bill Rogers and his dog,
Roy, and ask subjects to repeat it. Anna Morgan's retelling of the story
was very complete, as a videotape we made of the session shows:

> Bill Rogers went to Texas to do some shopping, and he left his dog with
> a friend while he was gone. His friend fed the dog four bones and tied
> him to a tree. Mr. Rogers bought himself a new suit and returned home

a few days later. He whistled to his dog, but the dog wouldn't acknowledge him. The dog smelled his new suit, and refused to acknowledge him. Then Mr. Rogers went and changed into his old suit and the dog came up and licked his hand.

"And they all lived happily ever after!" she added with a laugh.

To this day, our fellow neuropsychologists gasp when they see this tape of Mrs. Morgan repeating the details of a story she had heard only minutes before, with practically no hesitation and few errors. Even after having told the story hundreds of times, we ourselves have difficulty in recalling all its details. But Mrs. Morgan had mastered most of them after hearing it only once. It impressed us that, even at 100 years old, someone could perform better on some of the most demanding cognitive tests than the people administering them did. At times we felt that the centenarians should have been evaluating us!

After administering the tests, we combine the centenarians' scores with personal observations and a history given by family or caretakers on how individuals do with memory, self-care, household activities, communication, and social relationships. We count only deficits caused by cognitive problems; we don't tally those initiated by sensory impairment or disability. For instance, if Mrs. Morgan couldn't read because of her eyesight, we would not include difficulty with reading when considering the possibility of dementia. However, if her inability to read was due to a lack of comprehension, we would give such a finding significant weight in making a diagnosis.

Mrs. Morgan's score of 133 out of a possible 144 would have been normal for a mentally intact 74-year-old. We rated Mrs. Morgan on a 5-point scale where 5 is terminal dementia. Mrs. Morgan's score was 0; she had no signs of dementia, and in our estimation she was as engaged in and enthusiastic about life as a high school sophomore. Mrs. Morgan was a star in our study, a world-class athlete of aging who appeared to have a mind and constitution that would have ably served most people in their seventies. She seemed ageless, a woman who, at almost any time in her life, even her hundreds, could have been described as "in her prime."

Of the 74 centenarians in whom we performed detailed neuropsychological testing, 18 did not meet the criteria for dementia. Interestingly, the NECS had so far borne out the 25 percent rate of cognitively intact centenarians we had found in our initial survey at the HRCA.

A BEAUTIFUL BRAIN

We were becoming convinced that the phenomenon of demographic selection—by which some people were selected to live to extreme old age—dictated that centenarians would be a group of people who were relatively resistant to cancer, heart disease, and, as our study indicated, Alzheimer's disease. There were other hints that this was the case. Our patient's families reported that most of our centenarians were seldom sick; 95 percent of them had been free of major diseases into their nineties.

We got another hint of this overall resistance to disease when we used a computer program, called *Clinquiry*, to informally look at patient data from the Beth Israel Deaconess Medical Center. Among 145 centenarians involved in 220 patient admissions over a ten-year period, there were only ten cases of cancer. In the general population, cancer rates rise exponentially as the population ages, just like Alzheimer's disease. But our survey of the health status of NECS centenarians revealed a similar low cancer rate. Out of 169 centenarians seen thus far, only three have had a history of life-threatening cancer (that is, cancers other than relatively benign skin cancer or slow-growing prostate cancer).

The implication was clear that centenarians had the potential to completely escape some of the diseases associated with aging, like Alzheimer's disease, and perhaps escape dementia altogether. But we still couldn't be sure without results from the brain autopsies, and we were anxious to hear from our collaborators at Massachusetts General Hospital, Kathy Newell, E. Tessa Hedley-Whyte, and Bradley T. Hyman. This upcoming part of the study might begin to tell us how centenarians avoided or delayed Alzheimer's disease for so long. About 20 percent of the subjects agreed to brain autopsies. We retested these people frequently so we would know how well their brains were functioning near the time of their deaths.

Mrs. Morgan, at the age of 101, was one of the first of our centenarian brain donors to die. At a memorial service held in the First Congregational Church in Cambridge, people arrived from all over the country to attest to her strength, courage, and humor. Several friends had composed songs about her life and sang them at the service. We were asked to speak about Mrs. Morgan's contribution to the study. It was a true celebration of a life—just the way Mrs. Morgan would have wanted it.

A few months before her death, Mrs. Morgan's testing had shown that her mind was still very clear. We were particularly curious about the physical state of her brain. Would it show signs of Alzheimer's pathology? If so, we would have to conclude that the physical changes of Alzheimer's were probably inevitable, no matter how well one ages. At the same time, we would have to begin looking for explanations of how Mrs. Morgan might have compensated for the damage Alzheimer's disease did to her brain, so that she was able to remain so thoroughly functional.

But lack of Alzheimer's disease lesions would tell us that we had been correct all along; that centenarians were special in that they delay the disease, and in some cases avoid it. That finding would make them a new model for the study of Alzheimer's disease that no one could ignore. But until the autopsies were performed we would not know whether centenarians somehow compensated for Alzheimer's disease, or whether they were able in some cases to live their entire lives without it.

One spring morning, we received a call from Kathy Newell, the neuropathologist working on our project. She had just finished staining key areas of Mrs. Morgan's brain with a pink dye that would reveal whether they had the telltale neurofibrillary tangles of Alzheimer's disease. "What a beautiful brain!" Kathy cried. "There are very few tangles in any parts of the brain where we would expect to see them. It's like the brain of a healthy 50-year-old."

This was just the first of our extraordinary autopsy findings. Thirteen centenarians have undergone brain autopsies so far, and only four have shown signs of Alzheimer's disease. Some centenarians suffered from other, non-Alzheimer's types of dementia. Mae Vogel and Lucy Boring both showed minimal neurofibrillary tangles, and were probably impaired by a combination of depression and cerebrovascular disease; Myrtle March, who was moderately demented, suffered from Pick's disease, yet had fewer signs of neurofibrillary tangles than even Anna Morgan!

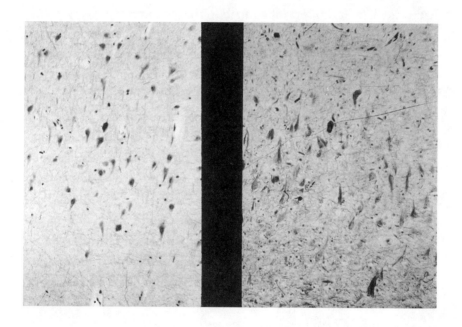

Above left, a microscopic slide of tissue from the hippocampus of Anna Morgan's 101-year-old brain shows no signs of disease. The hippocampus is key to the retrieval of short- and long-term memories, and is often one of the first sites destroyed by Alzheimer's disease. Detailed testing performed seven months before Mrs. Morgan's death confirmed that she was completely cognitively intact. This study marked the first time that such neurocognitive testing was correlated with postmortem pathological findings in centenarians. In contrast, the slide at the right shows the brain of a 52-year-old man with multiple neuropathological signs of Alzheimer's disease, including neurofibrillary tangles and neuritic plaques.

Researchers from around the world shared our exhilaration; this was the first time anyone had systematically followed up cognitive testing on centenarians with the neuropathological studies needed to determine whether they suffered from Alzheimer's disease. Even before Margery received her own advance copy of our report published in the March 1998 issue of *International Psychogeriatrics*, requests for reprints began to arrive from all over the world. In the same issue, Karen Ritchie, the internationally renowned neuropsychologist who studied Mme. Jeanne Calment, who lived to 122, said in an editorial on the value of studying centenarians that we had provided "an important contribution by examining the relationship between anatomical changes and cognitive performance in centenarians."

THE "MUSICAL VACCINE"

Having seen that a significant proportion of centenarians had avoided both the physical and behavioral manifestations of dementia, we became more and more curious about the full autopsy results and their implications. We considered that centenarians might simply have larger brains than other people. While a certain rate of brain cell loss is normal, Alzheimer's disease speeds the process of attrition greatly, usually beginning in memory and language centers, and eventually progressing throughout the brain.

In a study of geniuses, brain size varied as much as 40 percent, and a few genius brains weighed considerably less than three pounds. The Russian writer Ivan Turgenev's brain weighed in at an astounding 4.4 pounds, while American writer Walt Whitman's brain totaled a mere 2.8 pounds. We found similar results in our studies of brain weights. Among 13 centenarians whose brains we were able to autopsy, weights ranged from 1,314 grams down to 920 grams, all within the normal range. Josephine Lombardo showed no signs of dementia in our study, and her brain weighed 930 grams (just about 2 lbs.) the second smallest in the group. Myrtle March, who suffered from Pick's disease, had the smallest brain in the study but showed no signs of Alzheimer's disease. On the other hand, Alfred Benedetti, who had the highest brain weight in the study, also showed no signs of dementia. Size didn't matter.

As the neuropathology reports of other subjects were completed, new revelations greeted us. The autopsy of Fred Flagg, a former amateur musician with no signs of dementia who lived to 103, showed that he had suffered a severe brain injury. Despite complete blindness in his right eye and partial visual loss in his left, his visual-spatial abilities remained unimpaired. Like Mrs. Morgan, Mr. Flagg had performed his cognitive testing with the agility of a World Cup goalie, fielding each question and quickly tossing back the answer. Why hadn't he shown any signs of cognitive deficits?

Mr. Flagg had incurred damage to his left hippocampus, probably at some point early in his life. The hippocampus is involved in memory, and it was astonishing to us that anyone who had sustained this level of hippocampal damage would have been able to remember the long passages of music needed to play at the level Mr. Flagg had

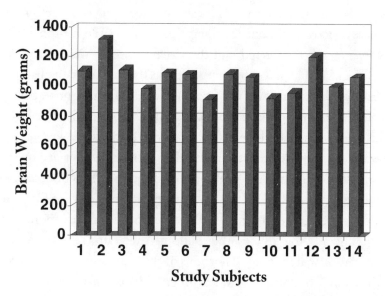

Brain weights of centenarians vary significantly. Brain weight does not appear to predict extreme longevity within this range (920 to 1,394 grams).

maintained throughout his life, much less perform so well on the verbal memory tests that were part of our evaluation.

Clearly, some important properties of the brain had given it the resilience to overcome this insult. First, Mr. Flagg's brain had adequate reserve capacity to handle the many complex memory tasks needed to perform music. Second, Mr. Flagg's brain probably compensated by involving his right hippocampus in picking up the slack for the damaged left hippocampus. This kind of compensation is by no means unique. Dr. Alan Gevins of the EEG Systems Laboratory in San Francisco studied a woman who had suffered extensive damage to her right brain, where the centers controlling movement of her left arm were located. Dr. Gevins showed that the woman's brain had rewired itself in a highly unusual way: The left brain took over control of her left arm, and she became able to move the limb again.

Many behaviors, rather than being controlled by a particular area of the brain, are initiated and carried out by complex networks of nerve cells. These networks are formed from input from our environment and our brain's activities. In his book *An Anthropologist on Mars*, Oliver Sacks tells the story of a blind patient whose sight was restored. Yet the patient still found it impossible to recognize certain objects—even something as familiar as a book—without touching them. His tactile neuronal networks were highly developed, but the visual networks were not yet in place. Because he had never before experienced visual input, he had not yet constructed the neuronal networks that told him what a book looked like, and was unable to make the association without feeling the cover and the pages, as he had done before he gained sight.

Neuronal networks constitute another protective capacity of the brain: Distributing the responsibility for important functions across several lobes increases the ability to compensate in the event that one of the lobes is diseased or injured. Active brains may create more new networks and add to old ones, thus building the brain's reserve. Activities like music, which link the portions of the brain involved in movement, memory, language, new learning, and vision, among others, may contribute to the ability to compensate in this way. Fred Flagg had a very intact right hippocampus, and we speculated that his many years of playing the flute, along with his avid reading in science, may have helped the right hippocampus compensate for the damage to the left.

Our subjective observation that a large number of centenarians played a musical instrument makes us think that such activities impart some form of protection, perhaps by increasing adaptive capacity and functional reserve. Mr. Flagg tangibly demonstrates for us the powerful immunizing role that complex activities like learning an instrument can play in compensating for damage that might occur due to processes such as strokes or Alzheimer's disease. For Mr. Flagg, music acted like a powerful vaccine against brain damage. The important thing to remember is that these vaccines are much more effective when employed preventively, before the onset of potentially dementing illness. Other activities besides music may prove to be equally effective.

The development of complex connections between neurons requires more than just "puttering around." Music, painting, poetry, sculpture, learning a language, and other challenging mental activities, some of which may bring in physical coordination as well, are much more stimulating and thus more protective for the brain. Self-expression and emotional involvement in the activity may be important as well. These multidimensional activities continually present new cognitive challenges that compel the brain to reinforce its defenses against deterioration.

Old age had suddenly begun to look very different. Living to 100, it appeared, did not necessarily mean living with disease and disability. In fact, it probably means a life lived in exceptionally good physical and cognitive health. But we needed to use very rigorous epidemiological research methods to determine just how many people live to become centenarians without dementia. To ensure that we were dealing with a representative sample, we included 34 age-confirmed centenarians who were all alive on one date: December 31, 1996. To our surprise, the prevalence of nondementia in this group was even higher than in the larger group of 74 cases collected over the previous two years. Eleven out of the 34 were dementia-free, a prevalence of 33 percent. Here was proof that aging and Alzheimer's disease were distinct, separate processes. No longer would we hear physicians say that a certain level of Alzheimer's damage was "consistent with age." Mrs. Morgan's 101-year-old brain had become a gold standard for healthy aging.

At a meeting of the Gerontological Society of America in 1997, we gathered together researchers studying centenarians in Japan, France, Sweden, Denmark, as well as from other parts of the United States. All of us were amazed to see that about one-third of centenarians had survived past the age of 100 without dementia. And more than 95 percent of these people were just like our centenarians: They had lived into their nineties without any loss of mental faculties. Around the world—whether you're in New Jersey or New Delhi—if you reach very old age, even if you live to 100, the chances of spending the greater portion of your later years without Alzheimer's disease or any other form of dementia are very good.

Our study—and the confirming research from around the world—literally gave people something to live for. We need not fear that a long life automatically implies lifelong confinement in a nursing home. Having seen centenarians such as Anna Morgan, Dirk Struik, Fred Flagg, and others attain extreme old age without any significant cognitive deficits, we had to conclude that normal aging does not imply loss of cognitive function. Our study indicates that, until proven otherwise, normal brain aging should be synonymous with disease-free aging.

While those findings inspired us, we also began to realize that there was something very important and mysterious about the people we had decided to study. Living to 100, we realized, was like a very fine filter. Our centenarians had arrived at this stage of life for very good reasons. Either they had lived a particularly healthy lifestyle and taken superior care of themselves, or were endowed with excellent genes for aging. Something had allowed them to escape many of the diseases that normally kill people at much younger ages. Exactly what that "something" was, we would spend the coming months trying to determine.

3

THE CENTENARIAN LIFESTYLE

MIT mathematics professor Dirk Struik came to the United States from the Netherlands in 1926 to lecture on Tensor calculus, which Albert Einstein used to construct his theory of relativity. At one time a theoretical mathematician, Struik later became a worldwide figure in ethnomathematics, the study of mathematics in primitive cultures. He is shown here at his desk in his home, at age 104.

While we were studying centenarians' cognitive function, we were also looking at their individual characteristics, hoping to find something that would account for their ability to live to 100. Our goal was to find out what made centenarians healthier than the vast majority of people. How did they avoid Alzheimer's disease, heart disease, cancer, and so many other chronic and fatal diseases for so long, and in some cases even escape them?

We felt in general that the genetics of aging was probably too complex to yield any really useful findings. Early research into some of the principal fatal diseases in Western countries suggested that their genetic determinants were too diverse and numerous to supply much information. How much could one gene tell us about aging if there were thousands more involved in the process?

On the other hand, some highly visible studies had indicated that environmental and behavioral factors—like diet, exercise habits, access to health care—were much more important than inherited abilities in coping with aging. Most researchers believed that studies of diet, lifestyle, and personality would yield more concrete, usable information about healthy aging.

DIET AND OTHER DEAD ENDS

Numerous studies suggested and in some cases confirmed that diet could play a role in many age-associated diseases. Long-term, meticulous examinations of heart disease in stable populations—such as the Framingham Heart Study, the Nurses' Health Study, and the Physicians' Health Study—had all detected relationships between dietary fat and heart disease. Other studies suggested that drinking one glass of red wine daily could protect people against heart disease. Epidemiologists had shown that a high-fat diet was associated with increased risk for several forms of cancer. International comparisons of cancer rates seemed to indicate that cultural variations in diet lay behind the high rates of stomach cancer in China and elevated rates of colon cancer in the United States. Diabetes, a major cause of heart disease, kidney disease, blindness, and nerve damage, can in the vast majority of cases be controlled with diet. Even osteoporosis, a chronic, nonlethal condition associated with aging, can be ameliorated to a certain extent by increased dietary calcium intake.

Was diet a determining factor in the longevity of our centenarians? In July of 1994, we tested the waters with a dietary questionnaire, provided by the Harvard School of Public Health's Dr. Walter Willett, who runs the Nurses' Health Study and Physicians' Health Study. This extremely detailed questionnaire depends heavily on the subject's ability to remember his or her typical diet over the past year, and measures levels of some 70 nutritional components.

After looking at responses from only 20 centenarians, it was clear that studying self-reported diet would not prove fruitful for several reasons. In the first place, we were interested in the conditions that allowed people to live to 100—what they were doing once they arrived at that age was often a different story. Many of our subjects had lost their robust appetites, and were no longer consuming full diets. We found a number of centenarians with deficiencies in important nutrients. They had to some extent migrated away from their lifelong dietary habits, and those potentially health-sustaining practices were the ones that interested us.

A chance incident made us even less hopeful of finding a dietary secret for living to 100. One morning we were at a lecture at Beth Israel-Deaconess Medical Center, where we happened to bump into Lester Steinberg, the son of one of our NECS subjects. At 79, Dr. Steinberg shows all the signs of slow aging we've become accustomed to seeing among centenarians' children, and he continues to practice medicine in the Boston area. Lectures such as the one we were attending are frequently accompanied by breakfast buffets; Dr. Steinberg reached out for a particularly sugary Danish.

"Do you really want to do that?" we said, surprised at Dr. Steinberg's choice of breakfast fare.

"Why not?" he replied. "I bet if you really knew what all the centenarians grew up eating, even my mother, you would be astounded. Back at the turn of the century, everyone ate fatty, salty foods. Storing food was the big problem, and people ate salted fish and meat, and pickled meat and vegetables. Everyone ate as much sugar and fat as they could find, because it was scarcer. I'm sure my mother grew up eating Danishes, and for all I know, they're probably good for me!"

Another complication of studying aging had risen up to bite us. The world had changed. Most processed foods had not existed during the centenarians' early formative years. Preserving was done by pickling, smoking, salting, and other means that have more or less lost favor. Fresh fruit was available at more limited times. And, as Dr. Steinberg pointed out, fat was a treat. Dietary habits have changed dramatically over the years. Not only would it have been very difficult to determine what our subjects had been eating when they were younger, it would be almost impossible to compare their consumption habits to those of today's population. The likelihood of a productive study of centenarians' lifelong dietary habits seemed slim.

The other striking finding was that our subjects' diets were so varied. Some ate very little red meat, if any; others ate red meat every day. One of our centenarians had been eating bacon and three eggs every day for breakfast for 15 years. Had he survived so long in spite of or because of this diet? Other centenarians swore by dietary concoctions they had invented, such as James Hanlon's breakfast combination of oatmeal, olive oil, raisins, apples, and other fruits. There was no rhyme or reason to the results we saw. About half of our centenarians were born overseas, and many more American-born subjects came from varied ethnic backgrounds. It was unlikely that we would find any discernible dietary patterns in this international welter.

The other possibility was that some centenarians—perhaps those in Dr. Steinberg's family among them—shared a peculiar, undiscovered advantage for dealing with excess dietary fat, cholesterol, or other predisposing factors for cardiovascular disease. If this were the case, their longevity would not be explained so much by their diets as by some genetically determined advantage in their metabolic and digestive systems.

We turned then to another important and easily measurable dimension of lifestyle: formal education. Some research has shown that better educated people tend to live longer and are less susceptible to dementia than those with less education. Higher learning has been associated with life expectancy up to two years greater than the general population. Some scientists have proposed that extended formal learning might lead to the formation of more dendrites, as we suspected we might find in our studies of centenarian brains.

But when we looked among our subjects for signs of higher learning, again we found a great variety of backgrounds and histories. Only two of our study subjects had earned advanced degrees: MIT mathematics professor Dirk Struik and psychology Ph.D. Lucy Boring. Some of our centenarians may have educated themselves extensively: Alfred Benedetti received only a sixth-grade education, but at age 103 he was able to draw a complex diagram of a ship's valve that he had invented and patented. Others may have been great readers, but were not followers of any professional discipline. Angelina Strandal received all her formal education in a one-room schoolhouse—to which she walked two miles each day—on Prince Edward Island. The average educational level our subjects attained was the tenth grade, which was completely consistent with the times they grew up in. Centenarians tell us it's not formal education that allows one to live to 100 in good cognitive and physical health.

Lola Blonder's Wars

Another avenue that lay open to us was the study of personality. Why did some people cope so well with aging and remain happy and engaged in life, while others with equal or perhaps even greater financial and health resources became miserable in old age? It was crucial to gather basic data about how centenarians interact with people and the world around them.

Characterizing centenarian personalities has been difficult because until recently there haven't been enough 100-year-olds to study. Researchers have instead contented themselves with looking at the "younger old." In 1961, based on a study of 700 Kansas City residents, the social scientists Elaine Cummings and William Henry proposed the disengagement theory of aging, which stated that older people gradually draw into themselves. Other social scientists, noting how many older people remain active with volunteer, family, and business activities, came to the opposite conclusion, that older people remain engaged in activity. They proposed a competing "activity theory" of aging.

Today, most psychologists believe that aging leads to neither increased isolation nor sociability, but rather that personalities after age 20 remain relatively stable. This isn't to say that adult personalities remain absolutely frozen, because they can and do shift in response to challenges, crises, and other events. But gerontologist Bernice Neugarten, who also studied the Kansas City subjects, concluded: "There is considerable evidence that, in normal men and women, there is no sharp discontinuity of personality with age, but instead an increasing consistency." In other words, as people get older, they become neither more nor less gregarious, but remain the same as they ever were, only more so. Psychologist Hans Eysenck basically agreed with these findings, stating that "older people are less variable in their conduct and their moods."

These observations were encouraging to us. They suggested that investigating our centenarians' personalities would not present the same problem we'd encountered in studying dietary habits, that people's diets often changed in old age. Rather, our centenarians would, by and large, have the same personalities they had had throughout their adult lives. Any commonalities among them could contain useful clues to our centenarians' longevity.

As we began interviewing our subjects, their stories of survival became more amazing and impressive to us. We had previously suspected that one of the reasons centenarians were able to live so long was that, just as they had avoided disease, they had also been lucky enough to skirt dangerous and stressful situations. But we quickly found out how wrong we were.

Sixty years ago, Lola Blonder lived in an elegant apartment in Vienna's first district. Five of the nine rooms looked out over the Ringstrasse, the city's tree-lined boulevard. When the French doors between the rooms were thrown open and the sun streamed in through the windows, there was a grand view of Oriental rugs and crystal chandeliers.

On March 13, 1938, aided by sympathizers who had already infiltrated governmental offices, the Nazi forces stormed into Austria, and Mrs. Blonder's life changed forever. The Nazis seized her apartment, with all the paintings, furniture, and art work inside. She endured hours of interrogation by Nazi officers attempting to determine the whereabouts of money she had deposited outside the country. As we listened to Mrs. Blonder, and her intensity came to the fore, it was easy to picture this small, gray-haired, wheelchair-bound woman as a courageous young mother, fighting for exit papers for her children, mother, and brothers.

Mrs. Blonder had already been through a significant emotional ordeal. Six months before the Nazi invasion of Austria, she had lost her first husband. She managed to bounce back from this early emotional blow, even though it is well known that the death of a spouse is one of the most stressful situations any of us can encounter, according to the widely used Social Readjustment Rating Scale. Death of a spouse can lead to all types of health problems, including headaches, nausea, insomnia, shortness of breath, and irregular heartbeat. The newly widowed use significantly more tranquilizers, alcohol, and tobacco after bereavement than before.

Bereavement inspires other behaviors in both man and animals that lead to ill health or accidents. People who have lost a spouse or child frequently neglect their own nutrition, grooming, even their financial affairs. Konrad Lorenz, the anthropologist who studied the lifelong monogamy of geese, noted that some animals demonstrate "searching" behavior after losing a mate. Humans frequently embark on the same kind of "wild goose chase" after an emotional loss and, in the midst of grief, become "lost" and vulnerable to accidents and tragedies.

Other events with high stress ratings include divorce, marital separation, jail, and death of a close family member, but many of the stressful situations Mrs. Blonder lived through are so unusual that they are not even included on the Social Readjustment Scale. What's more, she grieved the death of her husband under the most paralyzing type of anxiety: the fear that her children would be taken from her, just as her brother had been marched off to the Dachau concentration camp. Many Holocaust victims lost their will to live under similar conditions, or were so emotionally crippled by the experience that their health was permanently damaged.

There are many stories of Holocaust survivors whose lives were cut short by suicide, accidents, and stress-related illnesses like heart disease. But like many centenarians, Mrs. Blonder demonstrated a remarkable ability to cope with the stress of separation and bereavement. Although practically all centenarians have suffered severe bereavement—some several times—they are able to maintain their emotional focus and concentrate on survival.

A few months after the Nazi invasion, Mrs. Blonder and her family fled to Palestine, where she continued to show her courage and optimism. She worked for years to secure the release of her two brothers and her mother, who were still trapped in Austria. She went into business, making and selling cosmetics, creams, and lotions door-to-door. She married a watchmaker, whose late wife happened to be a distant cousin of Mrs. Blonder's own late husband. When Israel gained independence from Great Britain in 1948, Mrs. Blonder and the other members of her family served in the army that defended the newborn state against the combined Arab forces. Despite the loss of her second husband, she continued to find meaning in fighting for her children, her brothers, her mother, and the many Holocaust survivors who lived around her. Mrs. Blonder never became entrapped in anger or self-pity, nor did she expend undue energy on hatred toward the Nazis. All her resources were focused on engineering the survival of herself and her family.

Personality is one of the most important factors in survival. We see this in war, in treatment of disease, in sport, in academics, and in the type of terrible episodes Mrs. Blonder lived through. And we see it as an important component in the lives of centenarians. Something about centenarians allows them to accept the many losses of loved ones that occur along the road to 100, to live with limitations that come with growing older, and to deal with the feelings of impending mortality that certainly hang more heavily as time goes on. Not only do centenarians endure these upsets, but they frequently flourish despite them—writing poetry and autobiographies, learning to paint, winning golf tournaments.

In our experience with centenarians, we never find that their lives have been particularly easy or without disappointment. Centenarians don't live in ivory towers, free from stress and hardship. We heard many stories of privation, poverty, hardship, and oppression. Longevity is not a result of having avoided stress, but rather of having responded to it efficiently and effectively. Centenarians' personalities may insulate them from the kind of psychological and physical damage others incur through years of problems, losses, and emotional upsets. Although their lives may have been filled with just as much pain and woe as any of ours, their personalities may have helped keep them healthy.

Throughout life, Mrs. Blonder demonstrated the strength and resilience that helped her live to 104. Her essentially positive nature protected her from emotional stress, and created a calm internal environment that allowed her to keep her mind and body healthy. She was able to escape the crushing depression and loss of meaning in life that paralyze so many people who have undergone harrowing experiences. Her resilience and optimism were still evident in her nineties, when she began painting, and even into her hundred-and-fourth year, when she fought back from several life-threatening infections. As much as her genes, her immune system, or the heart that beat in her chest, her personality seemed to have contributed to her lifelong robust health.

STRESS-RESISTANT PERSONALITIES

Like intelligence and social status, personality is a widely used term that is extremely difficult to define. Personality refers to one's patterns of behavior and methods of adjustment to life. It is a key factor in a person's ability to survive life's most critical, stressful, and dangerous episodes. Positive personality traits can take people past their expected limits of physical strength or endurance, and can in fact mean the difference between life and death.

To identify lifelong personality traits that might lead to healthy aging, we administered personality testing to 60 centenarians. The NEO Five-Factor Inventory is a personality assessment tool that has been widely used to study neuroticism, extroversion, openness, agreeability, and conscientiousness in older individuals.

Personality testing had already produced interesting results about survival to old age. In the Terman study, which has followed a group of gifted California schoolchildren for more than 70 years, subjects who showed signs of conscientiousness and dependability were more likely to be longer-lived. Children—especially boys—who were rated as prudent, conscientious, truthful, and free from vanity were about 30 percent less likely to die in any given year than children without these personality traits. The finding seemed to indicate that these few characteristics conferred an advantage that increased these individuals' ability to reach old age.

We anticipated that the NECS, a population-based study, might yield very different results from the Terman study, which looked at an intellectually and socioeconomically select group over a period of time. This turned out to be the case. When we combined and averaged the results of the NEO Five-Factor Inventory, centenarians' scores were no different from the general population in most respects. But there was one domain in which they appeared significantly different: neuroticism. Centenarian women scored 15.5 on the neuroticism scale, while a comparison group scored 20.5, a statistically significant difference. We could not analyze the men's scores because there were so few, but a larger study might show that centenarian men are also low in neuroticism.

It was very revealing to find that centenarians, particularly women, are relatively immune to neuroticism. The term "neuroticism," the most important and pervasive domain of the five personality traits, is really a measure for what has been called "negative emotionality," or unhealthy feelings, like anger, fear, guilt, and sadness. It includes such emotional facets as depression, anxiety, hostility, self-consciousness (social unease), impulsiveness, and vulnerability. For example, older people who are high in neuroticism would see advancing age as a crisis, and might begin to worry about an unhappy retirement and poor health.

These anxious and fearful thoughts can themselves negatively impact health. Neurotic responses produce disruptive emotions that interfere with adaptation to unfamiliar environments and situations. High anxiety levels disturb heartbeat, immune function, and blood clotting in ways that increase the likelihood of heart attack. Stress and fear spark an all-body "alert" signal that induces the manufacture of both neurotransmitters—intracellular nervous system messengers—and hormones designed to aid the body in battle. When the "alert" signal is on

Can Personality Change?

Can we become more like centenarians, making changes in our approach to life so we can maximize our health? While research shows that personality remains stable throughout life, psychologist Erik Erikson and others tell us that change is necessary throughout the life cycle to meet the demands of new transitions and roles.

While these two notions seem contradictory, they are in fact two sides of the same coin. The Baltimore Longitudinal Study—which looked at personality in hundreds of individuals from ages 17 to 97—described a person's immutable characteristics as "Basic Tendencies, the core potentials of a person," which interact with environmental factors—including our families of origin and our education—over a lifetime.

An example of this dynamic can be found in the work of Harvard psychologist Jerome Kagan, who has shown that shy personalities are associated with particular patterns of brain activity that are present from birth. However, Kagan has also found that parental influence and teaching can modify shy behavior. Shy children whose parents teach them to cope in social situations and encourage social interaction can overcome a great deal of their shyness. Even adults with debilitating social phobias can learn to conquer some of their fears, according to psychiatrist Mark Pollack and psychologist Michael Otto of Massachusetts General Hospital.

all the time, these battle hormones can damage other important systems like digestion and the skin. Aging researcher Jay Olshansky calls emotional stress an "aging accelerator," and it is believed that stress may actually contribute to shrinking the hippocampus, a brain structure that is very important in memory. Coping with stress, or quickly getting over life's emotional setbacks, is therefore one of the most important factors in successful aging in centenarians, explaining how they keep their physical and mental functioning as long as they do.

High neuroticism has additional links to poor health, such as its relation to poor impulse control. People who rate high in neuroticism have trouble with resisting short-term gratification in order to reap

Centenarians are natural stress-shedders, but what comes easily to them because of their innate personalities may have to be consciously learned by the rest of us. This doesn't mean we can't do it with enough effort and practice, just as those of us without natural athletic ability have learned to hit a tennis ball or ski down a mountain reasonably well. Myer Saxe, a 100-year-old man who rose from newsboy to owner of a large shoe factory, attributes his abilities to shed stress not to an easy-going personality but to a conscious decision at a certain point in life that he was going to be a "fun guy." "I decided not to worry about anything. . . . I saw that worrying didn't do any good."

Although we may not be able to change our basic personalities, we can change how we respond to situations. For example, people with hard-driving, achievement-oriented personalities are probably not going to change their basic tendencies, mellow out, and avoid stressful situations. However, they can learn from centenarians that managing stress is important. They can learn the advantages of being adaptable and changing those aspects of their lifestyle that do not contribute to health. They can make conscious decisions to spend more health-enhancing time with family and friends. And they can gain a new perspective on their strivings by taking a humorous look at themselves.

long-term gains. They are therefore more likely to be smokers and alcoholics, two behaviors that also accelerate aging and reduce healthy life span.

Low neuroticism singles out centenarians as better than average at dealing with emotional stress. People low in neuroticism are calm and collected, even during crises. They are less prone to unrealistic thinking, and thus flexible enough to adapt to difficult circumstances. Persistent low neuroticism over the centenarians' lifetime not only helps protect them from the physical vulnerability associated with stress, but also insulates them from the loss of energy and focus that sends so many people on an emotional "wild goose chase" after a personal tragedy. Far from fitting the stereotype of the aimless, despondent, self-indulgent older person, centenarians are emotionally stable, flexible, adaptive, and seldom depressed.

This news challenges many of the widely held beliefs about aging. In "The Double Standard of Aging," Susan Sontag wrote, "Advanced age is undeniably a trial, however stoically it may be endured. It is a shipwreck, no matter with what courage elderly people insist on continuing the voyage." Unfortunately, Sontag's attitude is typical of our distorted, youth-oriented beliefs about old age as a time of negativism and hopelessness.

In fact, many people are extremely satisfied and happy in extreme old age. In *Why Women Live Longer Than Men*, Ball State University psychologist Royda Crose recounts the story of a centenarian woman who came to speak to her class of graduate students. One scholar asked the woman what age she would prefer to be right now. "Seventy," the woman responded. The class was stunned. Why would anyone want to be 70, when they could just as easily be 20? The woman replied that she wanted to watch her great-grandchildren grow up, and 20-year-olds don't have great-grandchildren. She was satisfied with having attained very old age, and enjoying her relationships with friends and family.

Healthy older people are not necessarily depressed about being old. More often, they are satisfied and happy with their current station in life. "They like their lives," Crose writes, "and only wish that they could live longer so they don't miss out on anything."

At 102, a year after we had first met her, Mrs. Blonder had every reason to feel depressed. First, she fell and broke her hip. Although her daughter, a nurse, preferred to keep her at home, they decided that it would be best for her to enter a nursing home. Initially, the environment proved disappointing; Mrs. Blonder felt ignored by the staff and missed her home life. While there, she also suffered a stroke that crippled her left hand.

Amazingly, her outlook remained upbeat and cheerful. She persistently worked to regain some function in her hand and held a toilet paper roll in her fist to keep it unclenched. She tried to teach her hand to work again by talking to it and "willing" it to move. Each morning, she and her daughter exchanged handwritten faxes about their plans and reflections for the day; they wanted to keep up their writing skills. She eagerly spoke with friends and strangers about her reminiscences, ideas, and painting. Although she recalled having been briefly depressed at various times in the past—especially after the deaths of her father and her two husbands—what she described was the sadness that is part of the normal grieving process following the death of someone of great personal importance. Most researchers believe that a normal grieving period—even up to three years—following the death of a spouse is usually healthier than keeping a "stiff upper lip." Mrs. Blonder concluded her grieving without derailing her own life and quickly returned to the business of living.

Currently, as many as one in six older people living in the community is thought to be depressed. Depression can complicate and exacerbate many conditions and may arise out of both mental and physical disorders. Harvard psychiatrist George Vaillant has shown that on average, people with depression die years earlier than nondepressed people. Yet because depression is so prevalent among older people, many physicians and researchers view it as "natural" to be dissatisfied with life in old age.

But centenarians completely contradict that notion. No matter how high the level of stress and disappointment, these people are able to weather it. Out of 74 centenarians, only four showed signs of severe depression on the Geriatric Depression Scale, a standardized questionnaire used to detect depression. The centenarians' stress-resistant personalities protected them from emotional strain and insulated them from internal and external conflict. Their personalities were a shield against depression.

Even the four centenarians whose test results indicated a high likelihood of depression did not manifest many of the classic symptoms. Helen Eckerly, who scored 23 out of a possible 30 on the Geriatric Depression Scale, had fought depressive tendencies her entire life, yet had never been immobilized by them. As her daughter put it, she "kept going." When we met Mrs. Eckerly, she was not unresponsive or detached as you might expect a severely depressed older person to be. We found out that Mrs. Eckerly had arranged her own admission to the nursing home so that she could live closer to her daughter. Taking charge of such a difficult situation is rare for a depressed older person.

It appeared to us that depression might have different implications for centenarians than for other people. Even in cases where they appeared to have been suffering from many of the symptoms of depression, they were often able to continue managing their lives successfully, without some of the health consequences that other people typically suffer. Perhaps maintaining emotional stability in old age is much more crucial for long-term physical and cognitive health than it is currently given credit for. Stress management may thus provide an important key to attaining extreme old age.

With their stress-resistant personalities and low risk for neuroticism and depression, centenarians are natural stress-shedders who shrug off life's slings and arrows with relative ease. Like natural athletes who can pick up a sport as easily as picking up a ball, most centenarians can handle a new situation without undue tension. Just as Nolan Ryan retained the ability to throw a 90-mile-an-hour fastball into his forties, centenarians retain their stress-fighting abilities from childhood into their hundreds. If people can emulate centenarians, either through stress reduction programs, alternative approaches like yoga, or a regular physical exercise program, we believe they stand a much better chance of coping with the mental and physical problems of old age.

He Who Laughs Lasts

Gratified as we were to have found one lifelong personality trait common to centenarians, we were still surprised to discover that they did not have more potentially modifiable traits in common. Gradually, we began to tease out behavioral characteristics that separated centenarians from other people. For instance, although we could not find any specific foods or nutrients that centenarians consumed, we could see that most of them ate moderately and sensibly. Our physical exams showed that 99 percent of our centenarians did not meet the criteria for obesity, an important risk factor for heart disease, diabetes, and perhaps other causes of mortality, such as cancer. About 80 percent of centenarians said that their current weight was close to what they had weighed for their entire adult lives.

We also talked with centenarians about their alcohol consumption. As for the daily glass of red wine that is supposed to provide some protection against heart disease, we found that alcohol consumption was uncommon among centenarians, although a few drank regularly: Mrs. Piazza drank wine at meals, and Isabelle Betts's doctor wrote an order for the nursing home staff to provide her with an ounce of Southern Comfort each evening before bedtime. But none of our centenarians revealed any history of alcohol abuse in their earlier lives. Smoking was practically nonexistent: The few centenarians who had smoked earlier in life had abandoned the habit quickly.

Most of our centenarians kept active, both physically and mentally. Anna Morgan, who at age 101 still read while riding a stationary bicycle, was the classic example. But there were plenty of others: William Cohen went to his office at the printing business he owned several days a week at the age of 101. Rena Gabella, who lived alone at the age of 100, still baked bread, cakes, and cookies for large family gatherings. Tom Spear played golf. Myer Saxe was a board member—not a resident—at the HRCA. Each one of our healthy centenarians had a full day of activity each and every day.

But some survival strategies of the centenarian lifestyle are unexpected. One of our centenarians' most effective self-protective devices comes from their ability to lighten their emotional load with humor. Many older people become sensitive about discussing illness, sex, and the prospect of death, or become preoccupied with troubles. In contrast, a visible and consistent component of the centenarian repertoire is humor.

At the age of 102, Angelina Strandal was interviewed by a network television news team interested in her longevity. Producers, reporters, and cameramen arrived at her home, and a long line of cars formed on the street outside. When asked what her neighbors would think, she replied with a laugh, "They'll think I died."

Mrs. Strandal was one of the most cognitively intact centenarians we studied, but even cognitively impaired centenarians reveal a sense of humor. Although afflicted by Pick's disease, Myrtle March received lots of attention from a niece who loved her sense of adventure and fun. Despite her waning mental function, she retained a sense of humor. Miss March had a mechanical raven in her room that would flap its wings and caw loudly. When we asked what it was saying, she interpreted with a smile, "It's saying 'Pack up and get out!'"

Most researchers agree that a well-developed sense of humor is a sign of mature psychological development. George Vaillant, who studied how a large group of male Harvard College graduates used emotional defenses, consistently found that a sense of humor is associated not only with good physical health, but also with superior psychological adjustment. Vaillant considers humor to be one of the best coping mechanisms available to us and "one of the truly elegant defenses in the human repertoire." We use humor both to recognize hard realities and protect ourselves from their inherent sorrow and hurt.

Humor not only helps us cope emotionally, it also helps us to think creatively and solve problems. It encourages and enables our minds to keep active, which is one of the most important defenses we have against aging. In a kind of cognitive reframing, it allows us to approach situations in a new way. As in the saying "If life gives you lemons, make lemonade," humor can turn an embarrassing situation, like accidentally stepping off a dock and getting soaked, into a hilarious and memorable story.

Humor often helps people put physical or psychological pain aside so they can get on with their work and lives. Doctors and nurses working with terminally ill patients can use humor as a way to "package and send off" the emotions they themselves feel while watching people die. In the same way, centenarians use humor to gain perspective on their own imminent deaths.

Anna Morgan once remarked that she wanted to make all her funeral arrangements before her death. "I don't want my children to be burdened with all this," she said. "They're old, you know." She used humor as a way of making a sad task appear somewhat normal, which allowed her to proceed with the funeral arrangements without the distraction of sorrow.

A sense of humor contributes to aging well physically. As William Fry, a Stanford University researcher, points out, the acts of smiling and laughing provide the same benefits as exercises like walking or swimming. Norman Cousins called laughter "internal jogging." Even the heart gets exercise, as laughter slightly increases blood pressure just long enough to provide tissues with increased oxygen. It also alters the breathing cycle in a way that increases both the amount of oxygen inhaled and the amount of carbon dioxide exhaled.

Laughing helps people relax and stay alert. During laughter, muscles throughout the body—in the head, neck, chest, and pelvis—tense and relax, in the same way that they do during stress reduction techniques like yoga. This helps keep muscles limber when in use, and also allows them to rest more easily. Laughter stimulates the release of certain neurotransmitters, called catecholamines, that raise alertness and mental functioning. A good joke may also help people prevent and recover from disease. According to Fry, laughter increases the concentration of disease-fighting antibodies in the bloodstream, thereby rendering the body more resistant to infection.

FRIENDS AND RELATIONS

The centenarians' durable sense of humor may also lead people to admire and want to be around them. This is part of the secret to centenarian charisma, which constitutes yet another protection against depression and stress. The popular conception is that the inevitable "shipwreck" of age leaves the older person marooned on a desert island of loneliness. Centenarians prove that this need not be the case. Despite the unavoidable fact that they have outlived numerous family members and friends, nearly all centenarians have many meaningful relationships. They are almost never "loners."

William Cohen, 101, who viewed independence as important to his longevity, realized that a close family was just as important. "The goal when you're older is to keep family close," he said, "to be independent, but to have them to help. As you get older, you need people, not dollars and cents."

Centenarians are almost never lonely; they have loyal supporters who provide emotional and physical support every day. In order to maintain these important relationships, centenarians need a certain degree of personal magnetism, and they must inspire the respect and affection that make these relationships endure. Few centenarians would pass for matinee idols, but they all seem to have one thing in common: They attract people. Psychologist Gina O'Connell Higgins has shown that traumatized children can develop into well-functioning adults because of their capacity to recruit others' invested regard. Centenarians, too, have this capacity to recruit the investment of family and friends, with similar beneficial results.

James and Florence Hanlon, the married centenarian couple, are protected by an exemplary rich and extended web of social networks. Their son and daughter-in-law live right next door and their daughter lives in the same house with them. Each week, when they go out for dinner at a local restaurant, they create a stir as they proceed to their table, chatting with well-wishers and patting familiar shoulders at every table. It is not just because they are both centenarians that they receive all this attention, reports their son: They were always very sociable people.

While many older people become lonely and isolated, even centenarians who are ill and live in nursing homes benefit more often from the attention of highly concerned and dedicated families. Although mentally fit, Mrs. Blonder had continuing health problems resulting from infections and strokes. Her daughter, Eva—a very young-looking 70-year-old—drove half an hour several times a week to see her mother. The two of them spent most of the day together, chatting in German about old times and new. Eva made sure that her mother had everything she needed and was well taken care of.

One of the more interesting paradoxes we found in the study was that a relatively high proportion of female centenarians in the study—about 14 percent—lack the most important social connection in our culture: marriage. A surprisingly large proportion of our centenarian women never married, even though marriage was an important goal for young women of this generation. However, these lifelong single women were surrounded by loving people of all ages. Marion Macdonald, a former Harvard Medical School chemistry instructor who never married, sent out nearly 150 greeting cards each year that she had painted and lettered herself. She received visits and telephone calls from former students across the country, who sought out her advice and conversation.

Thus, if centenarians do not have children, nephews, nieces, or cousins, they frequently have friends who do for them what children and other relatives normally do. We saw many examples of the charisma centenarians exude, and the kindnesses and respect paid to them by nonrelatives. Antonia Andrade, a 103-year-old former housekeeper, never had children of her own. Her former employers, the Johnston family, visited her for years, even after she had entered a nursing home.

Even cognitively impaired centenarians are able to maintain strong personal relationships. Celia Anderson's dementia showed on every possible test and she could not remember a single name. Still, she had nieces related to her only by marriage who visited her because, they said, "She has always been likable." Even after entering a nursing home, she was a favorite among the staff because of her sunny personality.

These relationships are an important survival tool. The protective web of social networks is vital to health, not merely because of the assistance some older people get from friends who drive them to the supermarket and doctor's appointments, or come to fix a leaky faucet. Researcher Marjorie Fiske Lowenthal has proven the importance of relationships through her studies of older women and their confidants. Dr. Lowenthal found that people who had an ongoing, close relationship with a confidant had better health and higher morale than those who did not.

Lisa Berkmann of the Harvard School of Public Health has found that older people with more friends are much more likely to recover from a heart attack than people with few or no friends or social supports. One study demonstrated that people with no friends were three times more likely to die than those with at least one or more sources of social support. These outcomes apparently have physiological underpinnings, since contact with friends and loved ones may also lower the levels of hormones like cortisol that are released in stressful situations. A friendly face may be just as health-giving as an aspirin or vitamin E.

Unfortunately, there are some situations so dire that a joke, a friend, or an aspirin is inadequate to heal the pain. In these situations, many centenarians fall back on another kind of relationship.

THE RELIGION FACTOR

One older woman who had never been very religious began to read the Bible every day. She spent more and more time perusing its pages, and her children and grandchildren began to wonder what was going on. "Why do you think Grandma spends so much time studying the Bible?" one of her grandchildren finally asked. "Maybe she's studying for the final exam," her cousin replied.

National polls show that religious behavior and attitudes are more prevalent in people over age 65. Half of these people go to church each week and three-quarters of them agree with such statements as, "I constantly seek God's will through prayer," and "I believe God loves me even though I might not always please Him." Among persons 65 and older, 82 percent say their religious beliefs are a very important influence in their lives.

Regardless of their observance of holy days and rituals, most centenarians have a lifelong awareness of their spiritual side and their relationship with God. When Mrs. Blonder's first husband died, she recalls having a conversation with God that helped put the loss in perspective: "I said, 'All right, God, you were very smart. You did the right thing.' He took Herbert away so that he would not be there when the Nazis came. I realized that it was his plan."

Being part of God's plan is a key part of centenarians' self-concept, allowing them to cope with the inevitability and proximity of death. "When he takes me, he takes me," many centenarians say. "Until then, I will keep living my life as I always have." Angelina Strandal often said that each day she asked God for another day, "and he always gave me one."

According to Sigmund Freud, the mythical figure of God was created by early man as a psychological shield against the insecurity and helplessness of living in a hostile world. Freud meant to disparage religious belief as an obstacle to the achievement of maturity and independence, but it turns out that piety has significant protective effects for older people. They consistently invoke religion as a way of dealing with illness, pain, and infirmity of all kinds. In a 1982 study of 1,459 persons aged 65 and over, religious attendance was more closely related to satisfaction with health than were gender, age, race, education, marital status, working status, alcohol use, smoking, or recent hospitalization. Advanced cancer patients with religious beliefs score significantly lower in pain perception than nonbelieving patients. Older men who get no comfort from religion have greater functional disability than those who do.

Harvard Medical School mind-body expert Herbert Benson has shown that frequent prayer, a feature of most religions, can lower blood pressure and reduce pain in cancer patients. Another study has found that frequent churchgoers have comparatively lower levels than nonchurchgoers of interleukin-6, an immune system substance associated with stress. Evidently religion and prayer, just like laughter and closeness, provide important health-giving effects that cannot be replicated by drugs or diet. This combination of stress-reducing personality traits and behaviors gives centenarians the freedom to adapt to the many changes and challenges they have experienced in their lives. It allows them room to change in a changing world.

ADAPTABILITY

The history of life on Earth is one of adaptation. New species evolve because of their ability to thrive in a shifting environment. Established species either persist or disappear, depending on their ability to gather food, defend themselves, and procreate.

Just as adaptation determines the survival of a species, it decides the longevity of individuals. In *Adaptation to Life*, George Vaillant in fact proposed that successful adaptation *is* health. From the moment we are born, leaving the comfort and sustenance of the womb behind, we begin a process of adaptation that is both instinctive and conscious. The process continues throughout the most advanced ages.

One of the key reasons for centenarians' longevity, we believe, is their adaptive capacity. Adaptation is not exclusively passive, nor is it limited to responses to environmental stimuli. The full repertoire of adaptation includes the ability to control the environment and to take charge of situations.

Centenarians demonstrate their adaptivity in different ways. To battle the loss of mental and physical abilities, they adopt strategies to keep their minds sharp and their limbs strong. In addition to his work as official historian for the town of Quincy, Alfred Benedetti ran three times a week well past the age of 100; at 101, Anna Morgan rode a stationary bike every day while reading newspapers and political pamphlets.

However, when centenarians see that they cannot continue an activity to which they have been accustomed, they quickly either find a workable new way to do the activity or substitute a more manageable one. After her nursing home admission, when Isabelle Betts's independence became more limited, she decided to take up crossword puzzles as a way of keeping her mind active. (This may also have kept her language skills sharp.) Centenarians are realists. Many other older people become concerned about appearances when decreasing leg strength and balance put them at risk of a fall, and refuse to use a cane or a walker. Centenarians will not resist such assistance if they can see that it will increase their mobility and safety. Centenarians are frequently assertive, as they often demonstrated when our cognitive and personality testing sessions ran too long. They are able to say "no" when they need to, and, like Myrtle March, warn people to "Pack up and get out!" when they push too hard.

One of the most remarkable examples of centenarian adaptation is the ease with which they adjust to new living environments. Several centenarians, such as Helen Pollycutt and Helen Eckerly, took the unusual step of arranging their own admissions to nursing homes and assisted living environments. Most older people fight fiercely against this loss of independence, and then deteriorate noticeably. Those who fail to heed the signs of growing dependency end up at home unattended, malnourished, and surrounded by unsanitary conditions. But centenarians see the writing on the wall. When the best solution is a nursing home, centenarians jump in and get comfortable.

Erik Erikson, the renowned developmental psychologist, wrote that, "The adaptation of individuals to the needs of the body, the community, and the environment in which they live is mandatory for survival." As we progress on the path from the crib, to school, to a home of our own, sometimes to the nursing home, and, one hopes, back to our own homes again, inexorable changes in our bodies, minds, and social status create confusion in how we view ourselves and our place in the world. Moving with the effortless ease of tightrope walkers, centenarians appear to adapt to these changes in an efficient, lasting way.

THE NINTH STAGE

Erikson was the first to describe a series of stages that take place during psychological growth from infancy into old age. He originally observed eight different stages of life. At each stage a person faces a particular developmental task or conflict between two opposing tendencies that must be resolved before psychological growth can take place. These developmental stages must be mounted like a ladder; each rung has to be taken in order. A successful struggle with each conflict results in a sense of coherence, wholeness, and the ability to move on to the next stage, while a failure to come to terms with these issues results in a lack of growth. Was it possible that centenarians might have progressed through these developmental stages more easily or with better results than others? Was there something unique or characteristic about their psychological development?

In Erikson's first stage, for example, helpless infants must develop a basic trust or confidence in themselves and others. This is a crucial issue for aging well. People must be able to place their trust in friends and family members in order to thrive in old age. Centenarians' close family ties, with the security they bring, are important for coping with stress and managing situations that require cooperation, coordination, and a certain amount of graceful letting go of responsibilities. Erikson compared it to a kitten that entirely entrusts its well-being to its mother, who carries the limp baby around in its jaws. "We human beings require a lifetime of practice to do this," he noted. People who have not developed trust have difficulty accepting the care they need when they become physically and mentally frail. They may put themselves at risk for hip fractures because they insist on walking without leaning on a helpful arm, or end up living in hellish conditions because they have refused help in their homes.

Having developed trust, young children must learn in the second stage to deal with shame and doubt and to act independently. Children who have negotiated this stage are able to act on their own, without relying on the support or approval of others. Centenarians have the self-reliance that comes from successful negotiation of this conflict. As much and as often as possible, they live independently. Adele Rogers, the oldest woman in Rhode Island, continued living in her own apartment at age 106, receiving only minimal assistance with housework.

In the third stage, or play stage, children must learn to cope with guilt and develop a sense of purpose. Centenarians frequently have a very strong sense of the importance of their activities. Mrs. Blonder demonstrated this conviction as she worked frantically to rescue her family from the Nazi occupation, and later when she joined the effort to defend the new state of Israel.

Between the ages of 7 and 11, in the fourth stage, children have an intense focus on learning, which is a highly socialized experience. When a child fails to achieve personal competence, he or she will develop a sense of inferiority. All centenarians, regardless of their level of education, have confidence in their learning skills. Alfred Benedetti, who had only a sixth-grade education, nonetheless became supervisor of the engineering drawing department at a shipyard. At age 103, he was still the unofficial historian of the town of Quincy.

At the end of childhood lies the fifth stage, adolescence, when the discovery of identity begins. The child who has been capable of carrying earlier tasks to completion can now focus on defining a role for him or herself. The adolescent begins to develop a consistent set of values. Centenarians like Anna Morgan, who sacrificed a great deal of time and money to actualize her belief in the rights of workers, retain such values.

These values give shape to the sixth stage, when young adults separate from their families and begin to explore intimate, loving relationships, developing their capacity for mature love. We had to accept that this kind of love may not necessarily mean marriage. As we've noted, many centenarian women never married, but they still found "families" with friends, relatives, students, or coworkers who made them feel needed and loved. We have observed centenarians' devotion to loved ones. At 106 and 101, James and Florence Hanlon have been married for 79 years. Dirk Struik's wife, Dr. Saly Ruth Ramler Struik, lived to age 99 and, after her death, he wrote a richly detailed biography of her. Most other centenarians referred to the death of spouses with deep regret, and we could often sense the richness and sincerity of their feelings.

The seventh stage is concerned with nurturing and guiding the next generation. Having children is the hallmark of this stage, but generativity can take many forms at different ages. We were reminded of Marion Macdonald, who never married or had children, but kept in touch with many of her students. Even years after she had entered a nursing home, they continued to visit her.

The eighth and last stage involves "the acceptance of one's one and only life cycle as permanent and inevitable," in Erikson's words. Inability to come to terms with one's life history results in despair, but those who resolve this conflict successfully emerge with the quality of wisdom or, as Erikson called it "an informed and detached concern with life in the face of death."

Centenarians appear to have negotiated all of Erikson's eight conflicts and to have attained a state of high psychological maturity, marking them as sages, role models, advisors, consultants, and, in a sense, icons. They are, as the ancient Greek historian Plutarch said of Lycurgus, "at the age where life is still tolerable, and yet can be quitted without regret."

Interestingly, centenarians appear to have entered another developmental stage, one that Erikson speculated about. When he formulated his theories in the early 1950s, only a small percentage of "elders" existed in society. Years later, as the percentage of older people increased, Erikson prophesied in his book *The Life Cycle Completed*, that "a universal old age of significantly greater duration suggests the addition to our cycle of a Ninth Stage of development with its own quality of experience. . . ."

In this Ninth Stage, the struggle for a balance between opposing qualities no longer exists. Contradictions such as the conflict between mortality and meaning in life coexist and are accepted. A profound peacefulness prevails; centenarians are ready for death but still engaged in life. They no longer think about past mistakes or losses, nor do they struggle to integrate the contradictions and ambivalences of their long lives. They don't ruminate about whether or not their lives had meaning—they are still actively finding meaning in their lives. They warm quickly to telling stories about their struggles and successes of the past, and often perceive and portray themselves as crucial characters in the events that unfolded around them, such as Mr. Bernays's tales of the growth of American roadways.

Our inquiry into the lifestyle of centenarians left us feeling that we had accomplished some important things. We had found several factors that appeared to help centenarians shed emotional stress and avoid the increased vulnerability to disease that comes with it. We had a valuable and increasingly detailed profile of the "typical" centenarian, a profile that drew from the ranks of all centenarians, rather than only the lucky few who managed to live to 100 in excellent physical and mental health.

Although our studies of personality had identified the importance of the centenarian lifestyle, we felt that there were still more basic issues that needed examination before we could say that we had determined what made centenarians different from other people. We had seen that more women made it to old age than men, but that men who lived to 100 had to be in excellent health in order to do so. We decided to turn our attention to one of aging's most crucial questions: why women outlive men. To many experts, the question had led to a dead end, but for us it proved to be an opening through which our speculations about the nature of aging grew and flourished.

THE LONGEVITY MARATHON

Women Versus Men

CREDIT: MICHAEL LUTCH

James and Florence Hanlon, ages 106 and 101, are that rare couple who have managed to succeed together in the Longevity Marathon. The odds against a married couple living to 100 are about 6 million to 1; however, they are improving.

MARIE KNOWLES was born into a close-knit farming family of five girls in 1894. When she was seven, her father decided that hay, straw, and oats didn't agree with his hay fever, and the family moved to the larger city of Bangor, Maine. Marie was not a particularly strong person, and she had scarlet fever at the age of 27, which resulted in a heart murmur that persists today. Although she was never poor and did attend college, unlike many women of her generation, Marie is certainly not wealthy. She recalls that the most she ever earned in a year was $7,200. In fact, she left her administrative position with the Visiting Nurses Association in Brooklyn because she felt that her fellow nurses cared too much about their take-home pay and pensions, and not enough about patients.

During most of the 1950s, she operated a small guest house in the town of Searsport, Maine, where she rented out rooms for $3.50 a night. Since 1960, she's shared a small house in Portland with a few other older women who help take care of one another. Today, at age 104, her philosophy is, "Pick out the fine things in life, and if you can't find them there, pick them out of your own head."

"STEEL MAGNOLIAS"

To a great extent, everyone working in the NECS has learned to believe in the strength of women, because our studies of centenarians have been primarily studies of the intelligence, durability, and resilience of women. Eighty-five percent of the centenarians in our study are women, which is consistent with the general centenarian population. Worldwide, centenarian women outnumber centenarian men by about nine to one. Not only do women have the advantage in numbers, they also hold the most important record in the longevity marathon: the longest life. As we've pointed out before, the oldest person in recorded history is a woman, Mme. Jeanne Calment, who died in 1997 at the age of 122.

In all developed countries and most developing ones, women have greater life expectancy than men, sometimes by a margin of as much as ten years. In the United States, life expectancy is about 79 years for women and about 72 years for men. The difference has become more pronounced in this century as female life expectancy has increased faster than that of males: Since 1900, the average national increase in life expectancy in developed countries has been 71 percent for women and 66 percent for men. Women over age 65 outnumber men by a ratio of three to two.

This phenomenon is neither uniquely human nor uniquely modern. In almost all animal species that have been observed in the wild, females tend to live longer than males. Female macaque monkeys, for instance, live an average of eight years longer than males, and female sperm whales outlive their mates by an average of 30 years. Women seem to have been outliving men for centuries, perhaps millennia. In Sweden, the first country to collect data on death rates nationally, the earliest records (1751–1790) show that the average life expectancy was 36.6 years for women and 33.7 years for men.

Only in a very few countries—India, Pakistan, Bangladesh, and some others—does the life expectancy for men exceed women's. One reason that these nations depart from the worldwide trend is particularly disturbing: All are known for long-standing sexually discriminatory practices, such as female infanticide and bride-burning, which dramatically cut into the average life expectancy for women.

The longevity of women is surprising, given that men enjoy numerous physical and cultural advantages over women. In most aspects of biological and social life, men appear to hold the trump cards. In worldwide competitions like the Olympics, men are stronger and faster than women. They are taller on average, and less likely to be overweight. Men typically have access to more money than women and receive more prompt medical care for certain potentially lethal medical conditions like heart disease. In contrast, older women are the single poorest group in America and often have no one to depend on: 35 percent live alone and 52 percent are widows, whereas among older men, only 14 percent live alone and 23 percent are widowers.

Even in the world of medical research, women are seldom regarded with the level of respect that ought to be accorded to the sex that composes two-thirds of the United States' over-65 population, and 51 percent of the world's general population. Basic studies of human physiology and psychology have often shunted women to one side. They have seldom been consulted as authorities on aging, as a 1998 article in the *Journal of the American Medical Association* pointed out:

> The issue of differences between the sexes is a relative newcomer to the hot-button issues on the nation's health research agenda. It was only in 1984 that the National Institute on Aging published its report on the Baltimore Longitudinal Study of Aging, using data derived only from men, and called it *Normal Human Aging* . . . . Although women were added to the study in 1978, they had been seen only once when the report went to press and were not included in it.

Now we were about to confront another paradox: One would expect that a group of people with comparatively lower access to wealth, employment, health care, and education would have a shorter life expectancy than another group with more of these privileges. In various societies the stereotypical image of women is one of delicacy and dependence, not one easily equated with survival over the long haul. Expressions used to describe strong women are often derogatory, or are simply paradoxical: "steel magnolia," for instance. The average woman is supposedly crippled in society without the support and companionship of a man. Indeed, when our study subjects were born, women did not yet even have the right to vote. Yet the disadvantages that have been women's lot seem only to have made them stronger. For the most part, women just age better.

Why, we asked ourselves, have women triumphed in that most important of endurance tests, the longevity marathon? Physiologically, genetically, and behaviorally something must help women compensate for their physical and social hurdles. Is it because of their ability to bear children, or in spite of it? Do their roles in society—as caregivers, communicators, peacemakers—help or hurt them? The answers won't be found in the body alone—they may also be rooted in the psychology, behavior, and social roles of men and women.

The idea behind the longevity marathon isn't to run faster or jump higher; people simply want to stay in the race as long as they can and with as much good health as possible. As we began handicapping the longevity marathon, it appeared to us that men and women were running two different races. Despite their size, speed, and strength, men just seem to die more easily and frequently than women—even in the womb. Boys are conceived far more frequently than girls—about 115 male conceptuses for every 100 females. From that point on, however, women quickly make up ground, and they soon surpass men handily. For some reason, male fetuses are miscarried, stillborn, or spontaneously aborted more often than female fetuses. Consequently, by the time of birth, the ratio of boys to girls has dropped to 104 boys for every 100 girls.

It doesn't stop there, though: Boys die more frequently than girls in infancy, during childhood, and during each subsequent year of life. On the male track, hurdles begin to appear almost immediately. The lungs of boys are less developed at birth than those of girls, and therefore more susceptible to infection. Boys are also more likely to have cognitive disorders, some of which are associated later in life with risk-related behavior like alcoholism, smoking, unprotected sex, and drug abuse.

Male mortality accelerates considerably during certain stages of the longevity marathon. Puberty brings on a flood of behavioral changes that can spell disaster for men. It is the beginning of what some call "testosterone toxicity." With the increasing production of the male hormone testosterone, boys start taking more risks than girls, thus increasing the odds that more of them will die. A similar phenomenon occurs in pubertal monkeys.

These hormonal changes have only been exacerbated by the proliferation and availability of drugs and technology, both licit and illicit:
faster and cheaper automobiles, and more automatic weapons, for
example. During and after puberty, the causes of death are much more
varied and visible among men than women. Alcoholism and death from
automobile or motorcycle accidents are each three times as common
among men. Accidents claim the lives of 45 of every 100,000 males in
young adulthood. Men also have higher rates of infection with HIV, the
virus that causes AIDS. Between the ages of 15 and 24, male risk-taking
and recklessness translate into a mortality rate three times higher than
women of the same age. By the time we've run two-and-a-half ten-year
laps of the longevity marathon, to age 25, the numerical male advantage
has disappeared, and surviving females outnumber males.

Although the male mortality rate falls closer into line with that of
females after maturity, men continue to suffer the consequences of their
self-destructive behavior and lifestyle choices. A new round of hurdles
appear after the fourth lap, when an increasing number of men in their
forties start to see symptoms of heart disease, due in large part to their
greater rates of smoking. Over the next two or three laps, men face huge
obstacles. Men aged 55 to 64 are twice as likely as women of the same
age to die from heart disease and accidents, and four times as likely to
commit suicide. Other illnesses related to smoking and alcohol consumption—like lung cancer and cirrhosis—also kill more men than
women in this age group.

Later in life, testosterone puts men at risk biologically as well as
behaviorally. It increases blood levels of the "bad" cholesterol (low-
density lipoprotein, or LDL) and decreases levels of the "good" cholesterol (HDL, or high-density lipoprotein), thus putting men at
greater risk of heart disease and stroke.

At the same time, testosterone's behavioral effects continue to create trouble. The increased heart-disease risk men incur due to higher
blood lipids is further complicated by aggressive feelings and behavior—also mediated by testosterone—that can raise blood pressure.
Hostility and anger can evoke the "fight-or-flight" response, which
leads to the release of adrenaline and other hormones that can help

someone outrun an enemy, a situation men would have encountered more often than women during evolutionary times. But frequent doses of these hormones can lead to hypertension and blood vessel damage. This is another example of how men's physiology is designed for the "sprint," while women are built to last for the "marathon."

THE ESTROGEN EDGE

Women, on the other hand, are still cruising around the track in their fifties and early sixties, with relatively few hurdles in their way. Since puberty and the beginning of menstruation, they have been producing large amounts of estrogen, which has beneficial effects on cardiovascular health, including lower total cholesterol levels, lower LDL cholesterol, and increased HDL cholesterol. John Hokanson and his colleagues at the University of Washington have found that the activity of a liver enzyme called hepatic lipase is 50 percent higher in men compared to women. Estrogen appears to lower hepatic lipase activity, which in turn leads to a dramatic lowering of LDL and an increase in HDL cholesterol.

The "estrogen edge" provides additional aging benefits as a potent antioxidant. Damage from naturally occurring byproducts of cellular metabolism, called free radicals, has been implicated in several neural and vascular diseases of aging. Antioxidants like estrogen mop up free radicals before they cause damage. Emerging evidence suggests that long-term estrogen replacement therapy after menopause reduces a woman's risk of dying from heart disease and stroke, as well as reducing her total mortality risk. Estrogen therapy has also been shown in some studies to delay the onset of Alzheimer's disease, in which free radicals also appear to play an important role.

Because of their estrogen edge, women don't hit the heart disease hurdle until after the sixth lap, when women in their sixties begin to experience the cardiac ramifications of menopause. As estrogen decreases, women's cardiovascular systems become more susceptible to disease. Still, female heart-disease risk never approaches that of males until the eighties and nineties. Although women face the hurdle of cancer alongside men, their risk of lung cancer has been historically lower because fewer women have smoked. This may change in the coming years, as male smoking has decreased. The incidence of lung cancer among women has increased 400 percent since the early 1970s, primarily due to an increase in the number of women who smoke cigarettes.

GETTING OVER THE HUMP

Men face the steepest hill of the longevity marathon during their sixties and seventies. These are the years when cancer, heart disease, diabetes, Alzheimer's disease, and stroke are most likely to strike and kill, and they drastically thin out the numbers of men who can go on to the next few laps. During these two crucial decades, women appear much healthier than men by almost all measures.

But during the ninth and tenth laps—the eighties and nineties—we saw a new pattern occurring. The hurdles women had to vault started to come thicker and faster. Alzheimer's disease, stroke, and heart disease frequently blocked the path to 100 for women. But for men, the opposite appeared to be occurring. These same diseases had menaced men in the earlier laps of the male track. For the men who encountered them, they had been insurmountable obstacles that caused them to drop out of the race. But the men who had not run into these obstacles in their sixties and seventies seemed somehow "immune." As we had seen in our earlier studies, if men hadn't developed heart disease or cancer around age 80, they probably had avoided these diseases completely. They had run the most treacherous part of the race unscathed. Now, in a sense, the track sloped slightly downhill for men, and became easier to negotiate. We began to speak of them as having "gotten over the hump."

We had already seen evidence of this phenomenon in our study of 5,000 older people in nursing homes and the community. As a group, men who had survived into their nineties had better average cognitive function than men in their seventies or eighties. We reasoned that this was because most men with dementia died before reaching extreme old age. Cognitive function appeared to be an important "demographic selection" factor that determined which men would get over the hump into old age.

In contrast, women in their nineties had not undergone the same demographic selection process. Women with all levels of cognitive function were able to survive past the end of the ninth lap, because declining cognitive health did not kill women as readily as it did men.

In early 1998, we decided to compare the women and men in the NECS and see whether there was a significant difference in health between the two groups. Using a small representative subsample of 5 men and 28 women, we found that 80 percent of the men were able to function independently, physically and mentally. Meanwhile, only 18 percent of the women were independent, and those remaining required anywhere from minimal to maximum assistance; 36 percent were very or totally dependent on their caregivers for help with activities of daily living. In fact, when we looked at the results of our cognitive testing, we found that none of the men in our study had severe dementia, whereas women suffered from all levels of dementia, mild, moderate, and severe. Almost a third of centenarian women suffered from severe dementia.

The field had reversed. While women were healthier than men from their fifties through to their eighties, during the tenth lap there was a "gender crossover." Now the remaining men, although significantly smaller in number, were much healthier than women, because all the unhealthy men had been culled out.

Men who "get over the hump" are aging stars, gifted with a much lower risk of heart disease, dementia, cancer, or other chronic diseases. They reach extreme age because they effortlessly vault over the obstacles that force other men out of the longevity marathon. Women, we were beginning to see, do not need to age quite as well as men in order to live to 100. They can survive with some illnesses. But for men to remain in the longevity marathon, they have to be all-star aging athletes.

MORE MYTHS THAN FACTS

We were getting used to the fact that so many of our assumptions about aging were turning out to be false. Most of the important issues of male-female differences were already clouded by myth and stereotype.

Some researchers have proposed, for example, that men's shorter lives were due to stress in the workplace and other battlefields, both real and metaphorical. Women, they argue, are comparatively sheltered from the physical and emotional damage wrought by "the real world." Others have suggested that, whereas men tend to shut themselves off from others emotionally, women gain strength from their ability to manage and maintain relationships. At one time, women's strong ties to family members and friends were viewed as pathological deviations from the male "norm" of isolated stoicism. Psychology textbooks preached that normal human development required the achievement of personal autonomy.

More recently, Jean Baker Miller of the Stone Center at Wellesley College and Carol Gilligan of Harvard University have proposed models of healthy female development that emphasize the maintenance of interpersonal connections and relationships. In this vein, contemporary health research has recognized that isolation from friends can be detrimental to your health throughout the life cycle and in old age may even be lethal. As their siblings and contemporaries begin to die, both men and women depend heavily on friends and younger relatives. Curiously, however, we noted that a healthy wife could pull her husband along for a lap or a lap-and-a-half. And once her spouse died, she was usually able to continue the race independently.

Men, however, seemed even more dependent on relationships than women. Any man who wants to live to 100 must be behaviorally suited to getting over the personal losses that women seem to survive more easily. If a man's wife lives along with him to extreme old age, that would probably improve his chances significantly. Although we had met several lifelong single female centenarians, all of the men in our study had been married at some point in life, and many of our oldest men had enjoyed 70- and 80-year marriages. This stable companionship probably helped these men age much more successfully. But the loss of a wife is usually too high a hurdle for men to clear.

We were willing to accept that women take better care of themselves. Some research has shown that women eat lower fat diets than men, which would tend to limit heart disease and colon cancer, and that they are more likely to use sunscreen, thereby preventing skin cancer. Although women get short shrift in the research arena, they may recognize and seek treatment for health problems sooner than men. A higher rate of early treatment could explain in part why women live with diseases that tend to kill men. Unfortunately, most of these behaviors, particularly diet, have been difficult to document. And a 1998 article in the *New England Journal of Medicine* demonstrated that when men's higher rate of mortality was taken into account, men and women actually spend about the same amount on health care. Another assumption falls by the wayside.

In our studies of the centenarian personality, we saw that centenarian women possess stress-shedding personalities, which we suspected were so important to successful aging. We also saw that many of them had religious beliefs that seemed to buoy spirits and help ward off despair. However, there were so many more women than men among the centenarians that it was difficult to make accurate, statistically meaningful comparisons between males and females.

We saw that only the most clear-cut, obvious differences between the sexes would help us come to any reliable conclusions about female longevity. First, we had to consider the effects of sex hormones. Men make significantly more testosterone than women, and women make more estrogen than men, at least until menopause. These hormones are responsible for a significant portion of the differences between male and female physiology, and temperament as well. They also appear to have a dramatic effect on how people perform in the longevity marathon.

Current studies, such as the U.S. Women's Health Initiative, have been designed to illuminate the relationship between estrogen, heart disease, cancer, Alzheimer's disease, osteoporosis, and death. The relation between sex hormones and mortality patterns is still speculative. However, menopause and the resulting loss of estrogen production may be associated with the onset of a variety of negative health effects, including cognitive changes, such as memory and concentration problems. Our cognitively intact centenarian women like Anna Morgan and Angelina Strandal indicated that at least some women can do just fine for 40 to 50 years with reduced estrogen levels.

LOW-IRON MAIDENS

Until now, researchers studying slow aging and cardiovascular disease resistance in premenopausal women have focused on the role of estrogen. However, we and a few other scientists are evaluating the potentially significant effects of menstruation, which may impact longevity in ways never before considered. With the monthly shedding of the uterine lining, premenopausal women typically have a significantly lower iron load in their bodies than men. Since iron ions are essential for the formation of free radicals, a lower iron burden could lead to a slower rate of aging, reduced cardiovascular disease, and decreased susceptibility to other age-related diseases in which free radicals play a role.

Iron is a vital nutrient required by red blood cells to transport oxygen throughout the body. Physicians have traditionally prescribed iron replacement for premenopausal women with "iron-poor blood." It's possible that higher iron levels, which may have been considered "normal" only because they are common in males, actually speed the aging process. In studies at the University of Kuopio in Finland and the University of Minnesota Medical School in Minneapolis, male volunteers who made frequent blood donations showed heightened resistance to the oxidation of LDL cholesterol—a key step in the development of atherosclerosis and heart disease. The blood loss of menstruation could be as important in combating oxidation as estrogen is, if not more so.

If our efforts and those of the Nurses' Health Study—which is now considering the link between iron levels and oxidative damage—bear out our theories, it could have important implications for iron replacement therapy, and treatment of diseases of aging. Although dietary iron is of great importance in children to ensure adequate red blood cell production, it may turn out that adults, and perhaps even adolescents, are speeding up their aging clocks by maintaining iron levels that are now considered "normal," but may in fact be excessive. Iron supplementation for premenopausal women may go the way of general anesthesia during childbirth. Regular blood donation, which lowers iron, may turn out to be more than an altruistic act; for men and postmenopausal women, it may actually improve chances of longevity by reducing the rate of oxidative damage.

A MARKER OF SLOW AGING

The link between menstruation, reproductive ability, and healthy aging became even stronger when an unexpected finding cropped up in our study. As we looked at centenarian family trees, we checked birth dates of centenarian mothers and their children. One child's birth date stuck out. We realized that her mother must have been 53 years old when she was born.

At first we were skeptical. We had only heard of one person giving birth at such an age: A 61-year-old California woman had apparently convinced doctors to give her fertility treatment by leading them to believe she was 50 years old. But our centenarian had given birth to a child in 1949, long before the advent of neonatal intensive care units and sophisticated fertility clinics. This woman gave birth to a naturally conceived baby at an age that was practically unheard of. This certainly represented the outer limits of fertility, but it *was* possible. To be sure we were right, we checked the woman's birth certificate and other records, and subtracted her child's age from hers several times.

The mother-at-53 appeared at first to be an anomaly. But in the context of centenarians' slow aging, it made perfect sense that their reproductive systems would age slowly, too. If anyone can have a child at an advanced age, it should be a centenarian-to-be.

As we began checking the birth dates of more centenarians' children, we saw a new pattern emerge: About 20 percent of centenarian women had borne children past the age of 40. With the help of Dr. Ruth Fretts, an obstetrician/gynecologist at Beth Israel Deaconess Medical Center in Boston, we began to investigate whether centenarians differed significantly from the general population. Using death certificates from the Massachusetts Office of Vital Records and obituaries from the *Boston Globe*, we identified 54 women who were born in 1896 and died in 1969, and compared them with 78 women in our study who had turned 100 in 1996. Both groups had contended with the same social and environmental conditions, and had been supported by the same health care system throughout their lives. The only major difference between the two groups was that one group of women had died at 73, which was the average life expectancy for women at the time, while the other was still living at 100.

We felt sure that centenarian women were more capable of having children in their forties than shorter lived women. But would the study bear out our suspicions? The results that came back were persuasive: Only 6 percent of the women who had died at age 73 had borne children past their fortieth birthdays. Twenty percent of the centenarian women had borne children beyond the age of 40, and they were four times more likely to have borne children in their forties than women who had lived to age 73.

Interest in the study was tremendous. We were invited to appear on several television programs, including the *Today* show with host Katie Couric. We spent three days in the hospital's media office, barraged by reporters wanting to understand what this meant for the enormous population of baby-boomer women who were considering having children later in their childbearing years. Should women try to have children later in life? we were asked. The answer is no; having children is normally much safer and healthier for mother and baby during the conventional childbearing years. It's having the *potential to bear a child later* that's associated with longevity—not actually having the child. A healthy reproductive system after 40 is a marker of extremely slow aging.

The more we thought about this relationship between slow aging and an extended reproductive period, the more it occurred to us that slow aging might offer an evolutionary advantage. Women who enjoy more childbearing years can potentially have more children. Evolution invariably favors organisms that have more young, since they stand a better chance of passing their genes down to the succeeding generation. A woman who was healthy enough to bear and raise children for an extended period of time would certainly have the potential to have more babies than a woman who aged more quickly.

THE ROLE OF MENOPAUSE

All the evidence seemed to indicate that the estrogen-related and possible antioxidant benefits that characterize the childbearing years were a veritable fountain of youth for women. Why, then, should menopause exist at all? Menopause is all but unique to human females; there are a few examples of it in the animal world, specifically pilot whales, though their ovaries may fail along with other organs toward the end of life. Most other female animals spend nearly their entire lives with the ability to bear young. Reproductively, there is very little difference between a 60-year-old and a 10-year-old female tortoise. Both are able to reproduce efficiently. But the reproductive phase of a woman's life usually ends by age 50. Thus, she may spend up to half her life in a postmenopausal state. Why would human females have evolved in a way that allows the gradual reduction in midlife of what appears to be a health-giving hormone?

If our genetic and physical attributes were shaped by current forces, humans would probably be born with cellular telephones built into their ears. But the development of our current human physiology has taken millions of years of evolution. When thinking about the role of menopause, we had to put ourselves in the place of evolving hominids living hundreds of thousands of years ago. How could menopause have provided a survival advantage?

Previous observers, such as Steven Austad, author of *Why We Age*, explained menopause as an evolutionary accident that ancient humans had not encountered because of their shorter life spans. At the time that the human genome we've inherited was being assembled, they said, female life expectancy was so short that there was no reason for the reproductive system to last more than 50 years; most women were dead by age 40. As life expectancy climbed, certain components of the body proved more durable than others, their reasoning continued. The female reproductive system, with its monthly renewal, was more difficult to maintain than, for instance, the gastrointestinal tract, and it "ran out of gas" earlier than the rest of the body. For the average prehistoric woman, the resulting postmenopausal changes would have had no effect on health status.

On the other hand, although women surge ahead in the longevity marathon thanks to factors like menstruation and estrogen, they are also associated with a significant health threat: bearing children. While it allows us to walk on two feet, our upright stature has left the female of the human species with a tortuous birth canal. Birth in other mammalian species is relatively uncomplicated and accomplished independently, in part because the birth canal is straight. In humans, the birth canal is shaped more like a question mark. When it is time for the relatively large head and shoulders of a human baby to exit through this tight passageway, the situation can become dangerous. A baby that isn't correctly positioned risks becoming stuck, and if the problem is not properly managed, it may kill both mother and child. Numerous other complications can arise in childbirth that are potentially lethal to the mother.

In prehistoric times, childbirth may have killed as many as one out of ten women. Although the development of the field of obstetrics has diminished the risk significantly over the past century, childbirth remains a struggle, particularly for older women: A woman in her forties is four to five times more likely to die during childbirth than a 20-year-old. When menopause evolved, maternal mortality would have been much greater than it is today. Menopause was a lifesaver.

Because human children are dependent on their mothers for such a long time, continued health and longevity may enhance older women's contribution to the gene pool even when they can no longer reproduce.

This argument was first developed in the 1950s by Doris and George Williams, now at the State University of New York at Stonybrook, and since then numerous anthropologists have debated the point.

A 1998 article in the journal *Nature* by Craig Packer, Marc Tatar, and Anthony Collins showed that in wild populations of both lions and baboons, mothers usually lived just long enough to raise their own offspring. Those grand-lionesses and grand-monkeys that survived might help, but their help did not determine whether their grandchildren thrived. It is difficult to apply these results to the human situation. The grand-lionesses and grand-baboons in the study were all still mothers themselves; only 6 percent of the grandparent animals had stopped ovulating prior to death, and none for more than two years. The remaining females died while they were still reproductively active. These grandparent lions cannot be compared to human grandmothers, who may spend up to 40 or 50 years of their lives in a postmenopausal state. It was hard to see how lions and monkeys could be equated with humans.

A more appropriate example is the pilot whale, one of the few animal species in which females are known to spend a significant proportion of their life span in the equivalent of menopause. Like women, pilot-whale females expend a significant amount of energy rearing offspring: mothers suckle their young for up to 14 years after each birth. Perhaps, we thought, the whale's "menopause" is also adaptive. A number of years without reproduction would allow an older animal to continue nursing a maturing whale without the effort and risks of bearing new offspring. Menopause would help to ensure the survival of the existing offspring.

Because the postreproductive period lasts so long in humans, grandmothers can contribute significantly to caring for children, too. In her studies of northern Tanzanian Hadza hunters, Kristen Hawkes found that grandmothers were instrumental in feeding and caring for their sons' and daughters' children. While men hunted for sporadic game, the grandmothers dug up tubers that were their grandchildren's most reliable food source. The nourishment and care grandmothers provided allowed their children to have babies at more frequent intervals. In this study, children and grandchildren of long-lived women had an advantage over children of women who died young.

Contrary to Austad's viewpoint, we saw that menopause provided a survival advantage for the woman herself, as well as an increased opportunity to ensure the survival of her children. It has been noted that a species' life span is roughly correlated with the length of time that its young remain dependent on adults. When a significant, long-term investment of energy is required to ensure the survival of offspring, evolution favors longevity—in particular, female longevity. If offspring require a significant maternal investment of time and energy to survive—which human children most certainly do—then there probably comes a point in a woman's life when it is more efficient to pass on her genes by caring for the children and grandchildren she already has than by producing and nurturing more children, thereby risking death and the death of her existing children in the bargain.

Longer life spans afford women an opportunity to bear more children, as well as to assure their survival. The need to insure the survival of more children to reproductive age led to the selection of genes that extended female life span. Longevity-enabling genes are inherited by men as well as women, but it is women who are evolutionarily responsible for the life span of the human species.

At first glance, it would seem to follow that longer-lived men would also have an evolutionary advantage in passing on their genes. But primate studies suggest that males' reproductive capacity is determined less by their length of life than by access to females. This stands to reason, since men can pass on genes to many offspring simultaneously, while women can only distribute their genes to children that they sequentially bear and successfully rear to sexual maturity. Consequently, ensuring that genes are passed on is a much more time-consuming activity for women, whereas men's ability to procreate is governed by opportunity. So the survival of a man's children depends not so much on how long he lives as on how long the children's mother lives. Males, it appears, are simply "carriers" of longevity-enabling genes; they may or may not achieve longevity themselves, based on their behavior and life circumstances. But the reason they've inherited the capability is primarily to pass it along to their daughters.

These findings correlate with studies that show a similar role for female longevity in fruit flies. Selectively breeding female fruit flies that bear young at later and later ages produces extremely long-lived flies. In contrast, selective breeding of long-lived male fruit flies has no cumulative effect on life span.

Perhaps chromosomal differences between men and women also affect their mortality rates. The X and Y chromosomes that determine sex can carry genetic mutations that cause a number of life-threatening diseases, including muscular dystrophy and hemophilia. Because women have two X chromosomes, a female with an abnormal gene on one of her X chromosomes can use the normal gene on the other and thereby avoid such diseases. Men, in contrast, have one X chromosome and one Y chromosome (which carries very little genetic information), and cannot rely on a backup if a gene on one of the sex chromosomes is defective. This disadvantage began sounding more ominous when, in 1985, researchers at Stanford University reported the discovery on the X chromosome of a gene critical to DNA repair. If a man has a defect in this gene, his body's ability to repair the mutations that arise during cell division could be severely compromised. The accumulation of such mutations is thought to contribute to aging and disease.

Women's second X chromosome may itself contribute to longevity. Though one of the two Xs is randomly inactivated early in life, this "dead" X chromosome seems to become more active with increasing age. It may be that genes on the "dead" X come to life and compensate for genes on the first X that have been lost or damaged over time. This compensation could have a sizable effect, as it appears that roughly 5 percent of the human genome may reside on the X chromosome. In recent years, the X chromosome has also become the focus of the search for genes that might directly determine human life span.

These genetic differences could explain why women attain extreme old age so much more frequently than men. Perhaps men need to be aging superstars to live to 100 because they lack some genetic push with which women are endowed. This sex-linked aging boost could explain why women had lasting power in the longevity marathon, while men seem unable to live to 100 and beyond without virtual freedom from disability.

We had shown that women aged better than men, and that they deserved our attention as models of how to progress to extreme old age, despite the depredations of disease, dementia, and social disadvantages. We had collected evidence indicating that women were perhaps genetically designed to age well. And, almost without realizing it, we had progressed through our studies of male-female differences, and into the very nature of aging itself. Suddenly, we were faced with the possibility of a new explanation for why and how we age. But in pursuing this line of inquiry, we were bucking some of the field's most entrenched orthodoxy. At the time we were conducting our studies, most researchers believed that aging was primarily determined by individual environmental and lifestyle factors. Our suggestion that evolution and genes had their hands on the aging controls were not to be readily accepted, and we had a difficult task ahead of us to prove that it could be true.

5

A REVOLUTIONARY DISCOVERY

From left, Betty Colleran, age 70, pores over family photos with her centenarian mother, Elizabeth Stanton, age 100. Mother and daughter both show the signs of slow aging that typify people who have the potential to live to 100.

I T WAS AN AMAZING SIGHT: Tom Spear stood in front of millions of television viewers, comparing his golf swing with Phil
Donahue's. Mr. Spear's stroke itself was impressive enough; featuring an accurate short game, he shot an 84 to win a 55-and-over
tournament in his home city of Calgary in Alberta, Canada. But what
really caused viewers to gasp was not Mr. Spear's long game, but
rather his long life. Mr. Spear is 102 years old, but looks a healthy 70
or 75. He plays golf, he walks for exercise, he lives independently, and
takes care of his own home. How can this man, who remembers practically every day of his upbringing that started in the Northwest Ter-
ritories in 1896, still be this lively and active?

In late 1996, we asked Mr. Spear and five other centenarians to
join us on the *Phil Donahue Show* to help challenge inaccurate and
stereotypical ideas about aging. Mr. Spear and his age-mates were living proof that, in fact, longer lived people are not destined for dependency and nursing homes (only about 5 percent of people over age 65
actually live in these settings); that aging is not synonymous with disease; that it's not shock and stress that "age" people, but the response
to stressful events that can accelerate aging.

THEORIES THROUGH THE AGES

The most basic questions continue to confound our understanding of
aging. What is its underlying cause? What is the nature of the link
between aging and disease? Why do some people appear to age more
slowly than others, and what can we learn from that?

The predominant view among researchers has been that aging is the
result of constant, cumulative damage caused by disease and by-products

of normal metabolism, as well as toxins in the environment. They also believe that genes have little or no influence on the rate of aging and the predisposition to associated diseases. However, we had become part of a dissenting minority of scientists who believe that genes and evolutionary pressures exert superior control over how quickly people age, when they begin to develop age-associated diseases, and how long they live.

The confusion surrounding aging is nothing new; it has been misunderstood for all of recorded history. The Papyrus Ebers, thought to be written around the sixteenth century B.C., hazarded that the origins of aging were coronary in nature. A supposed "purulence of the heart" released toxins that corrupted the entire body. With its basis in Greek philosophical thought, Hippocratic theory relied on direct observation in its efforts to formulate a rational explanation for the causation of disease. Among its conclusions were that each individual receives a finite amount of life energy, or "heat," and that aging was the result of gradual and inevitable "cooling." Susceptibility to disease was seen as a by-product of the decline of an individual's life force and was thought to be an inescapable part of the aging process.

Further east, the ancient Chinese looked to the philosophical doctrine of Taoism for answers about aging. The Yellow Emperor's *Classic of Internal Medicine*, written between 200 B.C. and A.D. 200, held that the health and well-being of the human body depended on a balance of opposite principles, yin and yang. Disease, the aging process, and their manifestations were seen as the result of disharmony between yin and yang, while health and longevity reflected optimal balance between them. Consequently, those interested in living a long and healthy life needed to anticipate carefully the vicissitudes of yin and yang and avoid destructive imbalances.

Longevity and sex have long been linked. Taoists focused on simultaneously balancing and increasing *chi*, an ethereal counterpart to seminal and menstrual fluids. Taoists observed that these "life-force" fluids decreased with aging, and concluded that efforts to retain *chi* would be rejuvenating. They believed they would increase their longevity by bringing many partners to orgasm while the Taoist adept would "return the *chi* to the brain," by manually blocking ejaculation.

All over the world, enemies of aging have at one time or another advocated the consumption of animal gonads as aging preventatives. In fact, the shopping list alone for these life-extending nostrums would daunt the most seasoned chef. Examples include the testicles and hearts of lions and tigers, the genitalia of a wolf, the semen of a crocodile, and cakes baked in the shape of genitalia with magic spices. Of course, no such recipe has ever been shown to work.

The relationship between aging and death became clearer in the seventeenth and eighteenth centuries when mathematicians took up the question of life expectancy. Although it was empirically obvious that death became more imminent as people got older, careful record-keeping by mathematicians began to show how powerful and accurate the budding science of statistics could be in predicting life expectancy at different ages. In 1692, Edmund Halley, the name behind Halley's Comet and one of several seventeenth-century astronomers who turned to demography, used vital statistics to compute a life expectancy of 33.5 years for residents of the German city of Breslau.

In 1825, Benjamin Gompertz, a self-taught mathematician, made the surprisingly simple observation that death rates for all species rise exponentially after sexual maturity; in the time Gompertz lived, when human life expectancy was about 45, the rate of mortality began increasing quickly at about age 30. The Gompertz equation suggested that after a person's procreative abilities are realized or exhausted, fitness for survival drops rapidly. In the late 1800s, August Weismann, another pioneer in the study of aging, wrote that "there is no reason to expect life to be prolonged beyond the reproductive period; so that the end of this period is usually more or less coincident with death."

MODERN THEORIES

Modern theories owe much to this widely accepted view of aging, which mirrors the Gompertz equation's approach to mortality. Weismann was the first theorist of aging to articulate the notion that aging was the result of accumulated insults to living tissues. First, according to this line of thinking, the cells and organ systems themselves are damaged; later, when the defense mechanisms intended to protect cells and organs become disabled, damage continues unabated until the organism dies. As the Gompertz equation predicts, death rates rise at later ages as damage erodes and finally overwhelms the resources of aging organisms.

Numerous environmental sources of damage could be involved in the aging process. Ionizing radiation, toxic chemicals in the air and water, and certain common components of food all could be delivering infinitesimally small blows to our bodies which, when added up, might account for the gradual decline we perceive as aging. But equally important, if not more so, may be the dangers from within—substances our bodies use or produce constantly as part of life-sustaining processes, such as nutrition and metabolism.

One potential intermediary of age-related damage is a seemingly innocuous substance: glucose, the principal form of sugar used by the body. Just as sugar and honey stick to many different surfaces, glucose adheres to, or glycates, a wide variety of tissues. Heavily glycated tis-

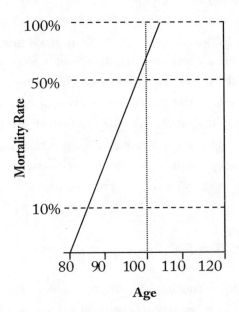

Gompertz predicted an ever-increasing rise in mortality with increasing age.

(SOURCE: RICHARD M. SUZMAN, DAVID P. WILLIS, AND KENNETH G. MANTON, THE OLDEST OLD (NEW YORK: OXFORD UNIVERSITY PRESS, 1992).)

sues become corrupted when glucose randomly binds masses of proteins. This "cross-linking" process—so-called because it binds protein parts that normally operate independently of one another—destroys the proteins' ability to function normally.

The effects of excess glucose are painfully apparent in diabetes, a disease that robs the body of the ability to control the level of sugar in the bloodstream. When people with diabetes fail to take the necessary measures to control their blood sugar, the excess glucose in the system plays havoc with vulnerable tissues, particularly in the eyes, nerves, kidneys, and heart. Diabetes researchers suspect that proteins in these tissues may suffer from the cross-linking that takes place as a result of high sugar levels.

A similar process may occur in aging, as, for many people, the body loses its ability to control blood sugar levels, and glucose accumulates over time. We've found that diabetes is almost nonexistent among centenarians, showing directly how important good blood sugar control is to longevity. Among 169 NECS participants, thus far there have been only six study members with diabetes.

Over the years, other candidate compounds have emerged as possible causes of aging. In the late 1970s, researchers began analyzing the composition of a yellowish pigment called "lipofuscin" that was originally found in brain cells. Every living thing seemed to have some of the pigment, from the prokaryotes and protozoa at the bottom of the evolutionary ladder, all the way to primates and humans at the top rung. Particularly intriguing was the observation that, in all known forms of life, levels of lipofuscin appeared to increase as organisms get older; thus it has been called "the aging pigment." A variety of metals have been found in lipofuscin, including mercury, aluminum, iron, copper, and zinc. Some or all of these metals may speed harmful oxidative processes. By accelerating the process of oxidation, lipofuscin may interfere with the efficient functioning of cells.

Oxidation begins when a molecule with an unpaired electron—a so-called "free radical"—attempts to bind an electron from another molecule. The free radical is like a roguish bachelor: Without a mate, it attempts to find another electron with which to bond. Dangling its unpaired electron in front of weakly bonded proteins, it eventually finds an electron that will break its bonds to pair with it. The protein that loses the electron to the free radical has been oxidized, or corrupted, just like a piece of rusted metal. Having lost one of its components, it may no longer be able to function optimally.

OXYGEN MENACE

Oxidation occurs constantly throughout the body, and many researchers have focused on it as a primary process in aging, for several reasons. Oxidative damage increases as organisms age. Raj Sohal and Sanjiv Agarwal found that three-month-old rats were better able to resist oxidation than 22-month-old rats. Species with longer life spans sustain lower rates of oxidation damage. When researchers compared five species, they found that the longer the life span, the more resistant the animal was to oxidative damage. One way to reduce the level of oxidative damage in animals is to feed them starvation diets. Coincidentally, such diets have been found to be one of the most reliable ways to increase animals' life spans.

A free radical can disrupt tissues throughout the body. Once it has destabilized one protein, a chain reaction occurs in which molecules "steal" electrons from one another, leaving many of them nonfunctioning. Proteins are the bricks and mortar from which the body is built. When proteins oxidize, they begin to deform and cease functioning normally, just as an old brick may start to crumble after years of exposure to wind and water. Frequently, free radicals will also degrade DNA, which acts as the blueprint for the body's proteins. When this happens, cells encounter increasing difficulty replacing damaged proteins, and their integrity drops even further.

Oxygen, probably the most crucial element required by living organisms, is also one of the most toxic because different forms of it so often carry free radicals. Cells generate these free radicals as waste products, but these potent substances also perform useful functions for the body. Macrophages, a type of white blood cell, generate hydrogen peroxide, a particularly toxic free radical, as a weapon for killing invading organisms. This is the same substance people use to bleach their hair; it works so well because it "cooks" protein, just like sunlight and heat. Sometimes, however, hydrogen peroxide and other free radicals leak out of damaged macrophages, and free radicals can damage the body they're designed to protect.

All plants and animals have developed mechanisms to ward off oxidative damage. Red blood cells, for instance, which ferry oxygen from lung membranes to cells throughout the body, contain hemoglobin, a molecule that acts specifically to prevent oxygen from harming other tissues. Cells are able to generate defenses against free radicals, such as superoxide dismutase, an enzyme that swallows up the unpaired electron without becoming destabilized itself. A number of components of a normal diet retard damage from free radicals, such as vitamin E and the mineral selenium. When researchers raise the level of these defense mechanisms in animals, their life spans increase.

Yet even this elaborate protective system has its flaws, and the free radical onslaught on proteins continues throughout life. Theoretically, damage from free radicals accelerates quickly as the body's defenses abate, along the same exponential curve described by the Gompertz equation. When considered together, the rate of accumulation of free radicals and the Gompertz equation present a nice, neat theoretical package: Mortality exponentially increases as damage increases.

As our study progressed, however, that package began to unravel. Our first indication of an inconsistency was the relative health of our centenarians, like Celia Bloom and Edward Fisher. We had already collected evidence showing that centenarians were, in many ways, healthier than people 20 and 30 years their junior. Rather than accumulating damage, they were shedding it like water from a duck's back. For instance, we had already found that men in their nineties were less likely to suffer from Alzheimer's disease than those in their eighties. Why hadn't they accumulated more brain damage than their younger counterparts?

By the same token, if we were to follow the theoretical Gompertz curve in death rates, we should see the curve rise sharply in extreme old age, as the agents of damage rapidly overwhelm the body's defenses. Mortality rates should increase by roughly three times between ages 95 and 110. However, demographers Vaino Kannisto, Robert Thatcher, and James Vaupel observed a different pattern in their analysis of mortality data from 14 European countries. Rather than an exponential increase in death rates between the ages of 95 and 110, they saw a more gentle upward slope.

The increase in mortality is only about half of what would be expected if an exponential increase in damage was the sole reason for aging and death. Mortality doesn't take the exponential leap; rather it slows down. Clearly there is a small but clearly defined group of people who are less vulnerable to the damage and diseases of aging.

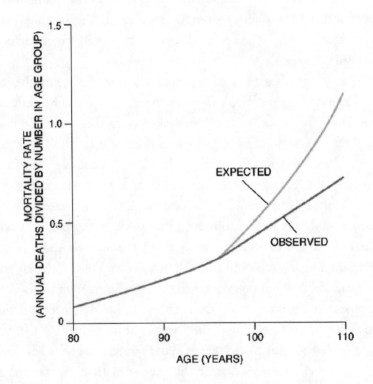

Mortality among the extreme old does not follow Gompertz's prediction, indicating that they enjoy some unique form of protection from the damage and diseases associated with aging.

This phenomenon is not limited to humans. The average life expectancy of fruit flies is about 17 days. In a population of millions of fruit flies all hatched on one day, the Gompertz function does a good job of predicting death rates for the first 20 days of life. Among flies that live longer, though, the same trend occurs that we observed among centenarians; mortality drops off, rather than rises. While the Gompertz curve predicts that all the fruit flies should die within 40 days of birth, a small percentage of fruit flies actually end up living for 100 days. Other researchers have seen the same phenomenon in experiments with worms.

When we called Dr. James Carey at the University of California, Irvine, to talk about the parallels between his work with fruit flies and

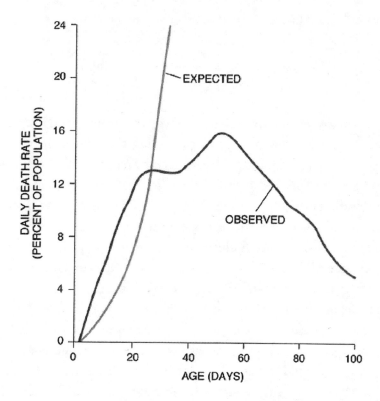

Gompertz's mortality predictions hold true for the majority of fruit flies, but fall short for those that achieve extreme longevity.

(SOURCE: FROM "THE OLDEST OLD," T. PERLS. COPYRIGHT © JANUARY 1995 BY SCIENTIFIC AMERICAN, INC. ALL RIGHTS RESERVED.)

our observations of centenarians, he was ecstatic. Carey agreed with the idea that, in any species, a small percentage of the population possesses superior protection from the damage we all incur as we get older. But what was that protective factor?

When we applied to government and private sources for funding, many of the researchers who reviewed our grant applications—and determined whether or not we would get support—were surprised that we weren't looking for the fountain of youth among centenarians. One scientist insisted that we measure centenarians' dietary intake of selenium, another that we ask centenarians about garlic.

Newspapers and magazines are full of fountain of youth prescriptions: hormones, extracts of gingko and garlic, yogurt. Fruit flies don't take any of these nostrums. Their variation in longevity did not appear to be linked to differences in diet or environment.

DESTINATION: CLEVELAND OR AUSTRALIA?

Something was clearly working in favor of the centenarians, paving their way to extreme old age by protecting them from the environmental and internal damage that afflicts the rest of us. Our experience with centenarians had revealed some common threads, but lifestyle choices did not seem to tell the whole story. People who made similar choices still died at average life expectancy. It seemed likely that genetic factors were also influencing the rate of aging.

Despite the popular belief that old age runs in families, many researchers have doubted there could be a specific set of genes that enable people to attain extreme old age. The argument goes like this: Genes don't "care" about longevity, because they're only concerned with procreation. Think of your genes as a convention of engineers who have all learned to build one airplane. Under ideal circumstances, they'd like the airplane to fly safely across the country, but their chief objective is to begin building copies as soon as their prototype demonstrates its ability to take off from one airport and land at another. The engineers build the airplane in Boston, board, and fly to Cleveland. Two engineers disembark and immediately begin building another airplane, more or less duplicating the craft they just left. They have no idea whether the airplane makes it to Pittsburgh, Chicago, St. Louis, Los Angeles, Hawaii, or Australia. They've reached the first stop, so they replicate the plane regardless of whether the design is sufficiently sound for a plane fit enough to fly across the country.

Evolution, the argument continues, isn't looking for airplanes that go to Australia. As long as the airplane successfully flies to Cleveland, the engineers can replicate it, and the same design will be used to fly to more cities and make additional planes. Similarly, as long as living organisms are sufficiently hardy to reach the point in life when they procreate, they and their genes will be duplicated.

According to this viewpoint, genes are not "interested" in what transpires after reproduction. There's no reason for them to care whether a person lives to 40 or to 100. Genes, the body's construction engineers, are not influenced by whether or how long the structure they have created is built to last. Consequently, there is no pressure to select for genes that confer longevity, and thus genes for longevity should not exist.

Researchers who believe there is no evolutionary role in aging cite examples of genes that are advantageous early in life, but become turncoats later. For example, type A personality, which is associated with driven, aggressive behavior, can be advantageous early in life; it spurs people to compete in work, in play, and in seeking relationships. Although a hard-driving personality is associated with heart disease, which is, of course, detrimental to longevity, it may also be useful in achieving the goals of job, success, and . . . having children. So genetic attributes that contribute to type A behavior would likely be passed on, despite their negative effect on length of life.

As persuasive as the "airplane" argument is, we had to reject it, or at least modify it considerably, because of the study of centenarians' fertility history we did along with obstetrician/gynecologist Ruth Fretts. As described in chapter 4, that study demonstrated that there could be an evolutionary advantage to longevity: A slowly aging reproductive system would offer the opportunity to bear more children, while a long, healthy postmenopausal lifetime would allow mothers and grandmothers to successfully rear their descendants to adulthood.

This was a signal that, contrary to popular opinion, there probably are genes that contribute to longevity, particularly in women, and the reason they exist is that they add to the number of potential childbearing and child-rearing years. To return to our airplane analogy, it is as though the aircraft engineers *do* know that a plane that lasts longer is a better airplane: An airplane that can reach more cities is more likely to be duplicated.

THE HAYFLICK LIMIT

Given the results of our study, we felt that we could not ignore the evidence for the role of genes in aging, which had been accumulating for many years. The first suggestion of a genetic role in aging arose from the experiments of biologist Dr. Leonard Hayflick. In 1962, Hayflick was a young researcher at Philadelphia's Wistar Institute. At the time, many scientists believed that normal cells could undergo an unlimited number of divisions when they were cultured in the laboratory, and Hayflick was curious about whether this was true.

In his laboratory, Hayflick observed a batch of human cells as they divided in a nutrient broth. When they approached 50 cell divisions, they began to slow, until they stopped dividing completely. The cells' last divisions were followed by a period without activity that Hayflick called "cell senescence," which then was followed by cell death.

Most scientists at the time believed that contaminants in the nutrient broth led to the cells' demise, so Hayfleck proceeded with additional experiments. He transplanted the nuclei of cells that had divided 50 times into younger cells, to see how many further divisions would take place. But when these older nuclei had been transplanted into them, younger cells would slowly divide only about ten times before halting. When Hayflick performed the reverse experiment, younger nuclei that had only undergone a few divisions before transplantation would allow older cells to undergo 50 or more divisions. The maximum number of divisions a cell can undergo came to be known as the "Hayflick limit."

Apparently, the cell's life span was regulated by a "clock" in the nucleus that lasted for a precise number of ticks. Hayflick suspected that this clock was located in the cell's DNA, and that what he had seen in the laboratory was not only a duplicate of what happened in the human body, but that it might represent the process underlying aging. Generally, the highest Hayflick limit among all the cell types of a particular species is an indicator of the species' life span. The mouse, for instance, has a life span of about one to two years and a maximum Hayflick limit of 30. Humans, with a maximum life span of 120 years, have a Hayflick limit of 70 or more.

The discovery inspired researchers to look for genes that control the Hayflick limit, and thus determine the dynamics of cellular aging and death. New information about telomeres may provide an answer. The telomere is a small tail of genetic material that lies at the end of each

It's Not Easy Being an Aging Researcher

Aging theories and skepticism appear to go hand in hand. Biologist Leonard Hayflick's observations about the nature of cellular aging began early in his career—so early, in fact, that he hesitated to publish his results for fear that he would be a laughingstock. In the late 1950s it was accepted that normal cells, which died and were replaced in the body, would divide an infinite number of times when cultured in the test tube. When Hayflick found that normal cells can undergo only a limited number of cell divisions, he was so concerned about his colleagues' skepticism that he sent cell samples to several of them and challenged them to replicate his results.

"They scoffed at the suggestion, but when they all telephoned us four months later to say that their cultures were dying, our trepidation vanished, and we decided to publish our findings," Hayflick later wrote in his book *How and Why We Age*.

chromosome, the large strands that organize a cell's DNA. Under a high-powered microscope, the chromosome looks like a twisted shoelace, with the telomere as the little protective plastic tip at the end.

THE TAIL WAGS THE CHROMOSOME

Chromosomes are filled with DNA, the most important function of which is to carry information. When a cell divides, chromosomes in the nucleus split in two, and each half carries one copy of the cell's genetic information to the resulting daughter cells.

Although telomeres are made from the same nucleotide base pairs that compose DNA, they have a distinct purpose, more closely involved with the process of cell division itself. Each time the cell divides, the telomere protects the chromosome as it unwinds, replicates and folds up again. Telomeres are also unlike the rest of the chromosome in that they are not copied in cell division. Chromosomal DNA is copied in full, while the telomere gets shorter and shorter until eventually, cell division and replication come to a halt.

There is a substance, however, called telomerase, that can maintain or lengthen the telomere. Some scientists believe that the gene for telomerase may play a pivotal role in how quickly or slowly cells, and people, age. In test-tube experiments, Andrea Bodnar from the Geron Corporation and Woodring Wright from the University of Texas have shown that adding telomerase to the nuclei of human cells increases their Hayflick limit and thus their life spans. Although we cannot conclude that administering telomerase to living humans will slow their rate of aging, this discovery illustrates the importance of genes to aging.

Interestingly, telomere shortening might actually increase life span rather than shorten it. Theoretically if we continued to have the same rate of cell division in our thirties and forties as we did in our teens, our cells would be more likely to become cancerous. Perhaps telomere shortening and, as a result, fewer cell divisions, developed evolutionarily as a defense against cancer. Consequently, increased rates of cancer are delayed into our forties and beyond, which is in fact when we observe that cancer becomes a predominant cause of death. If this theory is found to be true and telomere shortening does play an important role in aging, then aging itself may paradoxically allow us to live longer by protecting us from cancer!

The potential impact of genes on aging can be seen in a disease called Werner's syndrome, in which a specific genetic defect, discovered by George Martin and his colleagues at the University of Washington, leads to accelerated aging in children. These children are "anticentenarians": Very early in life they develop heart disease, cataracts, and other chronic diseases associated with aging.

If genes were involved in aging, especially in achieving extreme old age, we suspected that they would perform at least two crucial functions. First, they would allow people to age very slowly. In many interviews and testing sessions with centenarians, we had remarked to one another that not only did our centenarians look much younger than what we would have expected for their ages, but their children were extremely youthful-looking and vigorous as well. We had met a centenarian couple, James and Florence Hanlon, who were 106 and 101 years old respectively. Their son, Kevin Hanlon, was 70 years old, and still taking snowmobiling vacations above the Arctic Circle with his wife. His appearance was that of a man in his late forties or early fifties. Something was being passed from parent to child that retarded a predictable process in most people. A gene that preserved telomeres might fill such a role, but there was as yet no concrete evidence that this was the case.

Second, genes that allowed people to live to 100 would have to reduce the risk of contracting the common diseases of aging, such as diabetes, heart disease, cancer, and Alzheimer's disease. Heart disease and cancer are the two most common killers of people in industrialized countries. But we had already seen that centenarians lived so long, not by surviving these diseases, but by avoiding them until very late in life, if not completely. Some of the oldest centenarians in the study, those who lived to age 105 and longer, died of infectious diseases like pneumonia, or even household accidents, never having developed any of the chronic diseases of aging.

We were particularly intrigued by whether certain genes might protect centenarians from dementia, which has a dramatic effect on survival. The role of genes in Alzheimer's disease, which affects more than 3 percent of people over age 65, has long been debated. Some epidemiological evidence suggested that Alzheimer's disease is caused by environmental exposure to aluminum. Other research has implicated a mysterious infectious agent, called a "prion." Then, in 1987, Harvard Medical School researchers Rudolph Tanzi and James Gusella showed that a genetic defect was responsible for a rare, inherited type of Alzheimer's disease that affects only certain families. How the vast majority of Alzheimer's disease is caused remains unknown.

But in 1993, Alan Roses, then a researcher at Duke University, announced an interesting discovery about genes and the more common, nonfamilial form of Alzheimer's disease. Roses showed that certain variants of a gene, called "apo-E," were associated with greater susceptibility to Alzheimer's disease. Apo-E is the gene responsible for making apolipoprotein-E, a molecule that transports fats and cholesterol through the bloodstream. A person who inherits one copy of the e4 variant of the gene from each parent has eight times the risk of developing Alzheimer's disease than the general population. In Roses's study, these people began displaying symptoms at an average age of 68. The e3 gene variant was associated with a slightly lower risk of Alzheimer's disease than the e4 variant. Alzheimer's disease patients with two copies of this variant showed symptoms around age 75. People who possess two copies of the e2 gene variant may have the least risk. It was reasonable to assume that, although the e4 variant probably isn't the sole cause of Alzheimer's disease, it may significantly speed the disease process in comparison with the other apo-E variants.

Later that same year, we collaborated with Bradley T. Hyman, a Massachusetts General Hospital neuropathologist, in looking for this gene variant in the DNA of healthy people who were then 90 to 103 years old. We found that the e4 variant is rare among these long-lived people; only 14 percent had at least one copy of the e4 gene variant. These genes could have allowed these people to escape or at least delay Alzheimer's disease, one of the most common causes of death among the elderly. But how?

As our studies progressed, we theorized that apo-E variants represent a link between damage and genetic theories of aging. It seems likely that damage from free radicals plays a role in Alzheimer's disease, since vitamin E, an antioxidant, has been shown to delay the disease's onset. Perhaps the e4 variant of the apo-E gene codes for a protein that renders cells more susceptible to free radical damage. The e2 and e3 variants of the gene appear to code for proteins that are less susceptible to oxidation.

We began to consider other evidence for the role of genes in preventing the damage that leads to aging. Heat-shock genes were originally discovered because they are activated when cells are exposed to high temperatures. Further studies showed that different types of heat-shock genes respond to all different kinds of stress, like cold, low oxygen levels, and toxins. When these genes become activated, they produce heat-shock proteins, sometimes called "chaperone" proteins because of the function they serve. Heat-shock proteins shield other proteins from damage, preserving their individual three-dimensional shapes, which are vital to their function. These protective proteins ensure that other proteins are delivered to the cellular sites where they're needed.

One heat-shock protein, called HSP70, seems particularly important for longevity in fruit flies. Young flies produce a lot of HSP70, but as they age it appears that they express less and less. Brown University biologist Marc Tatar recently showed in controlled experiments that the more HSP70 fruit flies produce, the longer they live. Tatar implanted extra copies of the gene that produces HSP70 in some fruit flies, and compared their life span with that of normal fruit flies. The flies with more HSP70 genes lived longer, but only when they were exposed to mildly high temperatures (98°F) early in life, which activated the HSP70 gene. The protection provided by the HSP70 gene appears to be crucial to optimum cellular health.

We had evidence that genes preventing protein degeneration and loss of function, as well as those that decrease relative susceptibility to disease, are important determinants of aging. Still, we held little hope that we would ever be able to find all the genes important to longevity.

Genes are normally found by looking for specific traits in populations. A classic trait is tongue-rolling: Some people can do it, some can't. It's very easy to trace the inheritance pattern of a tongue-rolling gene through a family, and separate those who have the gene from those who don't. Finding a gene that causes disease has often been compared to picking a needle out of a haystack, but it can be done if the needle is sufficiently shiny; that is, if the disease trait and the gene both stand out from the background. In the case of most diseases, as with tongue-rolling, a person either has the gene or doesn't have it. In order to find such genes, scientists seek out families in which many members have one inherited disease. A thorough examination of the family's genes will often show how the people affected by the disease differ genetically from their healthy relatives.

But finding genes that *protect* people from disease, as we theorized longevity genes would do, would be extraordinarily difficult. First, we thought, most chronic diseases of aging are multifactorial, and each could depend on the activity or presence of many different genes. In fact, most researchers assumed that healthy aging would involve as many as 8,000 genes. The sheer number of genes would mean that each would make only a small contribution to aging; it would be very difficult to distinguish them as longevity-enabling genes. It might be relatively easy to find 8,000 needles in one haystack, but in this case, the needles—the genes that we were looking for—would be so difficult to differentiate from their surroundings that it would be as if they were all the color of hay. So we still held little hope for identifying genes that facilitate longevity.

FAMILY SECRETS

However, as centenarians began to enter the study, another unexpected pattern appeared: Now and then we would enroll centenarians who had a centenarian brother or sister. Slightly more frequently, a centenarian would enter the study and tell us about a brother, sister, or cousin who was 90 or older, and still healthy. Family clustering of centenarians such as this was extremely surprising. Although we had been discouraged from looking for genetic factors for longevity, it was hard to deny what we were seeing. The idea that two siblings would inherit the same 8,000 genes so frequently seemed highly unlikely. If longevity were so securely bred in these centenarians and their siblings, it would have to be passed along in the form of a much smaller number of genes, perhaps less than 50; otherwise, the probability of two siblings sharing a significant portion of them was too small.

This observation radically changed our ideas about the genetic control over aging. If, as was commonly believed, there were thousands of genes involved in the process, the likelihood of any one person reaching 100 would be random. It was as though the plans necessary to build an extra-durable airplane included about 8,000 additional and unrelated modifications, all of which had to be communicated from one engineer to the next. Making sure that the new airplane followed all the design specifications of its predecessor would be very difficult.

But what if only 50 major modifications—or even fewer—were responsible for making a more durable airplane? The longevity inheritance patterns we were seeing encouraged us to think that we might be able to identify genes that determine the rate of aging and susceptibility to diseases associated with aging. These were genes that could either protect people from or predispose them to a broad range of conditions. Such genes could represent very powerful tools for studying aging and illness. If indeed there were a very small number of genes responsible for allowing people to age slowly and avoid disease, we had to begin looking for them.

We consulted Brad Hyman, the neuropathologist with whom we had studied apo-E gene variants associated with Alzheimer's disease. He cautioned us that it would be difficult to mount such a study. The tools of genetics were designed to look at genes associated with diseases; no one had ever tried to identify genes that make people *healthier*, and it was not clear that the techniques existed to do so. Moreover, just to begin looking for a small number of genes that conferred longevity meant that we would have to locate at least 250 centenarian sibling pairs, a daunting challenge. The demographer James Vaupel had predicted that only one out of 400 centenarians would have a centenarian sibling. The typical centenarian lives less than a year after turning 100, often dying before one can find out whether any siblings will become centenarians. One of our frustrations was the more frequent case of nonagenarian siblings who were in excellent health and appeared well on their way to 100 but were too young to enroll.

As it turned out, it was precisely those healthy 90-year-olds who made us realize that the study could work. As we had learned, people who live to that age in good health are excellent candidates to become centenarians, and they have a similar genetic complement to that of their centenarian siblings. We had spoken with many centenarians who had healthy siblings aged in their early, middle, or late nineties. These younger brothers and sisters would be credible proxy centenarians.

This discovery marked the beginning of the Centenarian Sibling Pair Study, which was launched in 1997 in the hope of establishing whether extreme longevity could be determined by the presence or absence of just a few genes. At this point, we have enrolled more than 50 sibling pairs, the largest such group in the world. In order to qualify, one of the siblings must be at least 98 years old. The other must be at least 90 years old and must meet strict cognitive and physical health criteria that suggest the person has the significant potential to live to 100. Centenarians throughout the world are eligible, and it was through the Sibling Pair Study that we found golfer extraordinaire Tom Spear and his 98-year-old brother, Wallace.

Even as we were beginning the study, researchers discouraged us from looking for genes that determine longevity. When we traveled to New York City to describe the NECS and the Centenarian Sibling Pair Study to interested geriatricians, we met with a colleague who reminded us of the prevailing opinion among researchers about the role of genes. Urging us to drop this line of inquiry, he pointed to the Danish Twin Study, a frequently cited work in aging research.

The Danish Twin Study used Denmark's excellent birth and death records to compare differences in the life spans of identical and fraternal twins born between 1870 and 1888. This is a classic way of determining whether genetics or environment contributes more to a trait. If genes determine the trait, it will be more conserved among identical twins, which come from one set of sperm and ovum and have identical DNA, than among fraternal twins, who grow from two distinct sets of sperm and ovum and therefore resemble one another genetically only as much as any two siblings. If environment has more influence, then there will be very little difference between the two groups.

The Danish study examined whether parents' age at death could be used to predict their children's life spans, and whether identical and fraternal twins were significantly similar or different in their own life spans. As our colleague correctly pointed out, the Danish Twin Study showed that only about 30 percent of longevity was due to genetic factors. This was consistent with the idea of a weak genetic influence exerted by thousands of genes that only promoted longevity indirectly. The results of the Danish Twin Study had important ramifications for health education as well: It provided seemingly clear evidence that individual behavior was more important than genes in determining overall health and life span. Our colleague cautioned that the publication of research that confused this message would erode public resolve to assume healthier, more responsible lifestyles.

We agreed, up to a point. Although the Danish Twin Study has been instructive, there are problems in applying it to the study of extreme longevity. At the time the study began, there was still only a muted sense of the burgeoning importance of centenarians. *The Oldest Old,* an authoritative text on longevity by Richard Suzman and David Willis of the National Institutes of Health and Kenneth Manton of Duke University, concentrated on people aged 85, with relatively few aged 90 and older. This is understandable given the rarity of centenarians at the time. The Danish Twin Study itself had only a few subjects who reached their eighties; there was no one in the study over the age of 90.

But people aged 85 and older are no longer considered the oldest old: These are people who may still die on the same schedule as the Gompertz equation. There's no evidence that they share the special protection from environmental and metabolic damage possessed by centenarians. So while these were valuable studies of aging, they did not address whether genetics played a role in the ability to achieve extreme old age. Genes still had to be considered an important factor.

Not long after that conversation, our research took a dramatic turn that all but convinced us we were on the right track. Our close monitoring of local newspapers in the eight towns where we recruited centenarians for the NECS yielded a fortunate find. There, on the front page of the Quincy *Patriot Ledger* was a photo of a 108-year-old man blowing out the candles on his birthday cake. And right beside him, looking on, was his 103-year-old sister. To most readers, it was just a cute photo—to us it was a gold mine. We rushed off to recruit the two healthy centenarians for the Sibling Pair Study. An even greater surprise awaited us in the family of Mr. R., as this very healthy centenarian turned out to be named. As we arranged to meet with him and his sister, he asked whether we might want to meet his other sister, who was 97. We were astonished. The chances of finding centenarian siblings in the newspaper were extremely small, made smaller still by one of them being male. But the chances of identifying a family in which there were two living centenarians and a 97-year-old sister who appeared healthy enough to make it to 100 was just too small to be calculated. Imagine our reaction when they told us it was too bad we hadn't arrived two years earlier when their 101- and 102-year-old sisters were still alive.

Soon, two more spectacular finds came to light: the P and K families. Both these families had relatively high numbers of centenarians, as well as other long-lived individuals. According to current thinking about longevity, it would have been all but impossible to find three such centenarian-rich families. Demographers implored us to be extremely careful about verifying the ages of each individual family member, to ensure the validity of our findings.

One afternoon, as we were on our way to a television interview for a show on centenarians, we bumped into Louis Kunkel, a geneticist at Children's Hospital and Harvard Medical School. In the late 1980s, Dr. Kunkel had pioneered innovative techniques to identify the gene that causes Duchenne Muscular Dystrophy, a rare muscular protein defect that preferentially afflicts young boys. As we described our centenarian families, Kunkel grew more and more curious. These sounded increasingly like the large family pedigrees he had used to find important genes associated with diseases. If we could obtain more information about the R family, it might be possible to conduct a detailed genetic study.

A few weeks later, we met with Ms. R., one of the younger members of the R family and an amateur family historian. Ms. R. lived with her mother and son in a modest apartment on a quiet street in Boston. She was a very young-looking 35-year-old woman. Her mother, Mrs. D., looked much younger than her 68 years, and informed us that she still worked full time, taking care of "old" people at a nursing home. As we sat in her living room, Ms. R. told us how she had grown interested in family trees, and how she had been keeping track of the lives of her relatives. As we questioned her and her mother about brothers, sisters, cousins, aunts, and uncles, the scene became almost comical, as Ms. R. and Mrs. D. told us about more and more relatives who had lived or were still alive at extreme old age.

When we combined the family's information with what we had gathered on our own, an impressive picture emerged. We were able to trace the R family back four generations to an ancestor who lived to age 94. We eventually identified 220 descendants. The five siblings we first identified have nine cousins 90 or older and seven centenarian cousins. Several of these nonagenarians are still in good health, and may well gain the centenarian status of their relatives. The remarkable patterns of longevity in this family strongly suggested that a few longevity-promoting genes were being passed along from one generation to the next.

The same day we met with Kunkel and his colleagues to report what we had found. The excitement in the room was evident. Just the existence of the R, P, and K families indicated that there were relatively few genes that dramatically influenced longevity—genes that could perhaps be studied in mice and later used to combat important chronic diseases of aging.

As we briefed Kunkel on our afternoon conversation, we realized that we had found even more evidence of a limited number of aging genes: There was a strong likelihood of family intermarriage by cousins in two of the three families. Intermarriage has often been associated with the development of harmful inherited diseases. For instance, Tay-

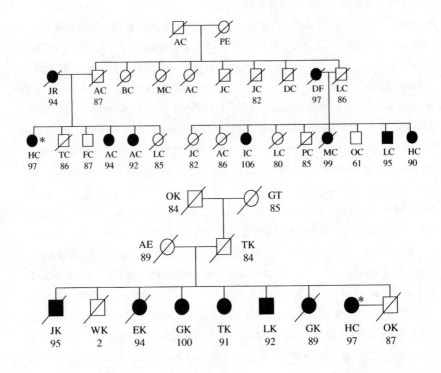

One of our key discoveries was the existence of families in which there was significant clustering of extreme old age, suggesting that it might be possible to identify genes associated with healthy aging. An abbreviated pedigree of the K family shows that seven out of eight siblings lived to very old or extreme old age. (Squares are men, circles are women, and a slash indicates that the person is deceased. Family members 89 and older are shaded.) As we collected more data on the family, we discovered that sibling O.K., at the bottom right of the figure, had married H.C. (noted by * in both pedigrees), a 97-year-old whose family also showed impressive clustering for longevity. Interestingly, these two families both originate in the same small region of Norway. We speculate that intermarriage at an earlier generation may have led to the predominance of a few longevity-enabling genes in these families, much in the same way that intermarriage can lead to the concentration of disease genes. We have observed such intermarriage in other families with clustering for extreme longevity.

Sachs disease, a debilitating neuromuscular disorder, probably resulted from continued intermarriage among Eastern European Ashkenazi Jews. We may have found a mirror-image case in which a positive trait, that of extreme longevity, has emerged as a result of intermarriage. This discovery reinforced our belief that a small number of genes—perhaps fewer than ten—might be responsible for extreme longevity in the R family. Our convictions were further bolstered when we met with Dr. Eric Lander, a geneticist and director of the Whitehead Institute in Cambridge, who suggested that if our observations were correct, we would be on our way to discovering extremely powerful and important longevity-enabling genes.

What we had seen on the *Phil Donahue Show* with Tom Spear had finally penetrated: Centenarians are different in a very fundamental way because of their genes. Although they are subjected to the same environmental and metabolic damage that the rest of us undergo, they manage to minimize it while avoiding the diseases of aging. And this accomplishment may be the work of only a few genes, perhaps fewer than ten. Did this mean that individual efforts to extend life span are worthless? That, until gene therapy can be provided, there is no point in adopting healthy lifestyles? We were left to ponder the significance of this for human health.

6

WHO WILL BE TOMORROW'S CENTENARIANS?

CREDIT: BRIAN WALSKI, COURTESY OF THE BOSTON HERALD

From left, Winifred Whynot, age 93, and her sister Catherine McCaig, age 102, are subjects in our Centenarian Sibling Pair Study. The study has already shown that siblings of centenarians have a markedly increased probability of living to their early nineties, in comparison with the siblings of people who live only to their early seventies.

IT WAS 1992 when we first met Celia Bloom at the Hebrew Rehabilitation Center for Aged. By the spring of 1994, we had begun enrolling centenarians in the NECS, and by the fall of 1997 we already had sufficient evidence to convince us that all our previous assumptions about the nature of aging had to be scrapped. In 1998, when the initial pedigree data from the Centenarian Sibling Pair Study arrived, we began our search for the genes involved in aging.

We knew there was much to be said about the importance of environmental and lifestyle factors in aging. Anyone who wants to live to 100 ought to leave the cigarettes in the pack. And the importance of occupational and environmental factors could not be denied; people working in proximity to ionizing radiation, toxic chemicals, or substances like coal dust would certainly feel their effects. Ample experimental and empirical data showed that toxic metabolites, particularly free radicals, inexorably degrade tissue over time. And most people in the field believed that genes played a limited role in aging.

By 1998, however, we had discovered the R, P, and K families. The appearance of heritable longevity in these families was enough to persuade us that the most important difference by far in a person's ability to reach extreme old age was genetic. We had met centenarians who ate unhealthy food, and some who had even been smokers for a time. Furthermore, if genes exerted little protective effect, we would not expect to see centenarians who had a history of significant toxic exposures. Yet, when we met Michael Makowski, the oldest man in Rhode Island, he told us that he had worked for years in a Pennsylvania coal mine and a Rhode Island shipbuilding foundry. Clearly, industrial poisons had not prevented him from reaching the age of 104.

THE POWER OF GENES

As our studies progressed, the picture became clearer. The strong influence of genes on aging that had been seen previously in a broad spectrum of organisms—yeast, flies, worms, and mice—had to be considered applicable to humans, since we had seen the power of genes in centenarians and their families. Certain genes, it appeared, helped people age more slowly and keep their health long after most older people began developing chronic diseases of aging or died. The few genes that conferred this ability had such a marked life-extending effect that we were able to see the pattern of their inheritance through multiple generations of family members. In some cases, the effect of these genes was so strong that it allowed people, like Mr. Makowski, to survive prolonged exposure to hazardous toxins.

We had to integrate our observations about centenarians and their families into an understanding of the interplay between genes and the environment. It was clear to us that even if a person was exposed to the worst of environments, the right combination of genes could still give

The Role of Genes

This graphic of The A.G.E. (Aging, Genes, Environment) Nomogram© illustrates how our research findings predict that genes play an essential role in the ability to achieve extreme old age. There are three crucial determinants of life expectancy: environmental exposure, genes, and the relative importance of environment and genes in determining life span. Lines A through E indicate a spectrum of this relative importance. If genes play the more important role (line E), a person endowed with an optimal set of genes (who would be found high on the scale at extreme right) would still be able to achieve relatively old age, despite exposure to a very poor environment (as noted by the scale to the extreme left). This would explain the longevity of persons such as Mark Makowski (represented by the dotted line) who was exposed to occupational toxins in mining and shipyard work. If environment played a more important role (as in line A), such a person would live a considerably shorter life.

the ability to achieve extreme old age. On the other hand, it would be very unlikely that a person without a minimum level of genetic advantage would be able to reach extreme old age, no matter how well that person controlled his or her environment.

Despite our evidence, the aging research community continued to have difficulty believing our results. It's not unusual for members of a scientific discipline to be skeptical about new discoveries, particularly when they contradict the prevailing dogma, as ours did. At one point, we were asked to write about our research on long-lived families for a textbook on aging. The editor admonished us not to include our data on the R family, in which we had found 21 first cousins over the age of 90; he told us that our academic readers would not believe such a finding possible!

Even some of our supporters were still afraid that the R, P, and K families were anomalies, freaks, or pretenders. Demographers working with us estimated that the chances of brothers and sisters living to the ages we found in the P family were about 1 in 1.5 million. The likelihood of the pattern of longevity we saw in the R family was ten

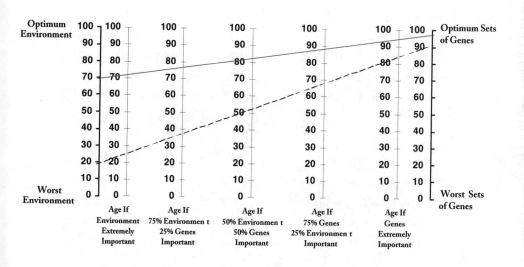

times greater. We had to show our colleagues that the potential for extreme longevity is genetically determined. We could support this assertion by showing that the blood relatives of centenarians also possessed a survival advantage. We needed to demonstrate the part that genetic inheritance played in these family constellations.

A stroke of good luck came our way when we were contacted by Dr. Leonid Kruglyak, a geneticist at the Whitehead Institute in Cambridge. Kruglyak is considered an expert in sibling pair studies, and he was eager to hear more about the Centenarian Sibling Pair Study and the R, P, and K families.

Kruglyak's spacious office overlooking the nearby campus of the Massachusetts Institute of Technology was not large enough to hold all the pedigree data we had amassed from our sibling pair study. We proceeded to a conference room on the institute's fifth floor, where we laid out sheets of paper on which were inscribed 40 centenarian pedigrees. Kruglyak was impressed. He concurred with our suspicion that the Danish Twin Study, which had supposedly established the subordinate role of genes in aging, had not enrolled sufficient numbers of extremely old subjects to draw conclusions about extreme longevity. We had collected more than 40 pairs of extremely old brothers and sisters in just a few months. Before Kruglyak sent us home, he suggested we analyze the statistical odds of such centenarian families occurring.

We compared the occurrence of centenarians in our families with the same set of families born in 1896 that we had used for the maternal age study. Again, we were encouraged by how strongly the analysis suggested a familial factor in aging. Centenarians were four times more likely than people who had lived to average life expectancy to have a brother or sister in their early 90s. In addition, the parents of these centenarians had lived an average of ten years longer than the average life expectancy of the population at the time they were alive. A striking 22 percent of mothers and 14 percent of fathers survived beyond 90 years of age. They consistently beat the survival odds.

We also attempted to determine the odds of a centenarian having a sibling who reached the age of 95 or older. Unfortunately, we continued to face the statistical problem of small numbers of siblings at such extreme ages in both the centenarian group and the group we were using for comparison. Nonetheless, we observed the trend that siblings of centenarians had ten times the chance of getting to age 95, and 15 times the chance of getting to age 100. These data were not statistically significant and were therefore questionable, but we are confident that as we enlarge both groups with more study subjects, we will confirm this observed trend. It appeared even clearer to us that centenarians had a much greater chance of having a sibling reach extreme old age than someone in the general population.

POSITIVE THINKING?

We of course were eager to use this data as proof positive that we had found families in which longevity assurance genes existed. When he saw our data, Kruglyak cautioned against doing so. The study showed that there was a *familial* factor in aging, he said, but genetics were not the only forces at work in families. Under most circumstances, siblings grow up together, go to school together, eat together, and share similar attitudes about life. Other longevity researchers would use that as a basis to dismiss our findings.

In the fall of 1997, we described the Sibling Pair Study and its early results at a meeting of the Gerontological Society of America. Skepticism was still apparent. Bernard Jeune of Odense University in Denmark, one of the strongest supporters of the Danish Twin Study, commented that he still believed that environmental forces were stronger than genes in extreme longevity. The strong familial connection we were seeing, he said, may have nothing to do with genes. Rather, he suggested the aging feats of centenarians had provided encouragement to their younger brothers and sisters that age 100 could be reached.

Of course, we had considered the possibility that an important component of the ability to live to 100 lay in attitudes and personality. But there was nothing in either the Danish Twin Study or our research to suggest that those effects would be limited to family members. The "encouragement" offered by a healthy centenarian should logically extend to everyone with whom that person makes contact, such as friends, coworkers (a few of our centenarians were still working), and health care personnel. We believed that the example of healthy aging would be more of a population-wide phenomenon—like Roger Bannister's four-minute mile—and less of a familial one. Like a rising tide, it should have affected the health and life spans of nongenetically related family members, too.

In fact, the people who would be most likely to share our centenarians' lifelong habits and benefit from their example were not necessarily aging well. These were the centenarians' spouses. If a shared diet or shared attitudes were responsible for the sibling's longevity, we should have seen at least some statistical difference in the spouses' length of life. But there was no visible correlation between being the spouse of a centenarian and living to extreme old age. As a group, the spouses' life spans were just average.

Our faith in the genetic explanation for longevity was further buoyed. In order to succeed in the longevity marathon, we saw, you need strong genes. Many people can get to the ninth and tenth laps through a combination of good genes and good "training"—a healthy lifestyle that includes exercise, proper diet, and antioxidant supplements. People who live to their seventies, eighties, and nineties in good health can make up for less protective genes by forming good health habits and by avoiding unnecessary hurdles, like smoking, excessive alcohol use, and sun exposure (as we'll discuss in chapter 7). But people who live to 100, particularly men, must have an extremely strong set of genes that protect them from damage from internal and external sources, such as free radicals and environmental hazards.

The families we had discovered, along with the sibling pairs, indicate not only a powerful genetic influence on aging, but also the involvement of a relatively small number of genes. The existence of a few powerful aging genes, and the possibility for identifying them, opens the door to discovering how these genes exert their influence, and even to understanding how the process of aging occurs.

In finding out how such genes might work, we were again probing new territory. In conventional genetic studies, scientists usually begin with a well-described disease, such as sickle-cell anemia, one of the first diseases for which a genetic cause has been found. Long before we had modern genetics, people were aware that sickle-cell disease runs in families. The symptoms and course of illness were well known. Physicians knew exactly what effect the disease had on the body, how the sickle cells affect circulation and retard oxygen distribution. Once it was understood that the disease was caused by a defective gene, it became simply a matter of finding it.

We decided to proceed in exactly the opposite direction. All that we had observed so far was that extreme longevity runs in families. We had observed some of the "symptoms" of extreme longevity: good health into the nineties; a notable lack of chronic diseases until just a few years before death; for women, the ability to bear children later in life; and a much higher rate of successful aging among women than among men. But, unlike our research predecessors who investigated sickle-cell disease, we had no idea what the "disease process" of longevity was. It was unclear to us how the ingredients of longevity-enabling genes would be transformed into a successful recipe for aging.

One recent discovery has given us a clue. In 1998, scientists at the California Institute of Technology reported their discovery of a gene that, when mutated in a certain way, allows fruit flies to live 35 percent longer than normal. In addition, flies born with a copy of this "Methuselah gene" live significantly longer than normal fruit flies when both are starved or exposed to the same levels of heat. Methuselah fruit flies also live longer than normal flies when both are exposed to the pesticide paraquat, which kills insects by generating free radical damage. This is further evidence that free radical neutralization may play a role in slower aging. But where would parallel genes be found in the human genome?

Obvious candidates were the mitochondrial genes. Mitochondria are the tiny organelles within cells that control energy production. Free radicals, the toxic by-products of metabolism we discussed in chapter 5, are involved in a wide range of diseases of aging, including Alzheimer's disease, heart disease, stroke, and diabetes. Free radicals have also been linked to the DNA damage that transforms healthy cells into cancerous cells. Research in Japan had actually found subtle, unique patterns in mitochondrial DNA among centenarians, although the group studied was small: 11 subjects. With our rapidly growing group of sibling pairs, we decided to create an arm of the study that would specifically look for mitochondrial DNA patterns that minimize the production of free radicals, or perhaps more quickly repair the damage they cause. This would help to explain why centenarians seem to be able to remain healthy longer than most individuals.

But what does this mean for the general population? If only a small percentage of humans have these genes, does that mean that individual efforts to live long and healthy lives are doomed to failure? Is each individual at the mercy of his or her genetic inheritance? We considered alternative interpretations of our study. Were we all born with an aging clock, just like Hayflick's cells? And were most people's clocks set to go off long before reaching 100 ticks? Or were our assumptions being clouded by the habitual view of aging, that extreme longevity was naturally rare and random? Perhaps the true image of human longevity would only emerge as other factors were removed from the picture.

Not long after we had begun collecting some of the more impressive centenarians of the R, P, and K families, Tom was explaining the study to soccer moms and dads at a Saturday afternoon party. One of the soccer moms looked to be in her early thirties. She was, in fact, 44, and had had her fifth child only two years earlier. A few of her aunts and uncles had lived into their nineties, she said, and her grandmother had lived to 101 in very good health. "Do you ever get faint in a hot shower?" Tom asked. This would be a sign that she had low blood pressure, a feature we consistently found in centenarians. The woman nodded. "Well, then, you're on your way," Tom said.

Tom's wife, Leslie, was also at the party. She had recently had a child, not long after her fortieth birthday, and remains in excellent health. Both her parents are still healthy in their eighties. She has low blood pressure, and she has always looked young for her age, which also seems to be a marker for potential longevity. Another woman at the party had borne a child at age 39, and her 80-year-old parents were in terrific shape. A fourth woman also had low blood pressure, and her grandmother had lived to age 90 in very good health.

It was an intriguing coincidence: Four women in one room, all of them showing, to some degree, the familial characteristics that we had begun to think of as predicting extreme longevity. This incident provoked even more questions about the implications of our genetic research, and the ease with which we had found the R, P, and K families. Was it possible that there were many more people with the genes for extreme longevity than we had anticipated?

Extreme longevity has been such a rare event because of the great attritional effects of neonatal death and infectious disease that were prevalent until earlier in this century. But public health measures, particularly vaccines and clean water supplies, have stripped away many of these causes of death. In doing so, they have unmasked the genes that facilitate longevity in more people. Many children who might have died earlier in life are now emerging into adulthood with longevity-enabling genes and may be able to live to old age, perhaps extreme old age.

The effect of improved public health measures and medical technology has not been to restart the genetic aging clock, but to allow it to wind down at a more appropriate time. In the past, the aging clocks of many children were stopped prematurely by infectious diseases and neonatal mortality. Earlier in our century, many more adults missed out on their later years or spent them in sickness or disability because of lifestyle habits.

Until we studied a cohort of people born just after the development of antibiotics and other lifesaving public health measures, we could not assume that longevity genes were rare. This was the first generation with the opportunity to live to its full genetic potential. We have yet to see how extensive that potential may be, but it's quite possible that we will see many more octogenarians, nonagenarians, and centenarians than anyone ever anticipated.

In 1997, the demographer James Vaupel predicted that one out of two girls born in Western countries from this time forward would live to 100. It seemed unimaginable. Now we were beginning to believe in the potential for many more people to achieve extreme old age.

COMPRESSION OF MORBIDITY

In our anticipation of a population explosion among the extreme old, we held a vastly different view of the future from that of other aging researchers. For years, longevity researchers and policymakers have warned that, based on the notion that people get sicker as they get older, increases of human life expectancy will result in an "expansion of morbidity"—a greater disease burden on the total population. The higher the percentage of older people in the population, the sicker the entire population will be, and the more expensive it will be to care for. In 1993, University of Chicago demographer Jay Olshansky wrote in a *Scientific American* article:

> Society will soon be forced to realize that death is no longer its major adversary. The rising threat from the disabling diseases that accompany most people into advanced old age is already evident.

What Olshansky seemed to be warning us about, along with Colorado Governor Dick Lamm, was that if we failed to face the natural limitations, we would become a nation of Struldbrugs. If we continued to push the outer limits of longevity, morbidity would expand to the point where it would overwhelm our country's financial and health care resources.

This image of older persons as "greedy geezers" sucking the lifeblood out of the economy drove important trends in medical practice and policy all over the country. In Oregon, legislation was proposed to put an age ceiling on some forms of health care. There was a strong undercurrent of opinion that we needed to "get real" about how much older Americans were costing us.

But a trend in the early 1990s put this idea of increasing illness with increasing age into question. Around the country, managed care companies had begun competing furiously for older patients, mounting huge campaigns, even hosting free dinner dances and handing out passes to golf and tennis clubs. Although clinicians and politicians were saying that hospital costs increase with age among older patients, these for-profit health care companies appeared to know otherwise. Why were HMOs climbing over one another to get at the older population? Perhaps they recognized that the resources needed to care for older persons had been overestimated and were trying to take advantage of Medicare reimbursement levels.

Then we saw something that confirmed our suspicions even further—a clear indication of not increased, but decreased health care costs in the oldest old. In a 1995 paper for the *New England Journal of Medicine,* James Lubitz of the Health Care Finance Administration looked at individual reimbursements received by 37.5 million Medicare beneficiaries up to age 95. As most longevity researchers might have expected, health care costs gradually rose as patients got older. This supported the notion that older people were sicker and more expensive to care for. Surprisingly, however, Lubitz found that proportionate health care costs plateaued at about age 75, or right around average life expectancy. From that age on, the older the patients were, the lower their proportionate lifetime health care costs fell. Average Medicare payment in the last two years of life for people who died in their sixties was $22,590, compared to an average of $8,296 for people who died at 101 years or older. Lubitz estimated that increased life expectancy could only be blamed for a

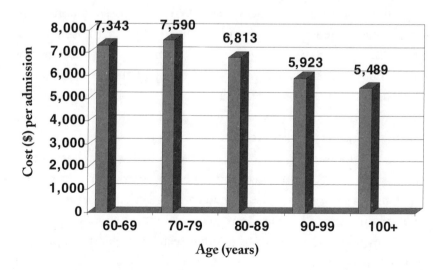

Contrary to expectations, acute hospital care costs actually decline after age 70 to 79 years.

small fraction of the rise in health care costs, about 3 percent. The much stronger influence on costs will not be the *age* of the baby boomers receiving Medicare payments, Lubitz predicted, but simply their *numbers*.

This study echoed exactly what we had seen in the academic long-term care facility where we met Mrs. Bloom and Mr. Fisher. They had experienced the vast majority of their lives in excellent health, only to suffer a brief period of poor health, or morbidity, near the end of their lives. We decided to investigate this compression of morbidity among the oldest old even further, to try to find some of the reasons for its occurrence. We looked at data from almost 679,000 hospital discharges in Massachusetts during 1992–1993. We found that the average total cost of a hospital stay was highest for patients between 70 and 79 years of age—bracketing the age of average life expectancy—and declined afterwards. The average total cost for patients in their seventies was $7,590 per discharge and for centenarians it was $5,489—a decrease of nearly 30 percent!

Why, contrary to popular opinion, did older patients appear to cost less to care for than younger patients? One main reason was that patients younger than 80 customarily receive or demand more intensive and thus costlier care than the oldest old. Younger patients were more likely to be referred to medical-school-affiliated teaching hospitals and tertiary care centers where the costs of treatment were substantially higher. Older patients were more likely to stay in cheaper community hospitals. Once in the hospital, patients aged 80 and over were also less likely to be sent to expensive intensive care units, or to receive heroic measures for heart attacks, strokes, or other acute crises.

We also found that expensive treatments such as coronary artery bypass surgery and organ transplantation were very rare or even nonexistent among nonagenarians and centenarians. Perhaps doctors are less willing to use the full medical armamentarium on frail, older patients. Or it may be possible, as we have often seen, that oldest old patients choose less aggressive treatment themselves, and more often instruct their physicians and nurses not to try to resuscitate them after a heart attack or stroke.

Several other factors may account for the decline in costs. Perhaps the oldest old were admitted for long-standing illnesses that had needed more aggressive testing and treatment at a younger age. For example, a 65-year-old with heart disease would probably undergo numerous tests to understand and characterize his or her condition. As time went on, subsequent hospital visits might not need to be so intensive, since the condition had already been diagnosed.

But it appeared that the most important reason for declining costs of care among the extreme old was that they simply were not as sick as younger patients. We compared patients' intensity of care using their ancillary costs as a measuring stick. These are any costs that the patients incurred—such as testing, drugs, physical therapy—that are not related to charges for room and board. Higher ancillary costs indicate that patients need more intense care.

Once again, our results contradicted what would have been predicted by the Gompertz curve. The percentage of total costs that were made up by ancillary costs dropped steadily from patients in their sixties onward. Among patients 60 to 69 years old, more than half the hospital costs came under ancillary care. For patients 100 and older, ancillary costs accounted for less than a third of their hospital bills. The centenarians didn't require as much hospital care as the 60-year-olds; they weren't as sick. This reminded us of the survival patterns we had heard about in fruit flies and the good health we had observed among centenarians. Now we had more concrete evidence of the oldest old's propensity to delay illness.

If a person has not developed certain diseases such as life-threatening cancer, diabetes, heart disease, stroke, and Alzheimer's disease, at the time when most others are prone to developing them, it becomes less likely with advancing age that the person will come down with these and other conditions. The oldest old are a select group of individuals who "get over the hump" because they are able to delay illness to a short period at the end of their lives—to compress morbidity.

In 1981, Stanford University's James F. Fries proposed the hypothesis that healthier lifestyles, improved medical care, and higher standards of living would compress, rather than expand, morbidity.

We had observed that most centenarians were healthy throughout most of their lives, that the vast majority remained healthy well into their nineties and sometimes into their hundreds, and that they frequently delayed chronic diseases of aging, if they hadn't avoided them completely. Almost none of our centenarians had suffered from life-threatening cancer. In fact, the only chronic disease we found commonly among centenarians was arthritis. A quick survey showed that, on average, our centenarians lived without disability until about age 97 and were taking an average of only one medication. When we asked families how long their deceased centenarian relatives had any form of disability before their deaths, their average answer was four years. This fit exactly with Fries's estimate that morbidity could be optimally compressed into 4 percent of the total life span.

From the first time we tried to slow Celia Bloom down long enough to take her blood pressure, we had been dealing with a fundamental challenge to the accepted notion that people get sicker as they get older. Fries's theories gave us an important insight into why we were seeing so many healthy people who were grazing the limits of the human life span. Their period of morbidity—the part of their lives spent in decline before death—had been compressed into the shortest possible time. They were living out the full extent of their genetic potential.

In other words, the mechanism for their longevity, or the closest we could come to defining it, was their compression of morbidity. Compression of morbidity is something centenarians do naturally in a variety of ways. Mme. Calment has been referred to as the Michael Jordan of aging because, despite some of her lifestyle choices, like smoking, she was still probably the longest-lived person in the history of the world. She was blessed with an incredible combination of genes that allowed her to attain this distinction.

If people want to emulate centenarians, they must imitate the centenarian ability to compress their period of morbidity into the last years of life. Not all of us are Mme. Calment, however. What centenarians do "automatically," we have to do "by hand." Therefore, we urge people to look into their family histories, determine whether their ancestors lived beyond average life expectancy, find the causes of death and disability, and make intelligent choices about how they can delay or even prevent the diseases that killed or disabled their predecessors. We include specific information in chapter 7 about how people can prevent chronic and disabling diseases of aging.

In fact, Fries recently demonstrated the ability all people have to compress their morbidity in the April, 1998, *New England Journal of Medicine*. Fries studied the health status of 1,741 college alumni who were first surveyed in 1962, when their average age was 43. Each participant's health status was rated from 1 to 3 on the basis of smoking, weight, and exercise habits. By 1994, when the group's average age reached 75, the importance of their health practices had become clear. People who exercised more, kept their weight down, and avoided smoking died later and became disabled an average of five years later than people with "high-risk" lifestyles. In imitation of centenarians, the "low-risk" subjects had compressed their morbidity, and given themselves more healthy years in the process.

People with an optimal combination of genes that affect aging can probably afford to relax and indulge themselves a little bit. They can place some trust in their genes' ability to slow their aging. But those who have family histories of cancer, heart disease, Alzheimer's disease, diabetes, and other afflictions should begin doing what they can now to compress inevitable illness into a small percentage of what could possibly be a very long life.

As average life expectancy increases, all of us must begin making important choices for ourselves. Will people be able to compress the morbid period of their lives, as centenarians do? Or will they end their lives in long periods of painful decline, the tendency we've seen among people who die in late middle age. If baby boomers want to avoid this fate, they must be prepared to use sensible measures to compress their period of chronic illness into the last few years of their lives.

7

YOU HAVE THE GENES, USE THEM!

What to Take and What to Do

Tom Spear, age 102, plays 18 holes of golf 3 times a week, and consistently shoots 15 strokes under his age. His club professional confirms that he can still hit a 3-wood 150 to 180 yards. Mr. Spear illustrates beautifully that aging is not a disease.

CREDIT: MARIANNE HELM

LIFE EXPECTANCY is lengthening, driven by new knowledge and prevention in heart disease, cancer, and other diseases, as well as by improvements in public hygiene, standards of living, nutrition, and other factors of modern life. But the gains society has achieved are still not as great as they could be. Average life expectancy *should* be 85, and it *would* be 85, if more people would take disease prevention seriously at a time when it is still possible to make an impact, and maintain good health habits for a lifetime. Unfortunately, the vast majority of baby boomers do a terrible job of preparing for old age. High-fat diets, smoking, excessive drinking, and lack of exercise not only reduce people's chances of achieving older age, they markedly increase the likelihood of a longer period of poor health in a shorter life. Yet many of us probably have the genes to get to old age and perhaps extreme old age. We just have to learn to use them.

The achievements of centenarians demonstrate that it is possible to avoid accelerating aging, and there may well be genes that slow down aging. Centenarians are the pioneers who have shown us the horizon of the human life span, and how to get there. But the prospect of such longevity presents an important challenge: Are people ready to do the work now to expand their healthy years, compressing their time of ill health into a very short period at the end of their lives?

The goal is not to make everyone a superbeing who can swim the English Channel at age 85. Rather, we want to help people gain more years of excellent health so they can do the things they enjoy or want to explore for the first time—like Tom Spear and his golf game, Lola Blonder and her painting, and Anna Morgan and her activism. But in order to do any of these things, body and mind must be kept intact. In this chapter, we're going to pass on suggestions, based on our experience and the latest research, for approaching the inevitable process of aging with care and foresight.

THE POTENTIAL OF ANTIOXIDANTS

Aging-associated diseases develop over many years. The damage caused by free radicals undoubtedly contributes to atherosclerosis and therefore heart disease and stroke, as well as to Alzheimer's disease, Parkinson's disease, vision problems associated with aging, various cancers, and rheumatoid arthritis, to name a few. The excellent research showing the effectiveness of antioxidants such as vitamin E and selenium in preventing or delaying many of these diseases has yet to make an impact on doctors' prescribing patterns. Unfortunately, the potential of antioxidants remains largely unrecognized by doctors and their patients.

Diligent use of these antioxidants, and others yet to be discovered, is our best chance right now to arrest or slow diseases of aging among people who are not endowed with excellent aging genes. Because they act in a preventive capacity, antioxidants should be used in appropriate amounts from early in adult life, to keep free radical damage at bay as long as possible. Most centenarians we studied did not have a history of using antioxidant vitamins or minerals, but it appears that their genes

Report Card on Baby Boomers

The Heart and Stroke Foundation of Ontario's Baby Boomer Report Card gives an indication of how few baby boomers are taking the necessary steps to compress their morbidity and live out their natural life spans. We need to improve our grades worldwide to live like centenarians.

Percent of Baby Boomers Who...	Men	Women	Both	Grade
Exercise Regularly	36%	35%	35%	F
Don't Smoke	63%	69%	66%	C
Are at a Healthy Weight	70%	65%	68%	C+
Have a Healthy Blood Pressure	72%	78%	75%	B
Have a Healthy Serum Cholesterol Level	42%	69%	55%	D

(SOURCE: COURTESY OF THE HEART AND STROKE FOUNDATION, 1996.)

allow them to age slowly and postpone the diseases of aging. Some of these genes may have potent antioxidant effects. The rest of us have no choice but to fight back with antioxidants and other sensible lifestyle choices to make up for our relative genetic disadvantage.

PRESERVE YOUR COGNITIVE ABILITIES

It is cognitive capacity, more than any physical disability, that most often determines whether people can attain extreme old age while remaining active. This is particularly true among men, as we saw in the Hebrew Rehabilitation Center for Aged (HRCA) study of 5,000 people between the ages of 60 and 90 (see chapter 2). No one achieves extreme old age without retaining a great deal of cognitive ability for the most of his or her life.

MEMORY

Several months ago, we were seated at a kitchen table with Alfred Benedetti, 102, and his 69-year-old daughter, Madalyn. He listened carefully through his amplifier as we administered a memory test involving numbers. After Mr. Benedetti rattled off the numbers, his daughter remarked, "I'm not sure I can do that. I wonder if I have a problem."

Madalyn worried about her memory. Many people fear lapses in memory and interpret them as the beginning of a decline into dementia and loss of ability to take care of themselves. In a recent study by Bruskin/Goldring Research, more than 80 percent of all physicians surveyed said their patients over age 30 complained of memory loss. And a recent study by the Dana Foundation found that nearly seven of ten adults have concerns about memory loss.

A surprising finding from our centenarian study is that worries about memory are greatly exaggerated. When we compared impairment in five major subcategories of cognitive function with ability to perform daily activities, like dressing oneself, we found that memory loss had less effect on independence than visual-spatial problems, abstract reasoning problems, or problems in what is known as *executive function.* Indeed, the factor that we found to have the greatest effect on independence is one of the executive functions known as "initiation," or the ability to plan and get started on a task. Retaining this ability was key to functional independence.

Also reassuring is that those occasional memory lapses are probably not a sign of dementia, but occur naturally throughout life. People often experience the tip-of-the-tongue phenomenon when a word won't come to mind, and this need not be interpreted as a warning sign of approaching dementia or Alzheimer's disease.

Another cause for optimism is that you can delay or halt processes that may lead to cognitive impairment. As we've found in our studies, genetics plays a significant role in determining the rate at which cognitive impairment progresses. However, there are a great number of things that can be done to preserve cognitive function as long as possible, delay the onset of dementia, and make the most of the cognitive function you retain. The time to start with this program is today, no matter how old you are.

MENTAL WORKOUTS

Dirk Struik is an example of how centenarians delay the onset of cognitive impairment. At age 100, the MIT professor traveled to his native Netherlands to lecture and to visit relatives. At age 101, he published an article on a new concept called ethnomathematics, and was writing his autobiography. Professor Struik is still studying, still thinking, still pondering old concepts and learning new ideas. He exercises his brain by organizing his ideas and explaining them to other people, either through writing or speaking. He and other centenarians practice instinctively what recent research on cognitive aging shows: Learning new things is the key to mental vigor. Learning stimulates the growth of dendrites and creates additional neuronal networks, which, as we saw in chapter 2, appears to be important for overcoming damage to brain tissue.

Centenarians preserve their cognitive function by engaging in mental activities that are interesting to them. Crossword puzzles (verbal functions), bridge (memory functions), and intricate jigsaw puzzles (visual-spatial functions) can help keep the mind sharp. Or you can follow the path of a centenarian like Mr. Barres, who, after retiring from a management job, started his own business and ran it until he was 101.

You can go beyond a daily "brisk brain walk" through the *New York Times* crossword puzzle and do mental strength training. Reading challenging books, learning foreign languages, or practicing a musical instrument can expand neuronal networks and build up functional reserve that will help compensate for aging changes. Even learning new dance steps can exercise the brain. In the Hawaiian city of Hilo, we met a remarkable group of elders who learned, practiced, and performed the traditional hula dance in a state-funded program. The intricacies of the beautiful complicated arm and hand movements that told a story were a challenging mind-building exercise. In addition, these elders enjoyed physical exercise, socializing, and the privilege of being the "wise ones," passing along tradition to the younger generation. These fortunate people glowed with health and well-being.

Activities that require coordination between multiple brain regions, like dancing, painting, learning a new language, certain sports, and particularly making music, produce multiple benefits for the brain, and make it more resistant to trauma and chronic damage as time goes on. Playing an instrument requires one to simultaneously read, listen, memorize, perform complicated manual activities, and in some cases innovate. This kind of complex activity gives the whole brain a workout and strengthens links between different brain regions. There is also a valuable relaxation component associated with playing familiar pieces that may reduce the impact of emotionally stressful situations.

We often discovered a piano in centenarians' homes. Many centenarians appear to keep these skills—music, art, writing—until very late in life; their ability to express themselves in these ways is often untouched by the passage of years. Playing an instrument has such potential importance that we have introduced questions into our study questionnaire that will help us determine whether centenarians are predisposed toward music.

In recent years, books that provide memory-improving exercises and strategies have begun appearing in stores. Several also provide programs for strengthening other cognitive functions. One of the earliest physicians to recognize the value of toning and strengthening the brain was neurosurgeon Vernon Mark, who has created a brain exercise program that challenges and motivates people. Based on techniques developed to help brain-injured individuals regain lost function, Dr. Mark's exercises can be easily incorporated into daily life. Here are a few examples:

- To keep *mathematics* abilities sharp, balance your checkbook without a calculator. Then use a calculator to check results.

- To exercise your *visual-spatial* abilities, draw the following geometric figure with your right hand, while timing yourself. Then draw it with your left hand. Again time yourself. Next try to draw it from memory. Keep practicing whenever you have a chance, like when you are on the phone. You'll notice substantial improve-

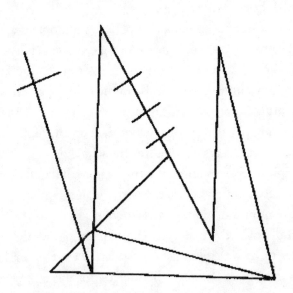

Copying this design (or other complicated shapes) can help maintain sharp visual-spatial abilities, like those of Anna Morgan.

ment, even with your nondominant hand. This activity also exercises your visual memory, as well as visual-spatial perception and construction (drawing) abilities.

GUIDED AUTOBIOGRAPHY

Several of our centenarians—Anna Morgan and Lola Blonder among them—were hard at work on or had recently completed their autobiographies when we met them. Autobiography is the essence of self-expression and lies at the core of all art forms, and there is no reason to wait until becoming a centenarian to begin. Writing an autobiography stimulates the mind by forcing one to integrate one's beliefs with past experiences and thus find meaning in life. Keeping a journal may serve the same function. It is among the most accessible forms of creative thought, and it is part of life review, which is a natural component of psychological development.

Originally conceived of by psychologist and gerontologist James Birren, "guided autobiography" is a group activity facilitated by a professional leader. The group provides feedback and support in facing biographical material that is painful to write about.

LATE-LIFE LEARNING

Learning never has to stop for anyone. Formal late-life learning can help preserve thinking abilities, and many older people are already doing this: Harvard recently granted a bachelor's degree to an 89-year-old woman. Adult education opportunities are numerous, and at least a third of American universities offer college and graduate level courses specifically for people over 65.

Educational travel programs are another source of new experience and knowledge. Elderhostel offers short-term residential learning programs worldwide to nearly a quarter of a million older students annually. Saga Holidays offers "Roads Scholar" programs that combine interesting destinations with lectures on history, botany, art, ecology, geology, and cultural traditions. (See the Internet Resources section at the back of the book for further information on these programs.)

MEDICATIONS

Besides brain exercises and continuous learning activities, there are a number of other preventive steps that maintain cognitive health later in life.

Nonsteroidal anti-inflammatory drugs (NSAIDs) like ibuprofen appear to prevent or attenuate the deterioration of brain cells. Over the last 15 years, researchers at John Hopkins University tracked the medications of 2,000 older adults. They found that people taking

Write What You Know

Although James Birren originally designed guided autobiography for people in old age, he has recently suggested that it would also be a useful exercise for baby boomers searching for ways to evaluate their life resources. People in midlife may want to use guided autobiography to decide how to allocate their time and energy in the future. For example, a person who spends 80 percent of his or her waking hours at work at age 40 might want to gradually increase the amount of time devoted to family activities and other pursuits.

Guided autobiography courses are offered at a number of adult education centers. However, Birren's guidelines can help people get started on their autobiographies now. Here are some themes to start with:

- Major transitions in life. Write about leaving home, going to college, fighting in a war, having a child.

- Your family. This could include your family of origin, and your current family. Note your family history, traditions, tragedies, and triumphs.

- Your major life work or career. This may be professional work or homemaking, whatever your primary focus has been.

- Your health. Detail your health history and include exercise, diet, and other elements.

- Your sexuality and intimate relationships. Write about your current love life and past experiences.

- Your friends and other social relationships. Describe who these people are, why they're important to you, and their special qualities.

NSAIDs had a 30 to 60 percent lower risk of developing Alzheimer's disease; NSAIDs prevent the characteristic inflammation of the disease from developing. Keep in mind, however, that large, regular doses of NSAIDs have significant side effects, including stomach ulcers and impaired kidney function, and it's important to talk to a doctor before starting to take NSAIDs on a regular basis.

New research will show whether aspirin, another anti-inflammatory drug with fewer side effects, can play a similar role in delaying

---

- The role of the arts in your life. Have music, art, and literature been important to you? Do you write, or play a musical instrument? Are reading, listening to music, and going to museums important parts of your life?

- Physical activities. Have you been an athlete, either as a professional or amateur? Do you participate in sports now? How important have sports been in your life?

- Leisure activities and hobbies. Has travel been important to you? Have you been involved in handicrafts or woodworking? Do you do a lot of home improvement projects?

- Volunteer work. This can include time contributed to organizations, serving on boards of directors, or helping at a hospital or clinic.

- Your experiences with stress. How did you handle stress in the past? Are you consciously pursuing stress-reduction techniques now?

- Your experience with death. Has someone close to you died? How did that affect you? What were your needs at that time? What were the needs of others close to the deceased? Were they met? How?

- Your financial resources. Do you have enough money? Have you ever made a lot of money? Or lost a lot of money?

Source: Adapted from J. E. Birren and D. E. Deutchman, *Guiding Autobiography Groups for Older Adults: Exploring the Fabric of Life*, pp. 67–79. © 1991. J. E. Birren.

the onset of Alzheimer's disease. Low-dose aspirin has the added advantage of having a demonstrated role in preventing heart disease.

VITAMINS AND MINERALS

Research on antioxidants such as vitamin E is also continuing. In a multi-institutional study based at Columbia University, 341 patients with moderate Alzheimer's disease took either 2,000 international units (IU) of vitamin E, 10 milligrams of the anti-Parkinson's disease drug selegiline, a combination of both compounds, or a placebo pill for two years. The results of the study, which were published in the *New England Journal of Medicine* in 1997, showed that treatment with any one of these substances significantly delayed some of the critical outcomes of Alzheimer's disease: death, institutionalization, loss of the ability to perform activities of daily living, or progression to severe Alzheimer's disease.

We strongly recommend the daily use of the antioxidant vitamin E for the rest of your life to help prevent or delay cognitive deterioration. As we explain further on in this chapter, vitamin E also helps protect people from heart disease and cancer. The majority of our healthy centenarians continue to consume diets rich in vitamins and minerals. But many people probably do not have the inherited, lifelong capability of centenarians to combat oxygen radical damage. We can make up for the difference in part by taking significant supplements of vitamin E (400 to 800 IU per day) and as we discuss later, selenium (100–200 mcg per day) as well. A significant amount of vitamin E can come from a healthy diet that includes wheat germ, dried beans, and leafy green vegetables. With a varied diet, you can get many of the vitamins you need for good brain functioning. However, achieving the levels we are recommending would be impractical through diet alone, and we therefore strongly recommend the use of an appropriate vitamin-E supplement.

Be careful when selecting your vitamin-E supplement. Some dietary supplements can give you all these vitamins and minerals, but many do not contain the full amount of vitamin E necessary to delay the onset of Alzheimer's disease. In addition, many multivitamins contain iron and copper, which, as we discussed in chapter 4, may actually speed the rate of oxygen radical damage.

Some of the B vitamins—B_1, B_6, and B_{12}—may also be important for cognitive function. Deficiencies in B_{12} can cause confusion and other symptoms of dementia, and severe B_1 deficiency may cause profound memory loss. All these vitamins are water soluble and therefore require frequent replenishing.

NATURAL REMEDIES

Gingko biloba, a herbal product, is a popular dietary supplement purported to help memory and mental sharpness by providing additional oxygen to the brain. A recent article in the *Journal of the American Medical Association* found that about 27 percent of subjects tested responded to gingko. However, there are debates over whether the response was great enough to make a difference in a person's everyday behavior, and whether or not gingko is safe. People with bleeding disorders and those who take any blood-thinning drugs, including aspirin, should be wary and take this herbal supplement only under a physician's care.

ESTROGEN

As we showed in chapter 4, centenarian women were more likely to have children later in life than a comparable group of women who died in their early seventies. Centenarian women apparently produce significant quantities of estrogen, the female hormone that plays a major role in reproduction and reproductive cycles, for a longer time than shorter-lived women. Estrogen also may protect brain tissue by acting as an antioxidant, and it appears to build synapses, allowing brain cells to communicate with each other more efficiently. Recent research has shown a 40 to 60 percent reduction in the prevalence of Alzheimer's disease in women who take estrogen supplements after menopause. A study of 1,124 mentally healthy older women by Columbia University neurologist Richard Mayeux and colleagues found that, after a period of one to five years, Alzheimer's disease developed in 16 percent of the women who were not taking estrogen, but in only 6 percent of women who were.

Men may have at least one advantage in their estrogen secretion pattern in later years: Although they produce only a small amount of estrogen, that amount remains relatively steady throughout their lives. Therefore, they do not experience the dramatic estrogen drop that women undergo, which may affect cognition. But the study of the impact of male hormones on the aging brain is in its infancy. The New England Research Institute in Watertown, Massachusetts, is looking at the effects of male hormones on cognition. The institute has examined three hormones: testosterone, estrogen, and dihydroepiandrosterone (DHEA), a hormone controlled by the adrenal gland. None of these hormones affected memory or attention. DHEA appeared to improve spatial ability in men over age 65, but the long-term effects of this drug are unknown. Until the frequency of adverse outcomes is better delineated, particularly in the case of DHEA and testosterone, we cannot recommend using these hormones to prevent cognitive deterioration.

EXERCISE

The three-decker, three-family house is typical of old Boston neighborhoods, so finding centenarians residing in them was not a surprise. The surprise was that many 100-year-olds lived on the second or third floor. But it made sense: Climbing stairs gave centenarians regular exercise. In the days before washing machines and vacuum cleaners many centenarians spent much of their time on physically demanding household tasks, although they would probably be amused to find that these activities were essential to their well-being. Leisure activities such as dancing kept many centenarians consistently active. Some centenarians, like Angelina Strandal, had no time for leisure; she raised a family and cared for her ill husband all through the Great Depression.

Active lifestyles contributed not only to our centenarians' overall health but to their alert and agile minds. People can exercise almost all their lives. Tai Chi, an ancient Chinese program of meditative movements, can be performed by people of almost any age or physical ability level. It has moderate steady aerobic effects, uses all the muscle groups, and builds flexibility. With its slow, repetitive motions, this form of exercise also has the effect of decreasing emotional stress and anxiety.

STRESS REDUCTION

As we saw in chapter 3, centenarians are natural stress-shedders. This contributes to their longevity in part by improving their cognitive health, since anxiety and depression have significant negative effects on brain function. Many cognitive researchers have noted that depression and anxiety cause chemical changes in the brain that disrupt thought processes and erode people's ability to manage their lives. Centenarians seem to be able to keep their train of thought on track, despite stress. When Angelina Strandal's husband died and the burden of raising two children fell exclusively on her, she met these challenges with her natural ability to handle stress. When her life settled down in her later years, she lived a life that was low in what Dr. Lyle Miller, a Boston psychologist, calls "susceptibility to stress." Every evening, at age 103, she sat down with her son and daughter to eat a home-cooked dinner. She slept regularly, took a daily walk, attended mass regularly, and was in constant contact with her two children.

People who have difficulty dealing with psychological stress, in particular, should use stress reduction techniques, such as meditation and excercise, to cope with problems. For those who struggle with high levels of stress, programs such as Beth Israel Deaconess Medical Center's Mind/Body Medical Institute offer intensive, monitored programs that teach stress reduction techniques, such as progressive relaxation, and physical-mental exercises like yoga. Biofeedback, which teaches people to control physiological stress responses, is another alternative to antianxiety medications, which pose physical risks as well as cognitive side effects. Some insurance plans now cover nonmedical stress reduction programs if they are prescribed by a physician.

The physiological effects of failing to deal properly with stress cannot be discounted. Just as stress affects physical functioning, so it diminishes the efficiency of the brain. Stress can exacerbate mild cognitive problems and eventually impair everyday functioning. Over the long run, sustained stress has even more dire consequences, causing actual damage to brain cells. With age, hormones called glucocorticoids, which are secreted by the adrenal glands in response to stress, play a role in the loss of neurons in the hippocampus, the seat of memory in the brain. Studies of animals and humans have shown that nonmedical interventions such as guided imagery and yoga, which emphasize psychological work as a route to physiological health, effectively influence the production of glucocorticoids. Herbert Benson, director of the Mind/Body Medical Institute, has demonstrated that circulating levels of stress-related hormones drop with the use of relaxation exercises.

BLOOD PRESSURE

Researchers have begun to suspect that untreated high blood pressure may play a role in cognitive decline. Scientists in Hawaii found that for every rise of 10 mm/Hg in systolic blood pressure in midlife, there was a 7 to 9 percent increase in the risk of impaired cognitive function. These results remind us that what we do in midlife may have health consequences when we get older.

Active minds, exercise, sensible eating habits, and rewarding social relationships play a part in keeping brains functioning well. These were just part of our centenarians' lifelong lifestyles. Adopting a centenarian lifestyle now can help you take advantage of your potential to live a long life and cope with the dramatic social changes that will affect all aspects of life—social, economic, and cultural.

AVOID ATHEROSCLEROSIS

Atherosclerosis (sometimes called arteriosclerosis) is a gradual process of damage to blood vessels that involves accumulation of fat molecules, clotting factors, scar tissue, and other blood-borne materials. When atherosclerotic plaques block blood vessels, the results can be serious. Heart attack, the number one cause of death in industrialized countries, occurs when coronary arteries, the blood vessels that feed heart muscle, become partially or completely clogged, leaving the heart unable to get oxygen and nutrients. The heart's overall function can be permanently impaired depending upon the amount of damaged heart muscle. Stroke, the third most common cause of death and the leading cause of permanent disability for Americans, occurs when particular areas of the brain die when they are deprived of oxygen and nutrient-carrying blood.

We found that centenarians seldom had long-term histories of heart disease. They were much more likely to have suffered from acute cardiovascular events like heart attack or stroke at the very end of their lives, which was typical of the pattern of compression of morbidity we observe among them. Angelina Strandal was such a centenarian. Until about three weeks before her death, she appeared extremely well, and gave every indication that she might continue living a few more years. Therefore, it was surprising to find that she had had a mild heart attack, which soon led to her death. Nonetheless, her long life ended with this brief period of illness—the trademark of compression of morbidity—which we believe is primarily determined by centenarians' genes. Genetic endowments aside, others can approximate the centenarian experience by taking early, decisive, and lasting steps to prevent heart attack and stroke, such as avoiding smoking, eating a heart-healthy diet, getting sufficient exercise, and achieving and maintaining an ideal weight.

Testing for high blood pressure, high cholesterol, diabetes, and other hard to recognize risk factors for heart disease is extremely important. The 1988 National Cholesterol Education Program (NCEP) panel recommended that cholesterol measurements should be taken in all adults over 20 years of age and at least once every five years thereafter. The 1993 NCEP panel further recommended that HDL cholesterol be measured at the same time as total cholesterol. Adults should also be tested regularly for hypertension. Signs of diabetes, such as excessive hunger, thirst, and urination, should be addressed with a visit to a physician.

Six important factors that increase a person's risk for developing or worsening atherosclerosis are: elevated LDL cholesterol (discussed in detail below), elevated triglycerides (a type of fat), high blood pressure, obesity, stress, close family (first-degree relative) history of early heart attack (before age 60), and cigarette smoking. Smoking is a particularly dangerous and potent contributor to plaque formation. You can reduce your risk for both heart attack and stroke through a combined program of avoiding tobacco, eating a low-fat diet, reducing stress, getting regular aerobic exercise, and having appropriate screening and treatment for other factors that increase heart disease risk.

CHOLESTEROL

Cholesterol is a waxy, fatlike substance found in all people, regardless of their dietary habits. It is produced in the liver and is an essential ingredient in hormones as well as cellular structures. The gram per day manufactured by the body is all most people need, but many people consume another superfluous half-gram a day in the form of egg yolks, meat, fish, poultry, and whole-milk dairy products. The body transports cholesterol in two principal forms: low-density and high-density lipoproteins.

About 70 percent of body cholesterol is carried in the form of low-density lipoproteins, or LDL-cholesterol. Excess circulating LDL-cholesterol can be deposited on artery walls, where it may be oxidized by free radicals, leading to plaque formation and atherosclerosis.

The other form, high-density lipoprotein or HDL-cholesterol, is frequently called the "good cholesterol." HDL-cholesterol scavenges stray cholesterol from the bloodstream and returns it to the liver, where it is reprocessed or excreted into the intestines, and thereby disposed of. High HDL-cholesterol levels are associated with decreased risk of heart disease. Women generally have higher HDL levels than men, perhaps due to higher estrogen levels. This may explain in part why women's heart disease risk rises later than that of men, as we described in chapter 4.

A total blood cholesterol level below 200 milligrams per deciliter (mg/dL) is generally agreed to be acceptable. When total cholesterol rises above 240 mg/dL, the risk for cardiovascular disease doubles. More specifically, an LDL reading of over 130 mg/dL and/or an HDL-cholesterol reading below 35 mg/dL for men or below 40 mg/dL for women signify increased risk. A high HDL-cholesterol reading, of 60 mg/dL or more, is an indicator of reduced heart attack risk.

The very high rates of heart attack in North America and Europe suggest that cholesterol standards are too lenient; many who comply with the standards may still be at significant risk for atherosclerosis. Average cholesterol levels and heart attack rates are significantly lower in Japan than in the United States and Canada, probably because the Japanese diet is based predominantly on fish and vegetables, which are low in cholesterol and fat. In 1996, the Cholesterol and Recurrent Events (CARE) Study showed that American subjects with cholesterol levels considered normal in this country could lower their heart disease risk by further lowering their cholesterol levels.

A cholesterol check should be part of a routine yearly physical; more frequent testing by your doctor might be indicated if there are other major risk factors, such as a history of early heart disease (younger than 60) among first-degree relatives.

DIET

The first step in lowering cholesterol levels is to begin consuming a reduced-cholesterol and reduced-fat diet. The American Heart Association (AHA) recommends that cholesterol intake should be less than 300 milligrams daily. (Keep in mind that this recommended level may need to be decreased even further, approximating at least the Japanese diet.) For example, an egg yolk contains an average of about 300 milligrams of cholesterol. Red meat should also be avoided. In addition, the AHA recommends restricting fat to no more than 15 to 30 percent of total calories, and to make sure that carbohydrates comprise 55 to 60 percent of all the calories consumed. Consuming 25 to 30 grams of dietary fiber each day is associated with decreased cholesterol levels. The easiest way to do this is to eat more fruits, vegetables, grains, and legumes, minimize meat and sweets in the diet, avoid processed foods, and use olive and canola oils rather than animal fat and butter whenever possible.

For years physicians and dietitians have warned us to sharply reduce our consumption of saturated fats, the leading source of fat calories in the American diet. Saturated fats like butter and cheese are notorious for increasing levels of serum cholesterol and LDL-cholesterol. But another equally if not more notorious culprit in heart disease are the transfatty acids, sometimes called hydrogenated fats. Hydrogenation of vegetable oils renders them solid or semisolid, and thus easier to use as margarine or shortening. These hydrogenated fats are commonly used in commercial bakeries to make cookies, biscuits, cakes, and white breads. Unfortunately, this hydrogenation process also creates transfatty acids, which contribute significantly to the formation of LDL-cholesterol in the bloodstream.

In the ongoing, national Nurses' Health Study, Harvard researchers calculated intake of transfatty acids from dietary questionnaires completed by 85,095 women who had no history of heart disease or stroke. During eight years of follow-up, the fifth of the group with the highest intake of transfatty acids had a 50 percent greater risk for heart disease than the fifth with the lowest intake. In a recent Dutch study, 25 male and 34 female students ate diets that varied nutritionally only in their composition of major fats. During the period of the study in which students consumed transfatty acids, serum cholesterol rose about 6 percent above the levels seen with a liquid nonsaturated fat diet and about half as much as the saturated fat diet. But this was just the tip of the iceberg. Consumption of transfatty acids caused a greater increase in LDL and a greater reduction in HDL than that of saturated fat. The HDL-to-cholesterol ratio, an important measure of risk, rose an average of 23 percent when students consumed transfatty acids and only 13 percent when they ate saturated fat.

Transfatty acids may seem like a tiny part of the diet, perhaps the small amount of margarine on the morning toast. But this is deceptive. Huge slabs of hydrogenated fat are used to make foods that grace the countertops of most fast-food restaurants around the world. Anything cooked with hydrogenated vegetable oil is full of transfatty acids—much of the more than 400 calories that make up a large order of french fries are from transfatty acids. Avoiding foods cooked in margarine and shortening can reduce heart disease risk substantially.

Transfatty acids are a prime example of the difficulty we have in studying the implication of centenarian diets for aging baby boomers. When centenarians were establishing their dietary habits, these transfatty acids didn't even exist. We found that many centenarians ate high-fat foods such as butter and cheese, but few of them consumed amounts of transfatty acids in their diets that would be comparable to our generation's adults. Maybe this translates into an advantage for our current centenarians in that they were lucky enough not be exposed to a food component that many of us consume on a weekly basis in visits to fast-food restaurants.

CALORIC RESTRICTION

Evidence from studies of rodents and primates suggests that cutting calories may be a powerful means of slowing aging and heart disease risk. In Japan, researchers found that death rates from cerebrovascular disease, heart disease, and cancer were 31 to 41 percent lower in the more traditional Okinawan region—where adults consume 17 percent fewer calories and children take in 36 percent fewer calories—than in the nation as a whole, which consumes a relatively Westernized diet. In the Netherlands, a study found that nonobese, middle-aged men who reduced their caloric intake by 20 percent for ten weeks enjoyed increased HDL levels, reduced blood pressure, and a beneficial 10 percent loss of body weight.

Most people would have great difficulty reducing their total caloric intake by 30 percent, particularly for an extended period of time. However, people from cancer-prone families or those with a family history of the early onset of aging-associated diseases might be suitable candidates for long-term dietary restriction.

VITAMIN, MINERAL, AND HERBAL SUPPLEMENTS

Various medications and dietary supplements, including aspirin, vitamin E, selenium, and medications that interfere with particular means of cholesterol transport, reduce the progression of atherosclerosis. Dietary supplements can play an important role in health promotion, but they should complement, not replace, a balanced diet.

Because the oxidation of LDL-cholesterol is an important step in plaque formation, there appears to be a role for antioxidants in combating atherosclerosis. The American Heart Association acknowledges the value of vitamin E in preventing heart disease by inhibiting lipoprotein oxidation. In 1996, University of California School of Medicine researchers found that the progress of coronary artery disease was substantially slower in men taking 100 IU of vitamin E daily than in a matched group not taking the vitamin.

In the Harvard-based Physician's Health Study, men who consumed at least 100 units of dietary vitamin E had nearly half the risk of coronary artery disease compared to men who consumed less than 7 units of the vitamin. No benefit was observed from increased intakes of either vitamins A or C. The Nurses' Health Study found that women who took vitamin E for two years bore half the coronary artery disease risk of women who weren't taking the vitamin.

It is not clear if too much vitamin E has any adverse effects. Supplemental vitamin E can have the benefit of boosting the immune system, but doses that are too high may create annoying side effects, such as hay fever, and other allergies. Daily doses of less than 1,000 IU per day may be wise until more definitive data indicate otherwise.

Vitamin E comes in several forms: In humans, the liver appears to prefer the alpha form (alpha-tocopherol) for binding with transport molecules in the circulation. Thus, even though the gamma form may be the more effective in the test tube, for humans, alpha-tocopherol is the better supplement.

Selenium, another potent antioxidant, has made headlines as a defense against cancer, but may also have a protective role in heart disease. A 1989 study from the Netherlands showed that low selenium levels were associated with an increased risk of heart attack. Suggested selenium doses range from 100 to 200 mcg per day.

Vitamin C has been controversial, with studies either attesting to its value as protection against heart disease or indicating no benefit. On the other hand, vitamin C deficiency is associated with numerous maladies that are certainly to be avoided. If your diet is not rich in fruits and vegetables, which are potent sources of vitamin C, then supplementing it with 500 to 1,500 mg per day is warranted.

Several herbal supplements also make good sense in the fight against cardiovascular disease, as well as cancer and other age-related illnesses. These should be used in reasonable dosages as additional supplements. Keep in mind the reputability of the company you are buying supplements from, since quality can vary widely. Choose a national brand with a broad base of products that have stood the test of time and consumer scrutiny.

The health benefits of green tea have been noted by the Chinese for more than 3,000 years. The black tea most Western people like to drink comes from leaves that have been withered, rolled, fermented, and dried. The advantage of green tea is that the leaves are steamed and dried, which preserves the green leaf polyphenols. These polyphenols have been shown both in the test tube and in animals to inhibit formation of cancer-causing nitrosamines. Japanese scientists have noted both decreased rates of cardiovascular disease and a decreased risk of precancerous lesions in the colon in association with green tea consumption. James and Dorothy Morré and their colleagues at Purdue University reported at the 1998 American Cell Biology annual meeting that another constituent of green tea, epigallocatechin gallate (EGCg), is also an antioxidant, but, more important, it shuts down quinol-oxidase, an enzyme required by cancer cells in order to divide. They observed that in the test tube, EGCg-inhibited cancer cells failed to obtain a critical tumor size and subsequently died. Green tea extract in daily doses of 300 mg imparts significant health benefits and has no reported associated toxicity.

Grape seed contains pyrocyanidines, which are known to be potent antioxidants. In particular, they inhibit xanthine oxidase, an essential enzyme in the production of free radicals, as well as lipoperoxidase, an important potentiator of arterial plaque formation. No toxicity has been reported for grape seed extract. It should be taken in dosages of approximately 50 mg per day.

A number of substances are thought to be even better antioxidants than vitamin E, selenium, and the herbal substances noted above, with as few side effects, but there is no reliable data to back up these claims. However, given that such substances may well prove to be our most effective means of compressing our morbidity, it is imperative that careful efficacy studies be performed as soon as possible.

The benefits of vitamins B_6, B_{12}, and folate regarding atherosclerosis revolve around research into the amino acid homocysteine. High homocysteine levels are associated with increased risk of cardiovascular disease, stroke, and peripheral vascular disease, and appear to exacerbate the effects of smoking and high blood pressure. Deficiencies in vitamins B_6, B_{12}, and folate appear to be associated with increased homocysteine levels. Canadian researchers John Peterson and David

Spence reported recently that treatment with 2.5 mg folate, 25 mg B$_6$, and 250 mcg B$_{12}$ reduced the amount of plaque in the coronary arteries of patients with elevated homocysteine levels. People who have a significant family history of coronary artery disease would be wise to ask their physicians to check their homocysteine level.

Exercise

Regular exercise can help prevent or markedly delay type-2 diabetes, obesity, and other factors associated with heart disease. Yet the *Harvard Health Letter* recently noted that only 10 percent of Americans over age 65 engage in vigorous exercise on a regular basis. The Heart and Stroke Foundation of Ontario, Canada, in its Report Card on Canadian Baby Boomers noted that only 36 percent of men and 35 percent of women exercised regularly. Sedentary people lose approximately 40 percent of their muscle mass and 30 percent of their strength between the ages of 20 and 70, in part because of lack of exercise.

Sports such as swimming, rowing, tennis, cycling, running, cross-country skiing, and other forms of aerobic exercise help trim fat and strengthen hearts. But among these activities, resistance exercises—those that require you to work against gravity, such as weight training or walking up hills or stairs—are the only known way to guard against age-related loss of muscle tissue. Preserving or increasing muscle mass indirectly benefits the heart by improving the ability to burn fat. Also, muscle is the most efficient burner of fat in our bodies, so resistance training is the key to losing excess fat. Despite engaging in a regular regimen of running or other aerobic exercise, many adult men complain that they cannot get rid of midriff fat. Adding muscle is the key.

But resistance exercise has another important effect as well: In a 1992 study of frail, very old volunteers who were prone to falling easily, Maria Fiatarone and her colleagues at the Hebrew Rehabilitation Center for Aged observed that, after adopting a regular resistance training program, men and women tripled their thigh muscle mass and dramatically lowered their risk of falls. At the University of Alabama at Birmingham, researchers found that nonathletic women between the ages of 60 and 77 who performed the prescribed exercises, improved their isotonic strength (the strength needed to move heavy objects) by an average of 52 percent. Isometric strength (the force needed to push against a stationary object) rose by 31 percent, while walking speed increased by 18 percent. Indeed, these studies show one is never too old to increase physical strength and improve quality of life.

MEDICATIONS

Some of the many cholesterol-lowering drugs available have the added benefit of raising HDL levels. These drugs are known to markedly decrease the risk of heart attack and stroke for those individuals who are predisposed to cardiovascular disease by virtue of elevated LDL or other factors. The best known of these medications are called the statin drugs (lovastatin, simvastatin, pravastatin). In numerous studies, these drugs have been shown to reduce cholesterol, as well as heart disease and death from heart attacks.

ASPIRIN

The Physicians' Health Study found that men who took one baby aspirin (81 mg) each day reduced their risk of heart attack by 50 percent. Researchers theorize that aspirin's protective benefit may be due to its interference with the platelet's key role in plaque formation. Also under consideration is the possibility that the anti-inflammatory properties of aspirin may combat virally based chronic inflammation. In 1997, Harvard researchers discovered that men with elevated levels of C-reactive protein, a marker for chronic inflammation, had a significantly greater history of heart disease. Other researchers have noted the presence of inflammation-causing virus-like particles actually in the plaque. A third study suggested that gum disease can be a potent source of the chronic inflammation that precipitates plaque formation, emphasizing the need for good dental care for heart disease prevention. No studies have yet indicated that taking antibiotics to treat these infections lowers the risk for heart disease, though trials are currently underway.

ESTROGEN REPLACEMENT THERAPY

Although women generally develop heart disease about a decade later than men, cardiovascular disease is still the number one killer of women in industrialized countries. Estrogen replacement therapy has been a popular weapon in the war against heart disease in women. In addition to combating osteoporosis, hot flashes, and other difficulties associated with menopause, its role in the prevention of plaque formation and established cardiovascular disease has been documented in numerous studies. However, estrogen use should be considered very carefully in women with a family history of breast cancer.

A study reported in the *New England Journal of Medicine* found that women who took estrogen had a lower mortality rate than women who had never used the hormone. Women with coronary risk factors had the greatest reduction in mortality with estrogen use, and there was little decrease for women at low risk of heart disease. Cardiovascular protective benefits disappeared within five years after estrogen use was discontinued. Protective benefits did not increase with duration of use and in fact decreased after a decade or more. While cardiovascular advantages continued, breast cancer mortality rates rose by 43 percent in the study population. However, despite this rise, the benefits of treatment in preventing heart disease outweighed the risk. A white woman's cumulative absolute risk of death from the ages of 50 to 94 years has been estimated to be 31 percent from coronary heart disease, 2.8 percent from breast cancer, and 2.8 percent from hip fracture. Thus, according to this study, it appears that the benefits of estrogen use far outweigh the risks.

However, for many women the benefits of hormone use may not compensate for the fear of acquiring breast cancer and living with its repercussions. Estrogen replacement therapy's risks may be unacceptably high for women at low risk for cardiovascular disease and at high risk for breast cancer. Unfortunately, these issues do not easily lend themselves to simple formulas for calculating who should take estrogen and for how long. Every woman must carefully weigh the risks and advantages in her own case.

Surprisingly, a more recent study of hormone replacement therapy suggests that not all women benefit from its cardiovascular effects, and that the risks may be higher than previously thought. In a 1998 study of 2,783 women published in the *Journal of the American Medical Association*, Stephen Hulley and colleagues from the University of California at San Francisco showed that taking estrogen and progestin actually increased the risk of heart attack by 50 percent within the first two years of treatment. Risk may be elevated in the first few years of postmenopausal therapy because estrogen may increase the blood's propensity to clot. Four years after therapy started, the estrogen-treated women's heart attack risk dropped dramatically, to below that of untreated women, but the high risk of heart disease in the early years of therapy appeared to outweigh the long-term benefit. Investigators need to resolve these disparate findings to clarify the role of estrogen in heart disease prevention. Several long-running Harvard-based epidemiological studies may shed light on this critical issue in the near future.

HYPERTENSION

Blood pressure is the result of two forces: systolic pressure is generated when the heart pushes blood into the arteries and through the circulatory system; diastolic pressure is created by the arteries' resistance to blood flow between heartbeats. Blood pressure readings are given as: systolic pressure "over" diastolic pressure. According to the American Heart Association, a blood pressure reading of less than 140 (systolic) over 90 (diastolic) is considered normal for adults. Readings higher than this are believed to indicate increased risk for cardiovascular disease, leading to heart attack or stroke.

Although kidney disease and other illnesses can cause high blood pressure, the causes of the vast majority of cases are unknown. There are usually no symptoms. Those at highest risk are African-Americans, middle-aged and older people, obese people, heavy drinkers, women taking oral contraceptives, and people with diabetes, kidney disease, or gout. The only reliable way to determine whether you have high blood pressure is to have it checked at least annually, if not more often. It is a sign that the heart is working harder than it should, and untreated it can accelerate atherosclerosis and lead to stroke and other serious health problems.

Some drugs can interfere with blood pressure medications or raise blood pressure. If you have hypertension, it is important to tell your doctor about all the prescriptions and over-the-counter drugs you are taking. Potential difficulties can occur with nasal decongestants and other cold remedies, steroids, appetite suppressants, and nonsteroidal anti-inflammatory drugs such as ibuprofen.

People whose blood pressure just meets or slightly exceeds AHA guidelines should be wary. American standards for healthy blood pressure may be too high. Examinations of centenarians generally revealed systolic blood pressures of no greater than 110 and diastolic pressures lower than 80. Our study of centenarians' children showed that their blood pressure was consistently lower than that of the comparison group, whose mothers had died at age 73. Some studies have suggested that extremely low blood pressures indicate a high risk of mortality in old age. However, these studies have often included frail older people with significant medical problems. We suspect that the low blood pressure we observed among centenarians and their children promotes longevity.

While certain people may be predisposed to high blood pressure, there are steps everyone can take to minimize or even prevent it. Losing weight, quitting smoking, and getting regular exercise are proven means to reducing blood pressure and promoting general health and well-being. Some people find that their blood pressure is under better control when they eliminate salt from their diet. A wide variety of drugs, some of them very new, are now available to safely reduce blood pressure. There are scores of cookbooks that teach people how to season with herbs as tasty alternatives to salt.

When we visit centenarians at home, we often see them salting their food. Some people have a high sensitivity to the blood pressure–elevating effects of salt. Researchers have noted that such "salt-sensitive" hypertensives have a much higher risk of heart disease than the general population. We have not observed centenarians with such salt-sensitivity, and it appears to us that people with low blood pressure who enjoy salt or even crave it should not feel the need to limit its use, particularly if their doctors can confirm that they are not salt-sensitive.

Last, but certainly not least, research has shown that stress management is an important part of high blood pressure control. Meditation and breathing exercises (such as those found in the practice of yoga) and the use of guided imagery are examples of the many relaxation techniques available to help people cope with stressful situations.

PREVENTING CANCER

Like Alzheimer's disease and cardiovascular disease, cancer causes increasing rates of disability and death at later ages, peaking in the seventies. In fact, in our analysis of over 750,000 admissions at Massachusetts hospitals, costs were highest among patients in their midseventies, in large measure because of the corresponding peaking incidence of cancer admissions.

Cancer is among the most expensive of illnesses to diagnose and treat. After the septuagenarian years, overall cancer incidence declines, and with it, hospital costs. People surviving into their eighties and beyond have either encountered and beat cancer, or they have successfully passed through the period of life when the danger of developing cancer is at its highest. Now that they are in their eighties, their cancer risk actually falls. The prevalence of cancer in the families of our centenarians is extremely low, indicating that most centenarians share some form of resistance to cancer that we do not yet understand.

If many of your ancestors and relatives lived into extreme old age, then your risk of cancer is probably low. However, if many of your forebears died at early ages of heart disease, accidents, infectious diseases, or other causes, they never reached ages of high cancer risk, and it would be difficult to say whether or not you have an unusually high susceptibility to cancer. Yet, even if several close relatives have suffered from cancer, your own risk is not necessarily high, because behavior can be extremely important to cancer incidence. A familial pattern of cancer means that you need to keep your guard up, begin cancer screening at a younger age than that recommended for the general population, and be particularly diligent about avoiding known carcinogens such as cigarette smoke. Whatever your predisposition to cancer, it is important to begin a prevention plan right now, in order to delay the likelihood of developing cancer as long as possible, and hopefully preventing cancer altogether.

Fortunately, our understanding of cancer prevention has progressed a great deal over the past few years. There are still no magic bullets, no surefire bets to eliminate cancer from our lives. But antioxidants like vitamin E and selenium are shown to have the capacity to retard the destructive cellular processes that lead to cancer, and other cancer prevention steps have received scientific endorsement.

Over the past few years, epidemiologists such as the Harvard School of Public Health's Graham Colditz and Leslie Frazier have come to the conclusion that the vast majority of cancers—at least 65 percent and perhaps as much as 80 percent—can be prevented using fairly simple means. Eliminating this fearsome, expensive, and disabling disease from our lives, or at least markedly delaying it, means a significantly happier and more productive aging period for all of us—not just for the older people who want to avoid cancer themselves, but for their younger friends and family members who would like to enjoy life with them.

TOBACCO

Cigarette smoking is by far the most important behavioral health hazard facing Americans today. None of our centenarians smoked at the time of the study, and the number of former smokers was extremely small: less than 5 percent.

Despite the measurable drop in smoking among Americans, lung cancer remains responsible for one out of three cancer deaths in the United States each year, at least 400,000 deaths annually. Data from the British Doctors' Study, the American Veterans Cohort Study, the Nurses' Health Study, and the Health Professionals' Study indicate that one out of four cases of colon cancer can also be attributed to smoking. Tobacco use is also associated with cancers of the larynx, esophagus, bladder, kidney, and pancreas. Cigarette smoking may also be related to uterine and cervical cancer.

Avoiding or quitting smoking is the first and most logical individual step to effective compression of morbidity. Studies show that while early smoking increases the risk of lung cancer, continued smoking later in life increases the severity and lethality of lung cancer cases. Quitting smoking at any time in life, however, immediately reduces the risk of cancer. Within 10 to 15 years of quitting, former smokers' lung cancer risk is close to that of people who have never smoked.

Numerous tools exist for those who wish to quit smoking. Nicotine patches and gum can help reduce addiction cravings. Behavioral programs may help people understand the social "needs" that smoking helps them satisfy, and find other ways to fulfill these. Hypnotism may also help alleviate some people's dependency on cigarettes. And many people are able to quit "cold turkey" when they realize just how bad cigarettes are for their health. The key is to keep trying until a method works.

People who quit smoking almost always find that it was worth the trouble. Tom recently hired John, a slim building contractor with ruddy cheeks who smoked two or three packs a day. Tom asked his age, expecting to hear that he was 45 or 50, and was surprised to hear that he was only in his late thirties. It was clear that smoking had accelerated his rate of aging. John's father, also a smoker, had died of heart disease at 58. Tom warned John that he might not see his three children graduate from high school, and urged him to find a smoking cessation program. A few weeks later, John reported that he had bought nicotine patches in an attempt to quit. Though he had gained weight, he felt much healthier. Over the next six months, his chronic cough disappeared, and he was surprised at his increased energy. John will undoubtedly live a longer, healthier life and lower his risk of cancer if he can keep up his resolve to stay away from cigarettes.

DIET

As we pointed out in chapter 3, determining the role of diet in extreme longevity is complicated. Diet reporting is notoriously inaccurate, and diets themselves are extremely varied. It is unlikely that we will identify a specific food that plays a strong role in cancer prevention. International comparisons of cancer rates, however, do provide some insight into the broad effects of diet and culture. For instance, rates of colon cancer are much higher in the United States than in China, where, on the other hand, rates of stomach cancer are relatively higher. This suggests that some broad features of diets in each country—perhaps fat content in the United States, perhaps commonly used spices in China—may play a role in certain forms of cancer. As yet it's extremely hard to say.

What we have seen from these international studies, and from studies of populations like Seventh-Day Adventists, who eat no red meat, is that consumption of a low-fat diet with lots of fresh fruits and vegetables appears to be associated with lower rates of many cancers, including colon, lung, and prostate cancers. Harvard's Colditz and Frazier estimate that if all Americans increased their intake of fruit or vegetables by only one serving each day, the number of lung cancer cases would fall by 10 percent, and if all Americans ate five servings of fruits or vegetables a day, there would be a 20 percent decrease in lung cancer. Replacing red

Simplified Dietary Suggestions

Physicians often suggest that a healthy diet should consist of no more than 30 percent fat, and that the total cholesterol intake for one day should not exceed 200 to 300 mg. However, such advice often seems impossible to follow, even if a calculator and ingredient chart are handy. It may be easier to avoid certain foods while emphasizing others in the diet.

Emphasize

1. Fish: Rich in polyunsaturated omega-3 fatty acids that lower cholesterol and triglyceride levels. Daily consumption can cut heart disease risk by half.
2. Fiber: Whole grain breads and cereals, peas, beans, prunes.
3. Polyunsaturated fats (PF): Found in liquid vegetable oils such as corn (56 percent PF),

Avoid

1. Saturated fats: Whole milk, cream, butter, cheese, white bread, meat, poultry skin.
2. Hydrogenated vegetable shortenings and margarines: Found in many store-bought breads, cakes, and cookies. Check ingredients carefully.
3. Cholesterol: Egg yolks, organ meats, tripe, cod liver oil,

meat in the diet with chicken, fish, vegetables, and grains can also have a substantial effect on cancer risk. One less serving of red meat each week would reduce the number of colon cancer cases by 11 percent. Red meat consumption may be a risk factor for prostate cancer. Alcohol consumption has also been linked with breast cancer. Two alcoholic drinks per day may raise the risk of breast cancer by as much as 25 percent.

ANTIOXIDANTS

The role of dietary supplements has recently gained significant attention from cancer prevention experts. Several studies in highly respected medical journals support the use of the antioxidants selenium and vitamin E to reduce cancer risk. One of the first studies to get the medical community excited about selenium, published in the *Lancet* in 1983, found that people with low selenium levels were at double the risk of developing cancer when compared to people whose

Emphasize	Avoid
cottonseed, safflower, soybean, and sunflower (72 percent PF), and also in the fat of fish and nuts (except cashews).	butter, bacon fat, cream, cheddar cheese.
4. Olive oil: Even though it contains only 8 percent PF, it appears to help lower heart disease risk, perhaps because of antioxidant properties. It is also a monounsaturated fat.	4. Sweets and foods containing refined sugar: In addition to avoiding ice cream, candy, cake, cookies, etc., limit your intake of bread, which also contains significant calories, to one to two slices per day,
5. Fruit and fruit juices.	5. Fast food restaurants: Often serve foods high in fat, cholesterol, and sugar.
6. Vegetables: Except avocado.	
7. Decaffeinated tea: Especially green tea.	6. Packaged foods that don't need refrigeration: Generally high in saturated fat and sugar.
8. Red wine: One glass daily appears to cut heart disease risk.	

selenium levels were at the high end of normal. Prostate and gastrointestinal cancers seemed most strongly related to lower selenium levels. Subjects with both low vitamin E and selenium levels were at even greater risk.

Credible evidence of selenium's importance is growing. A 1996 study in the *Journal of the American Medical Association* showed that when patients who had suffered a bout of skin cancer were given daily selenium, they were less likely to die from cancer than patients not given selenium. This multicenter, double-blind, randomized, placebo-controlled trial enrolled 1,312 patients with a history of basal cell or squamous cell skin cancers. Their average age was 63. In comparison with conventionally treated patients, subjects who received selenium had two-thirds the risk of developing any additional form of cancer and half the risk of dying from cancer. The findings were so dramatic that, in its sixth year, the study was stopped to give the subjects in the comparison group the opportunity to take selenium.

In a 1986 study published in the *New England Journal of Medicine*, Alan Menkes and colleagues measured blood levels of vitamins E and A and beta-carotene in patients who had developed lung cancer anywhere from one to nine years earlier. People who had developed a specific type of lung cancer, known as squamous cell lung cancer, were over four times more likely to be beta-carotene deficient compared to control subjects. Subjects in the lowest fifth of the group in terms of vitamin E levels were two-and-a half times more likely to have any form of lung cancer compared to controls. The Alpha-Tocopherol, Beta Carotene Cancer Prevention Study Group also published in 1994 in the *New England Journal of Medicine* that vitamin E decreased the risk of prostate cancer.

OBESITY

Obesity is not common among our centenarians. In fact, the majority of them have never been obese, which further explains their low rates of cancer. Obesity has been linked to colon, rectal, and prostate cancer in men, and to cancers of the gallbladder, breast, cervix, uterus, and ovaries in women. A 13-year study by the American Cancer Society

Weight / Height	100	105	110	115	120	125	130	135	140	145	150	155	160
5'	20	21	21	22	23	24	25	26	27	28	29	30	31
5'1"	19	20	21	22	23	24	25	26	26	27	28	29	30
5'2"	18	19	20	21	22	23	24	25	26	27	27	28	29
5'3"	18	19	19	20	21	22	23	24	25	26	27	27	28
5'4"	17	18	19	20	21	21	22	23	24	25	26	27	27
5'5"	17	17	18	19	20	21	22	22	23	24	25	26	27
5'6"	16	17	18	19	19	20	21	22	23	23	24	25	26
5'7"	16	16	17	18	19	20	20	21	22	23	23	24	25
5'8"	15	16	17	17	18	19	20	21	21	22	23	24	24
5'9"	15	16	16	17	18	18	19	20	21	21	22	23	24
5'10"	14	15	16	17	17	18	19	19	20	21	22	22	23
5'11"	14	15	15	16	17	17	18	19	20	20	21	22	22
6'	14	14	15	16	16	17	18	18	19	20	20	21	22
6'1"	13	14	15	15	16	16	17	18	18	19	20	20	21
6'2"	12	13	15	15	15	16	17	17	18	19	19	20	21
6'3"	12	13	14	14	15	16	16	17	17	18	19	19	20

Weight / Height	165	170	175	180	185	190	195	200	205	210	215	220	225
5'	32	33	34	35	36	37	38	39	40	41	42	43	44
5'1"	31	32	33	34	35	36	37	38	39	40	41	42	43
5'2"	30	31	32	33	34	35	36	37	37	38	39	40	41
5'3"	29	30	31	32	33	34	35	35	36	37	38	39	40
5'4"	28	29	30	31	32	33	33	34	35	36	37	38	39
5'5"	27	28	29	30	31	32	32	33	34	35	36	37	37
5'6"	27	27	28	29	30	31	31	32	33	34	35	36	36
5'7"	26	27	27	28	29	30	31	31	32	33	34	34	35
5'8"	25	26	27	27	28	29	30	30	31	32	33	33	34
5'9"	24	25	26	27	27	28	29	30	30	31	32	32	33
5'10"	24	24	25	26	27	27	28	29	29	30	31	32	32
5'11"	23	24	24	25	26	26	27	28	29	29	30	31	31
6'	22	23	24	24	25	26	26	27	28	28	29	30	31
6'1"	22	22	23	24	24	25	26	26	27	28	28	29	30
6'2"	21	22	22	23	24	24	25	26	26	27	28	28	29
6'3"	21	21	22	22	23	24	24	25	26	26	27	27	29

Determine your Body Mass Index (BMI) by matching your height (barefoot) and weight (unclothed). A BMI of 18 to 24 is associated with minimal premature mortality and disability risk; 25 to 26 (overweight) is low risk; 27 to 29 (obese) is moderate risk; 30 to 34 (significant obesity) is high risk; 35 to 39 (morbid obesity) is very high risk; and 40 or greater (extreme morbid obesity) is extremely high risk. Obesity markedly adds to the risks associated with other behaviors or medical problems, such as diabetes or smoking. If you have such a disease or engage in such behaviors, your BMI-associated risk would shift into the next category. According to the advocacy group Shape-Up America, half of Americans are overweight.

found that both men and women whose body weight was 40 percent greater than average for their height and age group bore dramatically increased cancer risks—33 percent greater than the general population in men, and 35 percent greater in women. However, it is possible that even smaller variations from ideal body weight could carry some risk of cancer.

As we discussed in chapter 5, drastic reductions in calorie intake have been associated with reduced cancer risk and longer life span in rats. But the nature of the link between obesity and cancer is unclear. Obese people may have a tendency to produce greater amounts of insulin, a hormone that allows sugar to gain entry to fat and muscle cells. Insulin is also a growth factor, and, as we know, cancer is a manifestation of uncontrolled cell growth.

To reduce cancer risk, people should try to maintain a healthy body weight by exercising regularly and eating moderately. Consider your own exercise needs and those of your children to be a health priority, and try to do your part to ensure safe and adequate facilities for exercise in your home or neighborhood.

EXCERCISE

As people get older, they often complain about the difficulty of keeping weight off. This may in part be due to normal slowing of the metabolism, but there is a way to speed your metabolic rate back up: building muscle mass. Muscle is exceptionally efficient at burning fat, but as your muscle mass decreases, fat tends to stay on board. Therefore, an important part of your strategy to combat obesity must include isometric exercises—like weight lifting, for example—that increase muscle mass.

In addition to helping maintain an ideal body weight, exercise has cancer-prevention properties of its own. Exercise exerts beneficial effects on hormone levels and immune system activity, both of which may contribute to cancer prevention. In the colon, where the cancer preventive effects of exercise have been well documented, exercise may increase the rate at which stool passes through, perhaps reducing the time that the inner lining of the colon is exposed to potential carcinogens.

Exercise has also been linked to lower rates of breast and prostate cancer. One study showed a steadily declining rate of breast cancer risk for each additional hour of exercise performed weekly. Four or more hours of consistent weekly exercise were associated with a 60 percent reduction in breast cancer risk. Studies suggest that prostate cancer risk may also be reduced by exercise during young adulthood.

Exercise need not be excessively strenuous. Fifteen to thirty minutes of walking or bike-riding each day may be sufficient to reduce cancer risk. Low-impact exercises like yoga or Tai Chi may be helpful for people with limited movement. Although four days of exercise each week may be sufficient to reduce cancer risk, greater gains can probably be achieved with daily exercise.

Occupational Exposure

People should be aware of the measurable risk posed by carcinogens in the workplace. It has been estimated that 5 to 15 percent of cancer in men, and from 1 to 5 percent of those in women can be attributed to carcinogens encountered while at work. Probably one of the most important workplace carcinogens is tobacco smoke, but many companies have eliminated smoking from public places.

The International Agency for Research on Cancer publishes lists of workplace chemicals that have been linked or may be linked to certain cancers. Workers should be aware of chemicals they work with, and take steps to make sure that they are protected from exposure, either by special equipment or design.

Viruses and Bacteria

Viruses disrupt the growth and reproductive processes of cells, and turn them to the production of viral proteins. As their genetic material is co-opted, cells may undergo some of the changes leading to the uncontrolled growth that characterizes cancer. Several relatively common viruses and some more obscure ones have been implicated in this process.

For instance, Epstein Barr virus (EBV) is involved in causing almost all childhood cases of Burkitt's lymphoma in Africa, and some 20 percent in all other cases. EBV is also involved in about 35 to 50 percent of all cases of Hodgkin's lymphoma. Cancer of the liver may be caused by the hepatitis B and C viruses (HBV and HCV). Human papilloma virus (HPV) is involved in causing cancers of the anus and genitals. Women who are exposed to this virus at young ages are at particularly high risk. To prevent these cancers, it is important to avoid exposure to these viruses. People with active sex lives should use condoms to avoid exposure to HPV, HBV, HCV, and other viruses. Chronic infection with *h. pylori*, a very common bacteria that causes the vast majority of gastric ulcers, may predispose people to stomach cancer. Symptoms of ulcers, such as chronic intermittent abdominal pain, heartburn, and a feeling of fullness especially after small meals, merit a visit to your doctor.

SUN EXPOSURE

Sun exposure is one of the most frequently encountered and avoidable causes of human cancer. Sunburn and overexposure are principal causative factors in melanoma, the most deadly skin cancer, which accounts for 34,000 new cancer cases in the United States annually, or about 40 percent of all new cases. More than 7,000 Americans die of skin cancer each year.

Inherited characteristics, such as skin color, are very important to skin cancer incidence. Skin cancer is about ten times more common among whites than African-Americans. People with fair skin and red hair are at even greater risk. In countries where light-skinned people encounter frequent and intense sun exposure, like Australia, skin cancers occur in practically epidemic proportions.

Fortunately, there is a great deal we can do to avoid skin cancer. The most important thing is to avoid sun exposure. Wear shirts and hats whenever possible, particularly if you are more vulnerable to sun damage. Sunscreen with a protective factor of 15 SPF or greater should be used when exposure cannot be avoided. Notably, recent concern has arisen over the fact that these sunscreens do not protect against one form of ultraviolet light: UV-A. Only creams, such as zinc oxide, that completely block out all ultraviolet light can protect fully against sun exposure. Everyone should avoid unnecessarily prolonged exposure to the sun's rays. And it is particularly important to protect children from sunburn, which may create a lifelong susceptibility to melanoma.

RADIATION

While many of the dynamics of cancer risk from radiation remain unclear, epidemiological studies suggest that as much as 10 percent of all American lung cancer cases are principally caused by radon. This is a weak form of radiation that frequently accumulates in houses and basements because of its natural presence in certain forms of rock, especially granite. Medical X rays and accidental exposure to radiation, such as occurred at the Chernobyl nuclear power plant in the former USSR, also account for a small percentage of cancers.

Americans who want to reduce their risk of developing cancer as a result of radon exposure can use structural methods to eliminate the gas from their homes. Since radon is most dangerous when combined with exposure to cigarette smoke, the first step in eliminating lung cancer risk ought to be smoking cessation. We do not recommend refusing X rays or other forms of medical imaging in order to reduce cancer risk, since the additional risk is very small and accurate diagnosis of diseases is much more important.

DELAY OSTEOPOROSIS

Bones are constantly being remodeled by the body. Cells called osteoclasts break down bone, while bone-forming osteoblasts rebuild them. Bones stop growing in length during adolescence, but continue to bulk up until age 25 to 35. Then they will often start to gradually lose calcium. People who fail to get adequate calcium during the crucial first 35 years of life are consequently at increased risk of osteoporosis.

Osteoporosis, a loss of bone density that can accompany aging, affects at least 25 million Americans, most of them over age 65. Anyone taking glucocorticoid steroids—such as prednisone, methyl-pred-nisolone, or solumedrol—or certain antiseizure medications is also at increased risk of osteoporosis.

The loss of bone density brought about by osteoporosis leads to an increased risk of fractures. It is estimated that more than 1.3 million osteoporotic fractures occur each year in the United States. Approximately one-half of these fractures are spinal (vertebral) fractures, one-quarter are hip fractures, and one-quarter are wrist fractures. Hip and wrist fractures usually occur in association with a fall. All these fractures can lead to loss of function and, particularly in the case of hip fracture, loss of life. A significant proportion of people who sustain hip fractures have partial or total loss of mobility that may be irreversible. This loss of mobility in an older, frail person can lead to lower muscle mass, and poor lung and cardiovascular function, all of which markedly increase mortality risk. About one-quarter of people who were living in the community before a hip fracture must enter a rehabilitation setting for at least one year, and about 20 percent of all people who suffer a hip fracture die within one year. Fewer than 10 percent of our centenarian women have a history of fractures, a fact which underscores the importance of avoiding or delaying the occurrence of osteoporosis in the quest for healthy aging.

Eighty percent of osteoporosis sufferers are women. Over the course of her life, a woman is three times more likely than a man to sustain a vertebral or hip fracture, and six times more likely to suffer a wrist fracture. Accelerated bone loss after menopause contributes significantly to this increased risk in women. Estimates are that as much as 75 percent of bone lost in the years after menopause may be related to estrogen deficiency.

For women who develop osteoporosis, the greatest and most accelerated bone loss occurs in the 10 to 15 years following the onset of menopause. Thereafter, the rate of bone loss slows and stabilizes. Many women have no warning that they are suffering from osteoporosis until their first fracture occurs.

When vertebral (usually in the midback) fractures occur within 20 years of menopause, they are often painful. Such fractures are not always brought on by falls, but can result from lifting or from a sudden turn of the shoulders or hips. Vertebral fractures that occur among women in their eighties and nineties are usually not painful and develop slowly rather than in association with trauma. This type of fracture is a common cause of reduced height in older women.

PREVENTIVE MEASURES

A number of strategies have been shown to help prevent or delay osteoporosis and thus avoid the fractures that may result from thin bones. Diet should include adequate amounts of calcium, as well as vitamin D, which is necessary to absorb and utilize calcium. Dietary sources of calcium include low-fat dairy products like milk, or foods such as broccoli, tofu, and calcium-fortified fruit juice. Most people should consume from 1,000 to 1,500 mg of calcium daily, as well as at least 800 IU of vitamin D daily. Postmenopausal women can benefit particularly from calcium: 1,000 mg per day can reduce bone loss by as much as 50 percent.

If these foods are not a regular part of your diet, take calcium supplements, which are often combined with vitamin D. The usual dosages are 500 mg of calcium with 400 IU of vitamin D with each meal. A relatively small number of people should not take extra calcium because of certain kidney or parathyroid gland problems. Women should discuss calcium and vitamin D supplementation with their doctors.

An exercise regimen of at least half an hour, three times per week, is another important component of osteoporosis prevention. Any reasonable exercise regimen that has been approved by your physician should help. Weight-bearing exercise, like weight-lifting or walking in the swimming pool, actually increases bone density. Exercise also strengthens muscles, which helps prevent accidental falls.

Smoking accelerates bone loss, so we strongly recommend giving up smoking to anyone concerned about osteoporosis, not to mention health in general. Excessive alcohol use—more than one drink per day—can also speed bone loss and should be avoided.

The prevention or treatment of osteoporosis is also one of the important reasons for perimenopausal and postmenopausal women to take estrogen. Estrogen may also provide some protection against heart disease, and it can be helpful in some women who suffer from urinary incontinence. A number of patients cannot tolerate estrogen, however, because of hot flashes, vaginal bleeding, or other medical contraindications. When osteoporosis occurs in men, testosterone replacement may be an effective treatment. This is one of the few conditions in which testosterone therapy is appropriate.

SCREENING AND TREATMENT

Because it appears that much of osteoporosis can be prevented or at least markedly delayed, and because it is potentially so widespread, it makes sense that everyone should be tested for osteoporosis before it causes enough bone loss for fractures to occur. The test, called bone densitometry, measures the density of your bones. It has little or no

Checkups

Many of our centenarians tell us that the only times they saw a doctor was when they gave birth, or when they first began to experience serious illness in their late nineties or early hundreds. They got away with this in large part, we believe, because of their genes. Most people cannot afford such an approach to health care. Screening for various illnesses that cause premature mortality should be a key part of a strategy to shorten the duration of illness in your life. The prevention strategy below is divided into three age ranges: twenties to thirties, forties, and 50 and older.

IN YOUR TWENTIES AND THIRTIES . . .
Examinations and Tests

HIV and Hepatitis B & C tests: whenever you engage in risky behavior (unprotected sex, needle-sharing, etc.)

Blood pressure: at least every two years

Skin exam: every three years

Cholesterol (total and HDL): every five years

Eye exam: at least once between puberty and age 40

Self-exams

Skin self-exam: every month

risk associated with it and exposes you to about the same amount of radiation you might get in the flight from Boston to New York City. If you are age 25 or older and haven't yet experienced menopausal symptoms, and you exercise regularly (especially resistance exercise), eat a healthy diet with enough calcium and vitamin D, and do not smoke, you probably do not need the test. However, in the same age range, if you have one of these risk factors or you are going through or have gone through menopause, you should have the test. Men age 25 and older who have one of the risk factors or have suffered fractures after only a light blow to the bone should undergo densitometry as well. All men 60 or older should be tested.

If osteoporosis is detected, the good news is that there are now several medications available, beyond estrogen, that not only stop the disease, but can even reverse the damage it has already caused. One

---

Immunizations
Tetanus booster: every 10 years

If you are a woman:
Pelvic exam: every year
Pap test: every three years
Clinical breast exam: every three years
Breast self-exam: every month

If you are a man:
Testicular self-exam: every month

In Your Forties . . .
Examinations and Tests
HIV and Hepatitis B & C tests: whenever you engage in
    risky behavior Blood pressure: at least every two years
Cholesterol (total and HDL): every five years
Skin exam: every three years
Eye exam: every two to four years
Fasting plasma glucose (diabetes) test: every three years,
    after age 45

medication, alendronate (Fosamax), has been found to increase bone mass by 7 percent. Such an effect can reduce the risk of fracture by 50 percent. Another medication is raloxifene (Evista), which acts much like estrogen in its effects upon bone but reportedly lacks the increased risk of breast and uterine cancer that has been associated with estrogen. The pros and cons of taking one of these medications must be fully discussed with your doctor.

An integral part of your battle against the age-related diseases we've outlined above is a screening and prevention program established with a health professional. What you need to do depends in part on your age. We've constructed a prevention strategy for major causes of morbidity and mortality, which can be found in the pages that follow.

Self-exams
Skin self-exam: every month

Immunizations
Tetanus booster: every 10 years

If you are a woman:
Pelvic exam: every year
Breast self-exam: every month
Pap test: every three years
Clinical breast exam: every year
Mammogram: every one to two years
Optional (e.g. if you are close to menopause): Bone mineral density test (bone densitometry)
Follicle-stimulating hormone (FSH) test (confirms if you are going through menopause)

If you are a man:
Digital rectal exam if you are African-American or have a strong family history of prostate cancer (two or more first-degree relatives): every year

GUARD YOUR SENSES

Vision loss is one of the most frequently reported disabilities among older people. It is estimated that one in nine persons age 65 years or older—or about 3.5 million people—suffers sufficient visual impairment to interfere with many aspects of daily functioning, such as simply reading newspaper print. Visual impairment affects many of the most enjoyable aspects of life: reading, exercising, and socializing with others. Protecting vision is a worthwhile goal that should begin long before signs of vision loss become apparent.

CATARACTS

Cataracts occur when the lens of the eye—normally clear and flexible—becomes stiff, cloudy, and opaque. The resulting visual effect is

---

Testicular self-exam: every month

Prostate specific antigen (PSA) test: every year at age 45 in men who are at high risk, including African-Americans or those with a strong family history of prostate cancer

YOUR FIFTIES ON UP . . .

Examinations and Tests

HIV and Hepatitis B & C tests: whenever you engage in risky behavior

Skin exam: every year

Eye exam: every two to four years; every one to two years if 65 or older

Fasting plasma glucose (diabetes) test: every three years

Thyroid-stimulating hormone test: every three to five years if 60 or older

Cholesterol (total and HDL): every five years; every three to five years if 60 or older

Colorectal cancer tests: fecal occult blood test every year; sigmoidoscopy at age 50; colonoscopy every ten years thereafter

Bone mineral density test (bone densitometry): men too! every ten years after age 60

Blood pressure: every year

like looking through a camera lens smeared with Vaseline or covered with tissue paper. The major symptoms of cataracts include blurred or filmy vision that is not correctable by glasses, and a need for brighter light for close activities like reading. About half of all people begin developing cataracts between ages 52 and 64, but probably won't notice vision problems until age 65 or later. Cataracts may cause more severe vision problems for people between the ages of 75 and 85.

Atherosclerosis and free radical damage are believed to be the major causes of cataract development. Roaming free radicals may damage the structural components (proteins, enzymes, and cell membranes) of the lens. Researchers now believe that antioxidants play an important role in slowing or even halting this process. Dietary supplements such as selenium and vitamin E may help you delay or avoid the development of cataracts.

Self-exams
Skin self-exam: every month

Immunizations
Tetanus booster: every ten years
Pneumococcal vaccine: once after age 65
Influenza vaccine: every year if 65 or older

If you are a woman:
Pelvic exam: every year
Breast self-exam: every month
Pap test: every three years
Clinical breast exam: every year
Mammogram: every year
Optional (e.g. if you are close to menopause): Follicle-stimulating
    hormone (FSH) test (confirms if you are going through menopause)

If you are a man:
Digital rectal exam (for prostate cancer): every year
Testicular self-exam: every month
Prostate specific antigen (PSA) test: every year

Refined sugars that are converted directly into glucose may also play a role in cataract development and should be avoided. Some people may have a genetic predisposition to converting more of the body's sugars into glucose, thereby increasing their risk of cataracts. Talk to your ophthalmologist about whether to cut your intake of refined sugar. Cataracts also may result from diabetes, injury to the eye, and use of long-term oral steroids, diuretics, and major tranquilizers. They also have been linked to the use of commercially available hormones—DHEA and testosterone—which have been touted for their "age-fighting" capabilities.

Researchers have been examining the possibility that certain dietary supplements (vitamins C, E, and beta-carotene) may provide protection against cataracts. In 1998, in the journal *Ophthalmology*, researchers from the University Medical Center at Stony Brook published results of a long-term study of 764 subjects in which vitamin E reduced the risk of cataracts by one-half. A broader-spectrum multivitamin reduced the risk by one-third.

Recent studies indicate that people who spend a lot of time in the sun or who live at high altitudes develop cataracts earlier than those who do not; wearing sunglasses and a wide-brimmed hat are easy, inexpensive ways to help minimize exposure to harmful ultraviolet rays.

MACULAR DEGENERATION

Macular degeneration is a condition in which the macula, a highly light-sensitive area of the retina, becomes damaged over time, resulting in fuzzy or blurred vision or even total darkness in the middle of the visual field. Macular degeneration is the leading cause of irreversible blindness among adults. Gradual thinning of the macula results in "dry" macular degeneration, which accounts for 90 percent of all cases. It is painless and generally causes slight vision loss experienced as a "dimming" of vision during reading. "Wet" macular degeneration accounts for the remaining 10 percent of diagnoses, yet represents a far greater threat to vision. New blood vessels grow beneath the retina, leaking blood and fluid, and can rapidly cause a large blind spot in the middle of the visual field. Smokers beware: People who light up have a greater risk of recurrent vessel leaks than their non-smoking counterparts.

Beta carotene, vitamin C, vitamin E, and selenium have all aroused researchers' interest in this area. Preliminary studies suggest that certain vitamins and minerals may slow or even stop the progression of macular degeneration. In a 1996 Johns Hopkins Study, researchers measured blood levels of vitamin E (alpha-tocopherol), vitamin C, and beta-carotene, and noted a significant protective effect with vitamin E in particular.

Zinc also has attracted some attention as a potential weapon against macular degeneration. Zinc is key to normal retinal functioning, leaving some researchers wondering whether low zinc levels in some people are linked to the disease. Although a small study in the 1980s indicated that the mineral might slow down the progression of the condition, subsequent studies have not substantiated early hopes.

In a 1994 study published in the *Journal of the American Medical Association*, a high dietary intake of carotenoids was associated with reduced risk for macular degeneration. Those in the highest fifth of the study group in terms of carotenoid intake had a 43 percent lower risk for macular degeneration compared with those in the lowest fifth. Certain carotenoids—lutein and zeaxanthin, which are primarily obtained from dark green, leafy vegetables—were most strongly associated with a reduced risk. The intake of preformed vitamin A (retinol) did not have an appreciable impact on the development of macular degeneration, nor did vitamins E or C.

The National Eye Institute currently is studying the potential clinical benefits of vitamin and mineral therapy in the treatment of both macular degeneration and cataracts. Results from the study are not expected for several more years.

If you have already lost some vision to macular degeneration, low-vision aids that combine magnification and bright lights might be of help. Normal activities such as reading and watching television will not worsen the condition. Ask your doctor how you can monitor your vision between visits.

DIABETES AND EYE DISEASE

Although many people do not realize it, diabetes is the number one threat to adult vision in the United States today. About 8 million Americans have diabetic eye disease, and the price tag for prevention, screening, and treatment is high: about $2.8 billion annually. Each year, some 24,000 people in this country lose their sight because of diabetes.

Diabetes is a metabolic disorder in which the body becomes unable to independently regulate the amount of sugar in the blood. Sometimes it is difficult to imagine what this has to do with eye disease—even top diabetes researchers don't fully understand the link. Nevertheless, within the past few years, several large studies have firmly established that if you have diabetes, your likelihood of developing eye disease—such as macular degeneration and a related disorder, diabetic retinopathy—is closely related to blood sugar management.

In 1993, the *New England Journal of Medicine* published the Diabetes Control and Complications Trial (DCCT), a national study led by researchers at Massachusetts General Hospital. The study showed that people with type-1 diabetes who keep their blood sugar closer to the normal range (70–120 mg/dL before meals and below 180 mg/dL after meals) reduce their chances of developing diabetic eye disease by 76 percent. Similar studies in people with type-2 diabetes have confirmed that tight blood sugar control can lower their chances of developing complications, too.

About 10 to 20 percent of people already show signs of eye disease at the time they're diagnosed with diabetes. For these people, it's very important to begin good blood sugar management as quickly as possible to prevent the progression of eye disease. All adults with type-1 or type-2 diabetes should have a dilated eye exam at least once a year. If you have a family history of type-2 diabetes, have your blood sugar checked each time you see your doctor.

HEARING LOSS

Hearing loss is another age-related process that starts relatively early, yet can become disabling in later years. As with most of the conditions we have discussed in this chapter, prevention may begin at any age, but the earlier the better.

In most cases, hearing loss is part of the natural aging process, increasing so gradually it may go undetected until it reaches an advanced stage. Unfortunately it is a common problem affecting 30 percent of adults age 65 and older. Most commonly the cause is a gradual loss of nerve cells in the inner part of the ear. This may lead to a decreased ability to pick up high-pitched sounds like the chirping of birds or a telephone's ring. A man's voice may be easier to hear than the higher pitches of a woman's. People with this problem have particular trouble when there are competing noises, for example, when trying to talk to someone in a noisy, crowded room.

The cumulative effects of repeated exposure to damaging noises such as lawn mowers, leaf blowers, woodworking machinery, alarms, and loud appliances are important causes of hearing loss. The loudness of sound is measured in decibels. Normal conversation's volume is about 60 decibels, the humming of a refrigerator is 40, and city traffic noise around 80. Loud noises that cause damage like motorcycles, firecrackers, amplified music at concerts or through earphones, and small-arms fire, produce noise ranging from 120 to 140 decibels. Sounds of less than 75 decibels, even after long exposure, are unlikely to cause hearing loss. Therefore, when the noise is so loud that it hurts, your body is telling you to cover your ears and move away for a good reason: The noise can cause permanent damage. Avoiding noises louder than 75 decibels and reducing the amount of time one is exposed to everyday noises are very important.

Some general strategies to preserve your hearing should include: Know which noises can cause damage, wear ear plugs or other hearing protective devices when involved in loud activities, and plug your ears if you know a loud noise like an ambulance siren is about to occur. You may want to protect children who are too young to know the risks. Hearing tests should be performed on babies, again when the child is in the first few grades of elementary school, and, if no symptoms of hearing loss emerge in the interim, at age 60. An audiologist can recommend how often auditory testing should be performed, depending upon the test results. If hearing impairment is detected, one should seek an otolaryngologist, a specialist in diagnosing and treating hearing loss, which can often be ameliorated with hearing aids. Today, these devices are incredibly small yet powerful, and can subtract unwanted noise, allowing one to hear only selected sounds, like conversation. Audiologists and otolaryngologists can help decide whether and which kind of hearing aid will be helpful.

THE LIVING TO 100
LIFE EXPECTANCY CALCULATOR©

An early and consistent investment in diet and lifestyle can lead to additional years of good health in later life. We designed the Life Expectancy Calculator to translate what we've learned from studies of centenarians and other longevity research into a practical tool for individuals to estimate their longevity potential. Better scores indicate a reduced risk of disability toward the end of life. Of course, no one can guarantee either continued health or longevity. However, everyone should be aware of the factors that increase or decrease mortality and disability risk. Some of these are under individual control, and people who want to live longer, healthier lives should try to fashion their lifestyles accordingly.

The average person is born with strong enough longevity genes to live to age 85 and maybe longer. People who take appropriate preventive steps may add as many as ten quality years to that. People who fail to heed the messages of preventive© medicine may subtract substantial years from their lives.

To use the calculator, add your negative and positive scores separately. Most of our centenarian subjects would score very high on this test.

Following the quiz is a key explaining why each item is related to your longevity potential.

THE
LIVING TO 100
LIFE EXPECTANCY CALCULATOR©

1. Do you smoke or chew tobacco, or are you around a lot of secondhand smoke? If yes . . . **−10**

   Do you smoke or chew tobacco, or are you around a lot of secondhand smoke? If no . . . **1**

2. Do you eat more than a couple of hot dogs, slices of bacon, or a bologna sandwich a week? If yes . . . **−3**

   Do you stay away from processed meats? If yes . . . **2**

3. Do you cook your fish, poultry, or meat until it is charred? If yes . . . **−2**

   Do you minimize the amount of meat in your diet? If yes . . . **7**

4. Do you use butter or cream regularly? Do you eat cheese or fried foods regularly? If yes . . . **−5**

   Do you stay away from butter, cream, and other saturated fats as well as fried foods (e.g. French fries)? If yes . . . **7**

5. Do you drink wine and liquor in excess? If yes . . . **−5**

   Do you drink one glass of red wine daily? If yes . . . **2**

6. Do air pollution warnings occur where you live? If yes . . . **−4**

   Do air pollution warnings occur where you live? If no/rarely . . . **3**

7. Do you drink more than 16 oz of coffee a day? If yes . . . **−3**

   Do you take an aspirin a day? If yes . . . **4**

8

8. Do you floss and brush your teeth every day? If no . . . **−4**

Do you floss and brush your teeth every day? If yes . . . **4**

9. Do you have a bowel movement less than once every two days?

Do you make a point of eating plenty of fruits, vegetables, and bran every day, preferably in place of foods that are bad for you? If yes . . . **7**

If yes . . . **−4**

10. Do you engage in risky sexual or drug-related behavior that increase your risk of getting HIV or a cancer-related virus? If yes . . . **−7**

Do you engage in risky behavior that would increase your chances of contracting HIV or a cancer-related virus. If no . . . **1**

11. Do you try to get a sun tan? If yes . . . **−4**

Do you avoid the sun and use sun block? If yes . . . **3**

12. Are there dangerous levels of radon in your house?

Have you checked and found that there is no detectable radon in your house? If yes . . . **1**

If yes . . . **−6**

13. Does your body mass index put you in the obese category? (See chart in chapter 7.) If yes . . . **−7**

Does your body mass index put you in the lean category? (See chart in chapter 7.) If yes . . . **7**

14. Do you live too far away from other family membersfor visits to be spontaneous? If yes . . . **−4**

Do you live near enough to other family members that you can drop by spontaneously? If yes . . . **5**

15. Does stress bother you to the extent that you can't seem to shake it off?

If yes . . . −7

Can you shed stress? This might be by praying, sports, meditation, being able to respond to humor or by other means.
If yes . . . 7

16. Does more than one member of your immediate family have diabetes? If yes . . . −4

Is there diabetes in your family?

If no . . . 1

17. Were both your parents dead or very frail by their seventies?

If yes . . . −10

Is there more than one of the following relatives in your family who have reached at least age 90 in excellent health: parents, aunts/uncles, siblings, grandparents? If yes . . . 10

18. Are you a couch potato (no regular aerobic or resistance exercise)?
If yes . . . −6

Do you exercise 20 minutes a day or more?

If yes . . . 8

19. Do you take vitamin E (800 IU/day) and selenium (200 mcg) daily?
If no . . . −5

Do you take vitamin E (800 IU) and selenium (200 mcg) daily?
If yes . . . 5

Divide the two scores (negative and positive) by 5:

75 = 15	50 = 10	25 = 5
70 = 14	45 = 9	20 = 4
65 = 13	40 = 8	15 = 3
60 = 12	35 = 7	10 = 2
55 = 11	30 = 6	5 = 1

Now, add the negative score to the positive score for an estimate of the number of years you should add or subtract from your life expectancy (for example, −30 + 45 = 15).

For most men reading this book, life expectancy is about 84 years, and for most women, about 87 years.

_____ years added or subtracted from your life expectancy

THE REASONING BEHIND EACH ITEM IN THE LIFE EXPECTANCY CALCULATOR©

1. Cigarette smoke contains toxins that directly damage DNA and subsequently cause cancer. Cigarettes are the biggest direct source of nitrosamines that humans are exposed to. These substances, along with other constituents of cigarette smoke, are potent oxidants and carcinogens that lead to accelerated aging, and diseases associated with aging.

2. Some studies suggest that 90 percent of all human cancers are environmentally induced, 30 to 40 percent of these by diet. Preserved and cured meats (bacon, sausage, lunch meats, etc.) are the largest source of nitrites in our diet. Nitrites lead to the formation in our bodies of nitrosamines, which are important environmental oxidants and carcinogens. For instance, there is a significant association between nitrosamines and stomach cancer.

3. Charring can change proteins and amino acids into substances called heterocyclic amines, which are potent mutagens, or substances that can alter your DNA. Cooking meats at very high temperatures for long periods of time is also risky. The Iowa Women's Health Study found that women who consistently ate meats very well done proved 4.6 times as likely to have breast cancer as those who ate meats cooked rare or medium.

4. High protein diets, and the combination of a high fat and protein diet, have been associated with increased risk of cancer of the breast, uterus, prostate, colon, pancreas, and kidney. An important mechanism is that these foods can be inefficient sources of energy and cause excess oxygen radical formation.

5. Excessive alcohol is toxic. It damages the liver and the mitochondria within most cells of the body. This leads to acceleration of aging and increased susceptibility to many diseases associated with aging. Ask your doctor what is a reasonable amount of alcohol for you.

6. A number of air pollutants are potent causes of cancer and contain oxidants that accelerate aging.

7. Excessive coffee can both indicate and exacerbate stress. Stress can lead to a hormonal imbalance that can physically damage and age many organs. In addition, coffee predisposes the stomach to chronic inflammation of the stomach and ulcers. Such chronic inflammation leads to release of substances that raise the risk of heart disease.

8. Research shows that chronic gum disease leads to the release of inflammatory and toxic substances into the blood stream, encouraging plaque formation in arteries and ultimately leading to heart disease. This process probably also increases the risk of stroke and accelerated aging.

9. Keeping gut transit time under 20 hours seems to decrease the incidence of colon cancer, probably by decreasing the contact time between the gut lining and carcinogenic substances in the diet. These substances influence DNA damage and repair and therefore probably also influence the rate of aging as well. Epidemiological studies in humans and animal studies suggest that increasing dietary fiber will reduce the risk of certain cancers perhaps by increasing the frequency of bowel movements.

10. Viruses such as HIV and others that are transmitted by risky behavior not only cause AIDS but also various cancers including lymphoma. These viruses change DNA and, as a result, probably also influence aging.

11. The association between sun exposure and accelerated skin aging is clear. The ultraviolet rays in sunlight directly damage DNA. More sun means more wrinkles, sooner. It also means a higher risk of deadly skin cancer. Excessive sun exposure may also have more toxic consequences for the body in general.

12. Radon is a gas emitted from various types of rock, especially granite. (New Hampshire, the Granite State, is known for its high incidence of radon exposure.) Radon is a potent carcinogen. Toxic levels of radon in the home are equivalent to smoking two packs of cigarettes a day.

13. Extended family cohesiveness and frequent contact is a notable feature of centenarian families. Researchers have noted that people who do not belong to cohesive families have fewer coping resources and increased levels of social and psychological stress. Psychological stress is associated with heart disease, various cancers, and increased mortality risk.

14. Centenarians shed emotional stress exceptionally well. Their stress-resistant personalities and their relationships with others are important stress-reducing mechanisms.

15. Obesity is associated with inefficient energy production and an increased production of oxygen radicals within cells, therefore leading to increased risk of various cancers, heart disease, and accelerated aging. It may also lead to diabetes.

16. Diabetes causes excessive exposure to glucose and, when uncontrolled, results in age-related problems such as cataracts, impaired nerve function, eye disease, heart disease, and other vascular problems.

17. Genetics plays a significant role in the ability to achieve extreme old age. If both sides of your family develop diseases associated with aging significantly before average life expectancy, then it behooves you to do all you can to maximize your health status. If you have significant extreme longevity in your family, this will help significantly in your own ability to achieve old age in good health.

18. Exercise leads to more efficient mitochondrial energy production and less oxygen radical formation.

19. Vitamin E is thus far the best scientifically proven antioxidant available either in the diet or as a dietary supplement. It has been shown in epidemiological studies to delay or retard the progression of Alzheimer's disease, heart disease, and stroke. It also boosts the immune system. Selenium appears to have dramatic effects in preventing cancer.

8

O PIONEERS!

Reclaiming the Future

CREDIT: MICHAEL LUTCH

Centenarians like Edith Blair Staton, age 102, have lived the history most of us only read about. Mrs. Staton was acquainted with a number of American presidents and met regularly with several First Ladies in her capacity as national director of the Girl Scouts of America. Her favorite was Mrs. Hoover, who had a girl scout troop of her own. She knew people who died aboard the Titanic, *and she herself made several trips to Europe aboard the* Lusitania, *the sinking of which drew the United States into World War I. Here she sits in her Cambridge home, which contains a couch on which Abraham Lincoln sat while writing the Emancipation Proclamation.*

EXTREME OLD AGE is a new frontier to which literally hundreds of thousands, perhaps even millions of pioneers will travel in the coming years. The explorations of voyagers like Anna Morgan, Dirk Struik, and Tom Spear further expand our self-understanding and illuminate the mysteries of human life. As centenarians explore new forms of self-expression and artistry, they teach us that this new territory, this portion of life that was largely unknown to previous generations, is a gift. A Bureau of the U.S. Census Report, *65+ in the U.S.*, predicts that the baby boom generation will make it to 65 in better shape than their parents, and that the number of Americans living to age 85 may reach 7 million by the year 2020. As Theodore Roszak, author of *America the Wise: The Longevity Revolution*, wrote in a recent article: "We have become richer than our forefathers by 10, 20, 30 more years of life. Think of those years as a resource reclaimed from death the way the Dutch reclaim land from the sea."

Those who wish to enter the new territory of extreme old age must begin preparing many years in advance. Baby boomers who are now just beginning the longevity trek will fare far better if they listen to the guidance of centenarians. This new region, which for so long appeared barren to younger people, can be rich and fertile. But society and its attitudes will have to change considerably to facilitate the flowering of extreme old age. As the United Nations General Assembly noted in proclaiming 1999 the International Year of Older Persons, the nations of the world must work toward "a society for all ages." The extreme old must not be regarded as a separate culture. Our nations must mend the economic, geographic, social, and cultural gaps between young and old. The wisdom of centenarians is a critical resource that will help younger generations prepare for the long lives that almost certainly lie ahead.

AN INTERGENERATIONAL ARMISTICE

Demographic prognosticators routinely predict that "intergenerational wars" will erupt as baby boomers age. In particular, they foresee struggles in the workplace. Baby boomers attempting to climb the corporate ladder, the forecasters warn, will find the higher rungs obstinately occupied by older people. What many of these predictions overlook, however, is that during the Great Depression, a sizable dip in births resulted in a "baby bust." Baby boomers are being preceded into senior management positions by a generation of Americans who number only 30 million. As a result, there will be a paucity of senior managers in front of the baby boomers, who number 75 million. Baby boomers will be more likely to compete with one another for top-rung jobs than with members of the previous generation.

Older people will continue to pull their own weight in the work-force. The Vita Needle Co. of Needham, Massachusetts, employs 33

International Year of Older Persons

Recognizing the rapid growth of the older population and the vulnerability of older people worldwide not only to physical disease but to poverty and discrimination, the United Nations has declared 1999 the International Year of Older Persons. The United Nations encourages governments to incorporate these principles into their national aging programs whenever possible:

Independence
1. Older persons should have access to adequate food, water, shelter, clothing, and health care through the provision of income, family, and community support and self-help.
2. Older persons should have the opportunity to work or to have access to other income-generating opportunities.
3. Older persons should be able to participate in determining when and at what pace withdrawal from the labor force takes place.
4. Older persons should have access to appropriate educational and training programs.

people, average age 73. The oldest needle-maker is 88. Vita demonstrates the increasing respect that older people are receiving as employees. They arrive on time, work hard, and provide an additional advantage to employers in that their health care is usually covered by Medicare. Ernie Garron, a Vita sales engineer, believes the company is ahead of its time and predicts that others will follow its lead. "It's a trend you're going to be seeing more and more of, jobs where old people don't have to do a lot of physical labor," he said.

In Japan, where life expectancy is the highest in the world (83 years for women, 76 for men) policymakers have heard the alarm and taken steps to encourage the hiring of older workers. In 1990, a "subsidy for the encouragement of the employment of older workers" was made into Japanese law. Japanese firms can also receive subsidies for retaining their currently employed workers until they reach age 65. In another national program, Japanese workers nearing retirement age are retrained and reemployed. Japan also has 661 Sil-

---

5. Older persons should be able to live in environments that are safe and adaptable to personal preferences and changing capacities.
6. Older persons should be able to reside at home for as long as possible.

Participation

7. Older persons should remain integrated in society, participate actively in the formulation and implementation of policies that directly affect their well-being and share their knowledge and skills with younger generations.
8. Older persons should be able to seek and develop opportunities for service to the community and to serve as volunteers in positions appropriate to their interests and capabilities.
9. Older persons should be able to form movements or associations of older persons.

Care

10. Older persons should benefit from family and community care and protection in accordance with each society's system of cultural values.

ver Human Resource Centers where older people are employed to do community work, such as sidewalk-cleaning, or light manual labor.

When older people do leave the workforce, their volunteer efforts and social leadership often create a more sustaining social milieu for younger people. Elders have traditionally been observers and repositories of information about a changing world. In the years to come, they have the opportunity, more than ever before, to pass on experience that will help make new generations of old and extremely old people healthier and better equipped to face the frontier of old age. Their political power and cultural influence will grow with their numbers. The growth in the older population thus represents an opportunity to restore their place in society as integral members of the extended family and important contributors to the health and welfare of the greater population. Older generations have always assisted their children in child-rearing, but with more married cou-

11. Older persons should have access to health care to help them to maintain or regain the optimum level of physical, mental, and emotional well-being and to prevent or delay the onset of illness.
12. Older persons should have access to social and legal services to enhance their autonomy, protection, and care.
13. Older persons should be able to utilize appropriate levels of institutional care providing protection, rehabilitation, and social and mental stimulation in a humane and secure environment.
14. Older persons should be able to enjoy human rights and fundamental freedoms when residing in any shelter, care, or treatment facility, including full respect for their dignity, beliefs, needs, and privacy and for the right to make decisions about their care and the quality of their lives.

ples in the workforce, a healthier group of older people will have the opportunity to participate more actively in raising their grandchildren—and great-grandchildren, if they wish.

People in their later years have also consistently demonstrated a penchant for volunteerism. For example, the International Executive Service Corps enables more than 13,000 American business executives, mostly retirees, to share their expertise with companies and individuals in developing nations. Already, 93 million Americans volunteer some 20 billion hours of their time annually, about 220 hours per person. In Japan, a society where the culture has traditionally stressed "family first," volunteerism is increasing, with the number of nongovernmental organizations growing from 186 in 1991 to 351 in 1995. Given how active older generations are already, the elder boom could constitute a volunteer force of amazing proportions, with the potential to benefit educational, cultural, political, and social welfare institutions of all kinds.

Self-fulfillment

15. Older persons should be able to pursue opportunities for the full development of their potential.
16. Older persons should have access to the educational, cultural, spiritual, and recreational resources of society.

Dignity

17. Older persons should be able to live in dignity and security and be free of exploitation and physical or mental abuse.
18. Older persons should be treated fairly regardless of age, gender, racial or ethnic background, disability, or other status, and be valued independently of their economic contribution.

Dire predictions have been made about business costs rising and productivity being dragged down by the increased costs of caring for the elderly. Our research, and that of many others, indicates, however, that a longer lived society will be one in which health is better and costs are lower. A 1997 study in the *Proceedings of the National Academy of Science* by Kenneth Manton and colleagues of Duke University shows that 1.2 million fewer older people were disabled in 1994 than would have been expected from the disability rates of 1982. In other words, disability rates are falling dramatically.

An older society need not be one characterized by dependence. Rather than hindering our progress into the twenty-first century, older people are more likely to advance it.

A Mature Market

When we look back 50 years from now (as we hope to do), we will see the explosion of the older population as a tremendous boon, rather than a burden, to the economy, just as the youth market has been in this century. Advertisers and marketers, who have long understood that young people represent an important consumer segment, have yet to recognize the older market in the same way. This, however, is only because the numbers and financial power of the baby bust generation have not been close to that of the baby boom. When baby boomers begin to retire in greater numbers, demand will follow them into retirement. Many older people will take advantage of the leisure of their retirement years to explore the world around them anew. They will acquaint themselves with new technologies and cultural movements, trends that those embroiled in the workaday world are too busy to investigate.

In every point along its passage through the longevity marathon, the baby boomer population has dominated society both culturally and economically. As this generation moves closer to 65, society's perception of aging is changing, and interest in the topic of aging is increasing dramatically. There will be more books, plays, movies, and songs about aging, and we can look forward to older "looks" becoming more widely accepted and attractive in advertising and in public. As positive images of age increase, youth ceases to be the sole standard of beauty, and the customary stereotypes of older people in advertising begin to disappear. They are replaced by more representative, heterogeneous images and personalities, so that wrinkles and gray hair (and even no hair) carry less stigma than they do now. New products and services are beginning to emerge for the aging market. Designer Anne Klein, for example, has already developed a fashion clothing line that fits the lifestyles of older working women. Baby boomers, many of them anticipating long, healthy lives, are planning now so they will be financially well equipped for retirement and old age. The older market is poised to finally come into its own.

Golf, swimming, cycling, resistance training, and walking continue to increase in popularity as aging boomers look for physical activities that are easy on the body and can be enjoyed throughout life. (Imagine high-impact aerobics going the way of the Pet Rock, to be replaced by Tai Chi and yoga.) In addition, the tourism industry is already beginning to tailor its attractions to older people who have the time and energy to travel. Companies need to respond by becoming much more "longevity-friendly," emphasizing prevention and good health, as they already have established smoke-free work zones. Grocery stores already reflect the trend by increasingly featuring healthy foods and antioxidant vitamin supplements.

When people fully realize that the route to a healthy old age lies not in curing disease but in preventing it, the strength of the market-place will have to go to work in earnest, providing innovative options for aging people to preserve their mental and physical faculties. They will turn away from what Marshall McLuhan called "cool media," like television, and toward interactive activities and entertainments that keep one mentally active: puzzles, word games, and active learning pursuits.

There is already a resurgence of interest in education for the older set. Institutions of higher education, realizing that older people will eventually make up a significant portion of their student body, are considering ways to attract older students, planning programs, for instance, that enhance cognitive function and therefore help prevent Alzheimer's disease. A few schools, such as Dartmouth College in New Hampshire and Lasell College in Newton, Massachusetts, offer housing options for older people directly on or near campus, thus making themselves more attractive to this age group.

COME HOME, AMERICA

Centenarians live intergenerational lives. Although some may reside in dependent-care settings, they almost always spend time regularly with younger people, either from their own families or the families of others. During our studies, we observed that many centenarians lived with their families, sometimes in separate apartments in the same building, sometimes next door to one another, and sometimes in the same house.

There is a mutuality in the way centenarians and their younger relatives contribute to each other's lives. Children may take their centenarian relatives to the grocery store, or perform household chores. Eva Rindner and her mother, Lola Blonder, fax each other detailed letters each morning, just a few minutes after they've awakened. Mae Vogel's daughter spent considerable time with her mother. She gratefully remembered the long hours her mother had spent working as a cleaning woman to keep her children in school and the family together.

If we truly want to change the image of aging and older people, we must fight their marginalization and ghettoization. Economically and geographically, we must enable and encourage older people to remain in contact with younger generations. Most older people desperately want to remain in their own communities. According to a 1996 study by the American Association of Retired Persons, 81 percent of the 1,300 Americans over 50 surveyed wanted to stay in their own homes and never move. And a considerable number are in a position to do so: Figures compiled in 1997 by the U.S. Census Bureau show that 79 percent of households headed by someone over

65 own their residences, and of that group, 80 percent owned their homes free and clear.

More aging parents, if they heed the message of the lives of centenarians, will be moving back in with their children, or in close proximity to them. There is already a "backward migration" among older "snowbirds" who have decided it is more important to be near their children than to stay warm. Families are breaking age barriers to come back together.

Communities are creating living situations where younger and older people can live together and help one another. For middle- and upper-class older people who do not mind, or who actively seek, an age-segregated living environment, continuing care retirement centers can offer an optimal balance of autonomy and support. Some older people are moving into these living arrangements while they are still working. Residents live in their own apartments and share at least one meal a day in a communal dining room. Such retirement centers provide housekeeping and transportation. On-site skilled nursing care facilities for medical care or rehabilitation mean that couples can maintain close contact, even when one requires prolonged medical care.

Another vehicle that enables younger and older people to live with and learn from one another is cohousing, a communal living model that was first developed in Denmark in 1976. In these homes, residents have private living quarters, not unlike condominiums, but share recreational amenities as well as housekeeping responsibilities, such as cooking. In 1996 there were 20 operating cohousing communities in the United States and more than 150 in development.

Established in 1993 in Washington, D.C., Brookland Senior and Child Daycare Center is another model for intergenerational cooperative living. A private, not-for-profit organization, the Brookland Center houses a Child Development Division and an Adult and Senior Daycare and Treatment Division under the same roof. The Senior Care and Treatment Division serves older people with Alzheimer's disease, Parkinson's disease, and other impairments. Children and older people enrich one another's experience at the center every day.

Although many centenarians depend heavily on their younger relatives, the children of our centenarians depend upon their parents too. Angelina Strandal cooked and kept house for her children right up until the year she died at the age of 103. Laurence Moffitt, age 102, makes his great-granddaughter breakfast each morning before sending her off to school. Something of a historian, he is often called upon to share political reminiscences and personal memories with a local men's discussion group. Thus, he continues to contribute palpably to the lives of those around him.

Each time we met with centenarians in the course of our research, devoted children or other family members stood close by, marveling at their relative's intelligence, health, and determination. To younger family members, centenarians were an inspiring reminder of the worth of a life well spent and, like Roger Bannister's four-minute mile, of the possibility of achieving something remarkable. "She's doing it, living to 100," they seemed to be saying. "I can do it, too. If I live right, I have many more enjoyable years ahead of me."

OUR WORST ENEMY

While a healthy old age is a real possibility for baby boomers and future generations, we want to make a clear distinction between the suggestions that come out of solid research and the seductive claims and promises of hucksters seeking to capitalize on the age explosion. Over the last few years there has been a boom in the sale and promotion of so-called "antiaging" compounds, many of them derived from human hormones, such as testosterone, human growth hormone (hGH), dehydroepiandrosterone (DHEA), and melatonin. Some of these substances are not regulated by the federal Food and Drug Administration (FDA), and most of them are sold directly to consumers by mail, fax, and Internet outlets, as well as in health food stores.

None of these drugs has been subjected to the rigorous animal and human trials that prescription drugs must undergo before being marketed. There are claims that significant numbers of scientific studies support the clinical utility of these compounds. In reality there is a paucity of sound information about the use of these drugs in healthy people. The use of any drug without reliable safety and dosage information is dangerous. Indeed, there are also reports that these substances may cause serious, life-threatening conditions. Evidence that DHEA has any measurable effects on cognition, sleep, bone loss, or even self-reported well-being is still sparse and inconsistent. And there is also countering evidence suggesting that it may cause liver cancer and may also exacerbate prostate cancer, which can otherwise be a mild disorder that older men live with for many years. DHEA can also cause significant side effects in women, ranging from potentially permanent masculinizing traits like facial hair, acne, and a deeper voice, to an increased risk of breast cancer. Testosterone accelerates the manufacture of red blood cells, thickens the blood, and lowers HDL-cholesterol levels, thereby increasing the risk for heart attack and stroke. An hGH regimen, which can cost about $20,000 a year, can trigger diabetes and heart disease. It is also a cause of bone and internal organ enlargement leading to joint problems, organ dysfunction, and carpal tunnel syndrome. Inappropriate production of growth hormone in animals and humans has been linked to various cancers. People with a personal or family history of cancer are at greatest risk. Melatonin, sold as a natural sleep aid, has been hyped by manufacturers as a stress fighter, immune system booster, and antioxidant, but many people taking the hormone suffer from headaches, nausea, and nightmares. Melatonin may also negatively affect pregnancy and the retina. Most doctors advise pregnant women, or women who want to become pregnant, not to take melatonin; in fact, it is being studied as a possible contraceptive. The only people who can be sure to benefit from these drugs are those who sell them and the stockholders in the companies that produce them. Use of these drugs as "anti-aging" agents should be halted until further research can be performed.

In some cases even well-grounded scientific findings about aging are hyped beyond credibility. In a recent study, researchers halted the shortening of certain cells' telomeres during cell division, thereby allowing these cells to continue dividing longer than they normally would have. The result was indeed a breakthrough in aging research, but led to extraordinary claims by scientists, many of whom held stock in a company investigating telomeres. Michael Fossel, a researcher and investor in the company said on the January 16, 1998, ABC broadcast of *20/20*: "I think what you'll see is life spans of several hundred years . . . healthy life spans." Reporters opined that the finding would lead to development of miraculous antiaging drugs within five to ten years. The stock shot up from the low teens to more than $80 per share. (As more realistic scientists began to question the idea that telomeres hold the key to immortality, the research company's stock price receded.)

In the quest to age well, the accessibility of antiaging agents may turn out to be the baby boomer generation's worst enemy. All these quick fixes—hormonal medications with known and unknown side effects, breast implants that cause immune reactions, or exotic skin creams that "smooth out" wrinkles—are sold on the premise that they provide the benefits of a healthy lifestyle with none of the work. In fact, compressing morbidity may require some of us to make drastic changes in the way we live. Living to be a centenarian takes 100 years of effort.

A New World

While interest in antiaging therapies like DHEA and hGH has been intense, comparatively little has been done to investigate the potential for preventing age-associated diseases and disability. Until recently we had insufficient numbers to study extreme old age. As unprecedented numbers of people reach this important time of life, they give us the opportunity to study more precisely how people can live past the years during which they are most vulnerable to heart disease and cancer, the industrialized world's two greatest killers. The ages from 85 to 100 hold additional genetic and behavioral secrets that may help other people to live out the full length of their potential life spans in good health, perhaps even living to 100. Here, in summary, are some of the most important things we've learned from centenarians so far:

Centenarian Lessons for AGEING

Attitude How you feel about aging is key to your ability to thrive. Centenarians rarely consider their age a limitation. Rather, they take advantage of opportunities and possibilities that may not have been available to them previously.

Genes We believe that the vast majority of people have genes that allow them to live to at least 85 years old. Take advantage of these genes; don't thwart them. Good health practices will help you make up for at least some of the genetic difference between you and centenarians and maximize the disease-free portion of your life.

Exercise With older and older age, resistance training becomes increasingly important for maintaining strength and muscle. Increased muscle tissue burns fat more efficiently, reduces your heart disease risk, and markedly enhances your sense of well-being.

Investigate new challenges. Keep your mind active with new and different activities to exercise different parts of your brain. Take advantage of opportunities and possibilities that may have not been available to you previously, such as a second career, volunteer activities, musical instruction, writing, or travel.

Nutrition Emphasize fruits and vegetables in your diet, and minimize meat, saturated and hydrogenated fats, and sweets. Eat moderately in order to avoid obesity. Supplement your healthy diet with the antioxidants vitamin E (400–800 IU daily) and selenium (100–200 mcg daily).

Get rid of stress. Centenarians naturally shed psychological stress. Humor, meditation, Tai Chi, exercise, and optimism are some of the important ways to manage your stress.

As the baby boomers scout the terrain on the trail to 100, they too can help us answer important questions about aging well. The role of formal education is a case in point. Just as involvement in learning increases the chances of living to 100, so may higher educational levels improve the chances of aging well. We have already seen significant changes in the educational level attained by people 65 and over. In 1993, only about one-third (32 percent) of the population aged 75 and over had an eighth grade education or higher. At the same time, two-thirds (67 percent) of the population aged 65 to 69 had attained at least eighth grade. In future research, baby boomers who have achieved even higher educational levels will help us investigate whether and what kind of formal education can help stave off Alzheimer's disease. By the year 2030, 83 percent of the population aged 65 and over will have at least a high school education. The next generation of older people will allow us to question the nature of education in its current form, and whether it contributes in any measurable way to longevity.

As the march into extreme old age continues, more older people will be participating in large-scale health studies, such as the Framingham Heart Study, the Nurses' Health Study, the Physicians' Health Study, and others. We will learn about the effects of air pollution on aging, through data collected in the Six Cities Study and its descendant studies at the Harvard School of Public Health. These epidemiological efforts will yield more information about the factors that lead to successful aging.

The millions of people who currently take cholesterol- and blood pressure–lowering drugs and estrogen to prevent heart disease will tell us much about the long-term implications of these therapies for a healthy old age. We will see whether these drugs forestall disability, compress morbidity, and delay mortality. We will see which approaches to cancer prevention and treatment give the greatest long-term benefit for successful aging.

Sociologists will continue to search for the effects of community, relationships, and family life on aging well. We have noted that a large proportion of female centenarians were never married, although they often have rich social lives. Studying these independent, single older people will help us find useful strategies for reducing the isolation of single and widowed older people.

Another key area for future investigation is the sexuality of older people. Although much is assumed, remarkably little is known about how or whether sexual behavior changes as people age. There is no reason to assume, for example, that sexual desire shuts down at 65, any more than other important physical or psychological processes do. This subject has been difficult to study until now because today's older people were raised in a culture in which there were prohibitions against discussions of sex. Baby boomers, who lived through the sexual revolution, may tell us another story entirely.

The dynamics of sexual behavior may also be totally different in an older population that is healthier than ever before, since illnesses, and the side effects of medications used to treat them, are the primary causes of sexual dysfunction among older people. Studies such as the *Starr Weiner Report on Sex and Sexuality in the Mature Years* have shown that the most common and important reason for cessation of sex among older people is the lack of a partner; this is particularly a problem for older women, many of whom are widowed. The impact of medications and devices used to facilitate sex in older people, as well as the sexual implications of the loss of a spouse, or remarriage during old age, all need to be studied in much greater detail.

Centenarians are opening our eyes to the powerful role genes play in aging. Our discovery that the genes that promote slow aging are relatively few in number suggests that there may be one or a few physiological functions of great importance to aging, a conjecture supported by a 1998 study by Richard Miller and colleagues of the University of Michigan, published in the *Journal of Gerontology*. Miller found that four different areas in mouse DNA were strongly linked to long life span; none were linked to disease. This further supports our suspicion that aging well is due to slow aging and the resulting delayed onset of diseases associated with aging.

The fact that so few genes may be involved suggests that aging is governed by one or a few mechanisms present in most or perhaps all cells, organs, and organisms. Evidence points to free radical production and the damage it causes as the underlying process of aging. Genes appear to be our inborn defense system against the aging onslaught of free radicals. A 1998 study in the *Journal of Gerontology* by Hiroshi Adachi and colleagues from Japan indicates that aging in the *c. elegans* worm is governed by genes that protect against free radical damage. Masashi Tanaka and his colleagues from the Gifu International Institute of Biotechnology in Japan have shown that centenarians display certain patterns in the genes of their mitochondria that may provide a survival advantage. These patterns may reduce the number of free radicals produced in their bodies. Diminished oxidative damage may thus be the sine qua non of longevity. This concept opens up an entire new world in the search for means of delaying or preventing the diseases commonly associated with aging. The central role of oxidative damage suggests that the wider and earlier use of antioxidant supplements is an important strategy for lifelong health.

Centenarians have inherited the best available versions of aging genes, but there are still some scientists who hope to improve upon near-perfection. Geneticist Michael Rose of the University of California, Irvine, has predicted that the human life span will be lengthened to 300 years. Such an objective should be regarded with caution and skepticism. Millions of years of evolution have been necessary to optimize the genes that reduce free radical production and damage. It is premature to suggest that our current understanding of longevity-enhancing genes will allow us to extend individual life spans. Tinkering with these genes risks upsetting a delicate balance. Although the mechanisms underlying aging may prove to be relatively simple, they impact a multitude of critical cellular and organ functions. Any intervention with the goal of significantly extending life span should be evaluated carefully before being used in humans.

The most immediate benefit of studying longevity-enhancing genes lies in understanding how they work and their influence on diseases associated with aging. We hope to discover why centenarians are such a cancer-resistant population and how they markedly delay or in some cases entirely escape Alzheimer's disease. Ultimately, we hope to discover these mechanisms of resistance and translate them into medications that will transmit the centenarian survival advantage to others. Rather than extending life spans to 300 years, we hope that our genetic studies will lead to people living a greater proportion of their lives, no matter how long, in good health.

It is critical to keep in mind that there are other forces that bear on aging, such as lifestyle and behavior. All the potential benefits of genes that promote longevity can be canceled out by accidents, risk-taking, smoking, or failure to preserve one's mental faculties with appropriate activities. One of the most pressing problems for coming generations will be obesity, an important risk factor for heart disease, diabetes, and cancer. High-fat diets and sedentary behavior have led to increased obesity throughout the developed world. Currently in the United States, the population aged 75 and over has much lower rates of obesity than the population aged 35 to 74, indicating that higher obesity rates in the younger generation may be a significant obstacle to attaining extreme old age.

Yet the majority of people can compress the period of ill health in their lives into a few years, whether those years come in their seventies, eighties, nineties, or hundreds—and the chances for doing so get better with increasing age. Even without the centenarian genetic advantage, emulating the centenarian lifestyle and taking preventive steps to maintain mind and body can still maximize good health.

Our journey began with a vision of health in old age. We observed Celia Bloom, a woman who appeared to defy everything we had been taught about aging and disease. As our curiosity grew, extensive and careful scientific study has led to findings that have radically changed our ideas about aging. We found that the extreme old are significantly healthier than we expected, and that the older a person is, the healthier he or she has had to be to achieve that age.

These findings have not come easily, nor without effort. Our scientific colleagues have been reluctant to accept many of them. Nevertheless, they represent the value of seeking out older people and learning from them directly. Had we been content with textbook representations of older people, had we accepted the implications of studies that purported to answer questions about aging without actually observing the behavior of the extreme old, had we failed to satisfy our curiosity about why Celia Bloom was never in her room, we would not possess the knowledge we do today. People of any age who wish to understand aging should take the time to talk with and listen to those who have proven themselves capable of doing it best. Many claim to know aging's secret—the substances that can halt it, the foods that counteract it, the genes that promise to extend life to 300 years—but the only real proof will be when these savants actually make the journey to 100 themselves.

In a sense, we are much more fortunate than the settlers who followed the pioneers to the West. The pioneers of aging are among us; we need only to acknowledge them and welcome them into our midst. The more time one spends with older people, the less forbidding the prospect of aging becomes. Disease is frightening, and death a vast unknown. But as we find out more about aging itself, its prospects and potential look broader and more optimistic. It can be a time of work, of family, of play, and of love. It can be a time when dreams materialize, and new goals are dreamed. And it will be a time that in coming years many, many more people will experience.

FURTHER READING

Chapter 1

THE SECRET OF CELIA BLOOM: SEARCHING FOR A CENTENARIAN

Conceptions of Aging

Bellow, S. *Mr. Sammler's Planet.* New York: Viking Press, 1970.

Butler, R. *Why Survive? Being Old in America.* New York: Harper and Row, 1975.

Rowe J. W., and R. L. Kahn. *Successful Aging.* New York: Pantheon, 1998.

Shaw, G. B. *Back to Methusaleh: A Metabiological Pentateuch.* New York: Brentano, 1921.

Shem, S. *The House of God.* New York: Dell Publishing, 1978.

Swift, J. *Gulliver's Travels.* Edited by P. Turner. Cambridge, Mass.: Oxford University Press, 1998.

Prevalence of Dementia

Drachman, D. A. "If We Live Long Enough, Will We All Be Demented?" *Neurology* 44(1994):1563–1565.

Ebly, E. M., I. M. Parhad, D. B. Hogan, T. S. Fung. "Prevalence and Types of Dementia in the Very Old: Results from the Canadian Study of Health and Aging." *Neurology* 44(1994):1593–1600.

Evans D. A., H. H. Funkenstein, M. S. Albert, P. A. Scherr, N. R. Cook, M. J. Chown, L. E. Hebert, C. H. Hennekens, J. O. Taylor. "Prevalence of Alzheimer's Disease in a Community Population of Older Persons." *Journal of the American Medical Association* 262(1989):2551–2556.

Fratiglioni, L., M. Grut, Y. Forsell, M. Viitanen, M. Grafström, K. Holmém, K. Ericsson, L. Backman, A. Ahlbom, B. Winblad. "Prevalence of Alzheimer's Disease and Other Dementias in an Elderly Urban Population: Relationship with Age, Sex and Education." *Neurology* 41(1991):1886–1892.

Hoffman, A., W. Rocca, C. Brayne. "The Prevalence of Dementia in Europe: A Collaborative Study of 1980–1990 Findings." *International Journal of Epidemiology* 20(1991):736–748.

Jorm, A., A. Korten, A. Henderson. "The Prevalence of Dementia: A Quantitative Integration of the Literature." *Acta Psychiatrica Scandinavica* 76(1987):465–479.

Perls, T. "Symposium: Cognitive and Functional Status of Centenarians. Reports from Four Studies." *Gerontologist* 37, no. 2(1997): 37.

Randall, T. "Is It 'Oldtimer's Disease' or Just Growing Old?" *Journal of the American Medical Association* 265(1991):310–311.

Sayetta, R. B. "Rates of Senile Dementia: Alzheimer's Type in the Baltimore Longitudinal Study." *Journal of Chronic Disease* 4(1986): 271–286.

Schoenberg, B. S., E. Kokmen, and H. Okazaki. "Alzheimer's Disease and Other Dementing Illnesses in a Defined United States Population; Incidence Rates and Clinical Features." *Annals of Neurology* 22(1987):724–729.

Skoog, I., L. Nilsson, B. Palmertz, L. A. Andreasson, and A. Svanborg. "A Population-based Study of Dementia in 85-year-olds." *New England Journal of Medicine* 328(1993):153–158.

Wernicke, T. F., F. M. Reischies. "Prevalence of Dementia in Old Age: Clinical Diagnoses in Subjects Aged 95 Years and Older." *Neurology* 44(1994):250–253.

Relationship Between Cognitive Function and Selective Survival in Old Age

Perls, T. T. "Demographic Selection's Influence upon the Oldest Old." *Journal of Geriatric Psychiatry* 28(1995):33–56.

_____. "The Oldest Old." *Scientific American*, 272(1995):70–75.

Perls, T. T., J. N. Morris, W. L. Ooi, and L. A. Lipsitz. "The Relationship Between Age, Gender and Cognitive Performance in the Very Old: The Effect of Selective Survival." *Journal of the American Geriatrics Society* 41(1993):1193–1201.

Demographic Trends and the Oldest Old

Suzman R. M., T. Harris, E. C. Hadley, M. G. Kovar, and R. Weindruch. "The Robust Oldest Old: Optimistic Perspectives for Increasing Healthy Life Expectancy." In *The Oldest Old*, edited by R. Suzman, D. Willis, and K. G. Manton, 341–358. New York: Oxford University Press, 1992.

Vaupel J. W., J. R. Carey, K. Christensen, T. E. Johnson, A. I. Yashin, N. V. Holm, I. A. Iachine, V. Kannisto, A. A. Khazaeli, P. Liedo, V. D. Longo, Y. Zeng, K. G. Manton, and J. W. Curtsinger. "Biodemographic Trajectories of Longevity." *Science* 280(1998): 855.

Wilmoth, J. R. "In Search of Limits: What Do Demographic Trends Suggest about the Future of Human Longevity." In *Between Zeus and the Salmon: The Biodemography of Longevity*, edited by K. W. Wachter and C. E. Finch, 38–64. Washington, D.C.: National Academy Press, 1997.

Prevalence of Centenarians

Capurso, A., A. D'Amelio, and F. Resta. "Epidemiological and Socioeconomic Aspects of Italian Centenarians." *Archives of Gerontology and Geriatrics* 25(1997):149–157.

Perls, T. T., K. Bochen, M. Freeman, L. Alpert, and M. H. Silver. "The New England Centenarian Study: Validity of Reported Age and Prevalence of Centenarians in an Eight Town Sample." In *Age Validation of the Extreme Old*, Odense Monographs on Population Aging 4, edited by B. Jeune and J. Vaupel. Odense, Denmark: Odense University Press, 1998.

Wilmoth, J. R., and H. Lundstrom. "Extreme Longevity in Five Countries: Presentation of Trends with Special Attention to Issues of Data Quality." *European Journal of Population* 12(1996):63–93.

The First Centenarians

Jeune, B. "In Search of the First Centenarians." In *Exceptional Longevity: From Prehistory to the Present,* edited by B. Jeune, and J. W. Vaupel, 11–24. Odense, Denmark: Odense University Press, 1995.

Lundström, H. "Record Longevity in Swedish Cohorts Born Since 1700." In *Exceptional Longevity: From Prehistory to the Present,* edited by B. Jeune, and J. W. Vaupel, 67–74. Odense, Denmark: Odense University Press, 1995.

Richardson, B. E. *Old Age Among the Ancient Greeks. The Greek Portrayal of Old Age in Literature, Art and Inscriptions.* Baltimore: Johns Hopkins University Press, 1993.

Vaupel, J. W., and B. Jeune. "The Emergence and Proliferation of Centenarians." In *Exceptional Longevity: From Prehistory to the Present,* edited by B. Jeune, and J. W. Vaupel, 109–116. Odense, Denmark: Odense University Press, 1995.

Wilmoth, J. "The Earliest Centenarians: A Statistical Analysis." In *Exceptional Longevity: From Prehistory to the Present,* edited by B. Jeune, and J. W. Vaupel, 125–156. Odense, Denmark: Odense University Press, 1995.

Supercentenarians (age 110 years and older) and Age Misreporting

Bennett, N. G., and L. K. Garson. "Extraordinary Longevity in the Soviet Union: Fact or Artifact?" *Gerontologist* 26(1986):358–361.

Coale A. J., and S. M. Li. "The Effect of Age Misreporting in China on the Calculation of Mortality Rates at Very High Ages. *Demography* 28(1991):293–301.

Leaf, A. "Getting Old." *Scientific American* (September, 1973), 29–36.

Mazess, R. B., and S. Forman. "Longevity and Age Exaggeration in Vilcabamba, Ecuador." *Journal of Gerontology* 34(1979):94–98.

Palmore, E. B. "Longevity in Abkhazia: A Reevaluation." *Gerontologist* 24(1984):95–96.

Other Centenarian Studies

Allard, M. *À la Recherche du Secret des Centenaires.* Paris: Le Cherche-Midi, 1991.

Allard, M., V. Lébre, and J-M. Robine. *The Longest Life: The 122 Extraordinary Years of Jeanne Calment, from Van Gogh's Time to Ours.* New York: W.H. Freeman, 1998.

Capurso, A., A. D'Amelio, and F. Resta. "Epidemiological and Socioeconomic Aspects of Italian Centenarians." *Archives of Gerontology and Geriatrics* 25(1997):149–157.

Karasawa, A. "Mental Aging and Its Medico-social Background in the Very Old Japanese." *Journal of Gerontology* 34(1979):680–686.

Louhija, J. "Finnish Centenarians" (Ph.D. diss., University of Helsinki, 1994).

Poon, L. W., ed. *The Georgia Centenarian Study.* Amityville, N.Y.: Baywood, 1992.

Samuelsson, S. M., B. B. Alfredson, B. Hagberg, G. Samuelsson, B. Norbeck, A. Brun, L. Gustafson, R. Risberg. The Swedish Centenarian Study: A Multidisciplinary Study of Five Consecutive Cohorts at the Age of 100. *International Journal of Aging and Human Development* 45(1997):223–253.

Special Issue, *International Journal of Aging and Human Development.*

Chapter 2
BEAUTIFUL BRAINS: DISEASE-FREE AGING

General Texts Referred To in This Chapter

Albert, M. S., and M. B. Moss, eds. *Geriatric Neuropsychology.* New York: Guilford Press, 1988.

Cohen, Gene D. *The Brain in Human Aging.* New York: Springer, 1988.

Horn, J. L., and G. Donaldson. "Cognitive Development in Adulthood." In *Constancy and Change in Human Development,* edited by O. G. Brim and J. Kagan, 445–529. Cambridge, Mass.: Harvard University Press, 1980.

Nussbaum, P. D., ed. *Handbook of Neuropsychology and Aging.* New York: Plenum Press, 1997.

Sacks, Oliver. *An Anthropologist on Mars.* New York: Vintage Books, 1995.

Epidemiological Tools for Testing Cognitive Function

Albert, M. S. "Cognitive Function." In *Geriatric Neuropsychology,* edited by M. S. Albert and M. B. Moss, 33–53. New York: Guilford Press, 1988.

Albert, M., and C. Cohen. "The Test for Severe Impairment: An Instrument for the Assessment of Patients with Severe Cognitive Dysfunction." *Journal of the American Geriatrics Society* 40(1992): 449–453.

Army Individual Test Battery. *Manual of Directions and Scoring.* Washington, D.C.: War Department, Adjutant General's Office, 1944.

Blessed, G., B. Torfflinson, and M. Roth. "The Association Between Quantitative Measures of Dementia and of Senile Change in the Cerebral Grey Matter of Elderly Subjects. *British Journal of Psychiatry* 114(1968):797–811.

Brandt, J., M. Spencer, and M. F. Folstein. "The Telephone Interview for Cognitive Status." *Neuropsychiatry, Neurophysiology and Behavioral Neurology* 1(1990):111–117.

Coblentz, J. M., S. Mattis, L. H. Zingesser, S. S. Kasoff, H. M. Wisniewski, and R. Katzman. "Presenile Dementia. Clinical Aspects and Calculation of Cerebrospinal Fluid Dynamics." *Archives of Neurology* 29(1973):299–308.

Folstein, N. T., S. E. Folstein, and P. R. McHugh. "Mini-Mental State I: Practical Method for Grading the Cognitive State of Patients for the Clinician." *Journal of Psychiatric Research.* 12(1975):189–198.

Freedman, M., L. Leach, E. Kaplan, G. Winocur, K. I. Shulman, and D. C. Delis. *Clock Drawing: A Neuropsychological Analysis.* New York: Oxford University Press, 1994.

Ivnik, R. J., J. F. Malec, G. E. Smith, E. G. Tangalos, R. C. Petersen, E. Kokmen, and L. T. Kurland. "Mayo's Older Americans Normative Studies: WAIS-R Norms for Ages 56 to 97." *The Clinical Neuropsychologist* 6, Supplement(1992):1–30.

_____. "Mayo's Older Americans Normative Studies: WMS-R Norms for Ages 56 to 94. *The Clinical Neuropsychologist* 6, Supplement(1992):49–82.

Jorm, A. F., and P. A. Jacomb. "The Informant Questionnaire on Cognitive Decline in the Elderly (IQCODE): Sociodemographic Correlates, Reliability, Validity and Some Norms." *Psyhological Medicine* 21(1989):1015–1022.

Kaplan, E., E. Caine, and P. Morse. "Boston-Rochester Neuropsychological Screening Test.: Lexington, Mass.: Boston Neuropsychological Foundation, 1983.

Lawton, M. P. "Scales to Measure Competence in Everyday Activities." *Psychopharmacological Bulletin* 24(1988):609–614.

Lezak, M. D. *Neuropsychological Assessment,* 3rd ed. New York: Oxford University Press, 1996.

Mack, W. J., D. M. Freed, B. W. Williams, and V. W. Henderson. "Boston Naming Test: Shortened Versions for Use in Alzheimer's Disease." *Journal of Gerontology: Psychological Sciences* 47, no. 3(1992):154–158.

Mattis, S. M. "Dementia Rating Scale." Odessa, Fla.: Psychological Assessment Resources, Inc., 1988.

Mirra, S. S., A. Heyman, D. McKeel, S. M. Sumi, B. J. Crain, L. M. Brownlee, F. S. Vogel, J. P. Hughes, G. van Belle, L. Berg, and participating CERAD neuropathologists. "The Consortium to Establish a Registry for Alzheimer's Disease (CERAD). Part II. Standardization of the Neuropathologic Assessment of Alzheimer's Disease." *Neurology* 41(1991):479–486.

Mitzutani, M., and H. Shimada. "Neuropathological Background of Twenty-seven Centenarian Brains." *Journal of the Neurological Sciences* 108(1992):168–177.

Montgomery, K. M., and L. Costa. *Neuropsychological Test Performance of a Normal Elderly Sample.* Paper presented at the International Neuropsychological Society Meeting. Mexico City, Mexico, 1983.

Morris, J. C., A. Heyman, R. C. Mohs, J. P. Hughes, G. van Belle, G. Fillenbaum, E. D. Mellits, C. Clark, and the CERAD investigators. "The Consortium to Establish a Registry for Alzheimer's Disease (CERAD). Part I. Clinical and Neuropsychological Assessment of Alzheimer's Disease." *Neurology* 39(1989):1159–1165.

Pantoni, L., and D. Inzitari. "Hachinski's Ischemic Score and the Diagnosis of Vascular Dementia: A Review." *Italian Journal Neurological Sciences* 14(1993):539–546.

Pfeiffer, E. "A Short Portable Mental Status Questionnaire for the Assessment of Organic Brain Deficit in Elderly Patients." *Journal American Geriatrics Society* 23(1975):433–441.

Ritchie, K. "Mental Status Examination of an Exceptional Case of Longevity: J. C. Aged 118 Years." *British Journal of Psychiatry* 166(1995):229–235.

Spiers, P. A. "Acalculia Revisited: Current Issues." In *Mathematical Disabilities: A Cognitive Neuropsychological Approach,* edited by F. Deloche and X. Seron, 1–25. Hillsdale, N.J.: Lawrence Erlbaum Associates, 1986.

Weintraub, S., and M. M. Mesulam. "Mental State Assessment of Young and Elderly Adults in Behavioral Neurology." In *Principles of Behavioral Neurology,* by M. M. Mesulam, 71–123. Philadelphia: F. A. Davis, 1985.

Yesavage, J. A., T. L. Brink, T. L. Rose, O. Lum, V. Huang, H. B. Adey, and V. O. Leirer. "Development and Validation of a Geriatric Depression Rating Scale: A Preliminary Report." *The Journal of Psychiatric Research* 17(1983):37–49.

Correlation of Neuropsychological Evaluation with Neuropathological Findings

Braak, H., and E. Braak. "Neuropathological Staging of Alzheimer-related Changes." *Acta Neuropathalogica* 82(1991):239–259.

Morrison, J. H., and P. R. Hof. "Life and Death of Neurons in the Aging Brain." *Science* 278(1997):412–418.

Riley, K. P., D. A. Snowden, and W. R. Markesbery. *Age and Cognitice Function in the Absence of Neuropathologically Confirmed Dementing*

Disease. Paper presented at the annual Scientific Meetings of the Gerontological Society of America. Los Angeles, Calif., November 1995.

Silver, M., K. Newell, J. Growdon, B. T. Hyman, E. T. Hedley-Whyte, and T. T. Perls. "Unraveling the Mystery of Cognitive Changes in Extreme Old Age: Correlation of Neuropsychological Evaluation with Neuropathological Findings in Centenarians." *International Psychogeriatrics* 10(1998):25–41.

Snowden, D. A. "Aging and Alzheimer's Disease: Lessons from the Nun Study." *The Gerontologist* 37(1997):150–156.

Chapter 3
THE CENTENARIAN LIFESTYLE

Popular Texts Referred To in This Chapter

Cousins, N. *Anatomy of an Illness as Perceived by the Patient: Reflections on Healing and Regeneration.* New York: Bantam Books, 1979.

Kagan, J., N. Snidman, D. Arcus, and S. Reznick. *Galen's Prophecy: Temperament in Human Nature.* New York: Basic Books, 1997.

Sontag, S. "The Double Standard of Aging." In *The Other Within Us: Feminist Explorations of Women and Aging,* edited by Marilyn Pearsall. Boulder, Colo.: Westview Press, 1997.

Large Epidemiologic Studies of Factors That Influence Longevity

Giovannucci, E., M. J. Stampfer, G. A. Colditz, D. J. Hunter, C. Fuchs, B. A. Rosner, F. E. Speizer, and W. C. Willett. "Multivitamin Use, Folate, and Colon Cancer in Women in the Nurses' Health Study." *Annals of Internal Medicine* 129, no.7(1998): 517–524.

Glynn, R. J., J. E. Buring, J. E. Manson, F. LaMotte, and C. H. Hennekens. "Adherence to Aspirin in the Prevention of Myocardial Infarction. The Physicians' Health Study." *Archives of Internal Medicine* 154, no. 23(1994):2649–2657.

Kannel, W. B., W. P. Castelli, and T. Gordon. "Cholesterol in the Prediction of Atherosclerotic Disease. New Perspectives Based on the Framingham Study." *Annals of Internal Medicine* 90, no. 1(1979):85–91.

Shock, N. W., R. C. Greulich, R. Andres, D. Arenberg, P. T. Costa, Jr., E. G. Lakatta, and J. D. Tobin. *Normal Human Aging: The Baltimore Longitudinal Study of Aging.* U. S. Department of Health and Human Services. NIH Publication No. 84-2450. Washington, D.C.: U.S. Government Printing Office, 1984.

Psychology of Aging

Erikson, E. *Childhood and Society.* New York: Norton, 1950.

_____. *The Life Cycle Completed.* New York: Norton, 1982.

Erikson, E., J. M. Erikson, and H. Q. Kivnick. *Vital Involvement in Old Age: The Experience of Old Age in Our Time.* New York: W. W. Norton, 1986.

Personality and Aging

Cumming, E., and W. H. Henry. *Growing Old: The Process of Disengagement.* New York: Basic Books, 1961.

Eysenck, H. J. *The Structure of Human Personality.* London: Methuen, 1960.

Friedman, H. S., J. S. Tucker, J. E. Schwartz, C. Tomlinson-Keasey, L. R. Martin, D. L. Wingard, and M. H. Criqui. "Psychosocial and Behavioral Predictors of Longevity: The Aging and Death of the 'Termites.'" *American Psychologist* 50(1995):69–78.

Gould, R. A., S. Buckminster, M. H. Pollack, M. W. Otto, and L. Yap. "Cognitive Behavioral and Pharmacological Treatment for Social Phobia: A Meta-Analysis." *Clinical Psychology Science and Practice* 4(1997):291–306.

Higgins, G. O. *Resilient Adults: Overcoming a Cruel Past.* San Francisco: Jossey-Bass, Inc., 1994.

Lowenthal, M. F., and C. Haven. "Interaction and Adaption: Intimacy as a Critical Variable." In *Middle Age and Aging,* edited by B. L. Neugarten, 390–400. Chicago: University of Chicago Press, 1968.

McCrae, R. R., and P. T. Costa, Jr. *Personality in Adulthood.* New York: Guilford Press, 1990.

Neugarten, B. L., R. J. Havighurst, and S. S. Tobin. "Personality and Patterns of Aging." In *Middle Age and Aging,* edited by B. L. Neugarten, 173–177. Chicago: University of Chicago Press, 1968.

Saltus, R. "Mind and Body: Afraid of the World." *Boston Globe Magazine* (October 11, 1998).

Vaillant, G. E. *Adaptation to Life.* Boston: Little, Brown, 1977.

Personality Tests

Costa, P. T., Jr., and R. R. McCrae. *NEO Five-Factor Inventory.* Odessa, Fla.: Psychological Assessment Resources, Inc., 1991.

Costa, P. T., Jr., R. R. McCrae, and A. H. Norris. "Personal Adjustment to Aging: Longitudinal Prediction from Neuroticism and Extraversion." *Journal of Gerontology* 36(1981):78–85.

Humor

Berk, L. S., S. A. Tan, W. F. Fry, B. J. Napier, J. W. Lee, R. W. Hubbard, J. E. Lewis, and W. C. Eby. "Neuroendocrine and Stress Hormone Changes During Mirthful Laughter." *American Journal of the Medical Sciences* 298(1989):390–396.

Fry, W. E. "Humor, Physiology and the Aging Process." In *Humor and Aging,* edited L. Nahemow, K. A. McCluskey-Fawcett, and P. E. McGhee, 81–98. New York: Academic Press, 1986.

Fry, W. F., and W. M. Savin. "Mirthful Laughter and Blood Pressure." *Humor: International Journal of Humor Research* 1(1988):49–62.

LaRoche, L. *Relax—You May Have Only a Few Minutes Left: Using the Power of Humor to Overcome Stress in Your Life and Work.* New York: Villard, 1998.

Nahemow, L., K. A. McCluskey-Fawcett, and P. E. McGhee, eds. *Humor and Aging.* New York: Academic Press, 1986.

Spirituality

Benson, H., with M. Stark. *Timeless Healing: The Power and Biology of Belief.* New York: Simon & Schuster, 1997.

Blazer, D., and E. Palmore. "Religion and Aging in a Longitudinal Panel." In *Aging and the Human Spirit,* edited by C. LeFevre and P. LeFevre, 171–180. Chicago: Exploration Press, 1981.

Koenig, H. G. "Research on Religion and Mental Health in Later Life: A Review and Commentary." *Journal of Geriatric Psychiatry* 23(1990):23–53.

Singh, B. K., and J. S. Williams. "Satisfaction with Health and Physical Condition Among the Elderly." *Journal of Psychiatric Treatment and Evaluation.* 4(1982):403–408.

Social Relationships

Berkman, L. F. "The Role of Social Relations in Health Promotion." *Psychosomatic Medicine* 57(1995):245–254.

Seeman, T. E., L. F. Berkman, D. Blazer, and J. W. Rowe. "Social Ties and Support and Neuroendocrine Function: The Macarthur Studies of Successful Aging." *Annals of Behavioral Medicine* 16, no. 2(1994):95–106.

Depression Prevalence

Callahan, J., et al. "Mental Health/Substance Abuse Treatment in Managed Care: The Massachusetts Medicaid Experience." *Health Affairs* 14, no. 3(1995):173–184.

Evans, S. and C. Katona. "Epidemiology of Depressive Symptoms in Elderly Primary Care Attendees." *Dementia* 4(1993):327–333.

Stress

Benson, H. *The Relaxation Response.* New York: Avon, 1975.

Miller, L. H., and A. D. Smith, with L. Rothstein. *The Stress Solution: An Action Plan to Manage the Stress in Your Life.* New York: Pocket Books, 1993.

Sapolsky, R. M. *Why Zebras Don't Get Ulcers: An Updated Guide to Stress, Stress-Related Diseases, and Coping.* New York: W. H. Freeman and Co.

Chapter 4
THE LONGEVITY MARATHON:
WOMEN VERSUS MEN

Reviews
Crose, R. *Why Women Live Longer than Men.* San Francisco: Jossey-Bass Publishers, 1997.
Perls, T. T., and R. Fretts. "Why Women Live Longer Than Men." *Scientific American Presents* 9(1998):100–103.

The Gender Crossover and Getting Over the Hump
Perls, T. T. "The Oldest Old." *Scientific American.* 272(1995):70–75.
Perls, T. T., J. N. Morris, W. L. Ooi, and L. A. Lipsitz. "The Relationship Between Age, Gender and Cognitive Performance in the Very Old: The Effect of Selective Survival." *Journal of the American Geriatrics Society* 41(1993):1193–1201.

Psychology
Chodorow, N. *The Reproduction of Mothering: Psychoanalysis and the Sociology of Gender.* Berkeley: University of California Press, 1978.
Gilligan, C. *In a Different Voice: Psychological Theory and Women's Development.* Cambridge, Mass.: Harvard University Press, 1982.
Miller, J. B. *Toward a New Psychology of Women.* Boston: Beacon Press, 1976.

Evolutionary Theories for Menopause
Austad, S. N. "Menopause, an Evolutionary Perspective." *Experimental Gerontology* 29(1994):255–263.
Perls, T. T., L. Alpert, R. C. Fretts. "Middle-aged Mothers Live Longer." *Nature* 389(1997):133.
Williams, G. C., and D. C. Williams. "Natural Selection of Individually Harmful Social Adaptations among Sibs with Special Reference to Social Insects." *Evolution* 11(1957):32–39.

Maternal Age and Risk of Fetal Death

Fretts, R. C., J. Schmittdiel, F. H. McLean, R. H. Usher, M. B. Goldman. "Increased Maternal Age and the Risk of Fetal Death." *New England Journal of Medicine* 333(1995):953–957.

Ventura, J. S., J. A. Martin, S. C. Curtin. *Report of Final Natality Statistics, 1995.* Centers for Disease Control and Prevention/National Center for Health Statistics. 45(1997):11.

Correlation Between Maternal Age and Life Expectancy: Humans and Other Species

Hutchinson, E. W., and M. R. Rose. "Quantitative Genetics of Postponed Aging in Drosophila Melanogaster I: Analysis of Outbred Populations." *Genetics* 127(1991):719–727.

Packer, C., M. Tatar, and A. Collins. "Reproductive Cessation in Female Mammals." *Nature* 392(1998):807–811.

Perls, T. T., L. Alpert, and R. C. Fretts. "Middle-aged Mothers Live Longer." *Nature* 389(1997):133.

Torgerson, D. J., R. E. Thomas, and D. M. Reid. "Mothers and Daughters Menopausal Age: Is There a Link?" *European Journal of Obstetrics and Gynecology* 74(1997):63–66.

Clinical Causes of Menopause

McKinlay, S. M., N. L. Bifano, and J. B. McKinlay. "Smoking and Age at Menopause." *Annals of Internal Medicine* 103(1985):350–356.

Napier, A. D. L. *The Menopause and Its Disorders.* London, Scientific Press, 1987.

Tharapel, A. T., K. P. Anderson, and J. L. Simpson. "Deletion (X)(q26.2–q28) in a Proband and her Mother: Molecular Characterization and Phenotypic-karyotypic Deductions." *American Journal of Human Genetics* 52(1993):463–471.

Veneman, T. F., G. C. Beverstock, N. Exalto, and P. Mollevanger. "Premature Menopause Because of an Inherited Deletion in the Long Arm of the X-chromosome." *Fertility and Sterility* 55(1991):631–633.

Estrogen Use and Alzheimer's Disease

Tang, M. X., D. Jacobs, Y. Stern, K. Marder, P. Schofield, B. Gurland, H. Andrews, and R. Mayeux. "Effect of Oestrogen During Menopause on Risk and Age at Onset of Alzheimer's Disease." *Lancet* 348(1996):429–432.

Chapter 5
A REVOLUTIONARY DISCOVERY

The Gompertz Curve and Deceleration of Mortality At Extreme Ages

Carey, J. R., P. Liedo, D. Orozco, and J. W. Vaupel. "Slowing of Mortality Rates at Older Ages in Large Medfly Cohorts." *Science* 258(1992):457–461.

Gompertz, B. "On the Nature of the Function Expressive of the Law of Human Mortality." *Philosophical Transactions* 27(1825): 510–519.

Horiuchi, S. and J. R. Wilmoth. "Deceleration in the Age Pattern of Mortality at Older Ages." *Demography* 35 (1998):391–412.

Kannisto, V. *Development of Oldest-Old Mortality, 1950–1990*, Odense, Denmark: Odense University Press, 1994.

Kannisto, V., J. Lauritsen, A. R. Thatcher, and J. W. Vaupel "Reductions in Mortality at Advanced Ages." *Population and Development Review* 20, no. 4(1994):793–810.

Thatcher, A. R. "Trends in Numbers and Mortality at High Ages in England and Wales." *Population Studies* 46(1992):411–426.

Thatcher, A. R., V. Kannisto, and J. W. Vaupel. *The Force of Mortality at Ages 80 to 120*. Odense, Denmark: Odense University Press, 1997.

Vaupel, J. W. "Trajectories of Mortality at Advanced Ages." In *Between Zeus and the Salmon: The Biodemography of Longevity*, edited by K. W. Wachter and C. E. Finch. Washington, D.C.: National Academy Press, 1997.

Vaupel, J. W., and J. R. Carey. "Compositional Interpretations of Medfly Mortality." *Science* 260(1993):1666–1667.

Theories of Aging, Reviews

Finch, C. E., and R. E. Tanzi. "Genetics of Aging." *Science* 278 (1997):407–411.

Hayflick, L. *How and Why We Age*. New York: Ballantine Books, 1994.

Jaswinski, S. M. "Longevity, Genes and Aging." *Science* 273 (1996):54–59.

Perls, T. T., and R. Fretts. "Why Women Live Longer than Men." *Scientific American Presents* 9, no.2(1998):100–103.

Oxygen Radical Damage

Adạchi, H., Y. Fujiwara, and N. Ishii. "Effects of Oxygen on Protein Carbonyl and Aging in Caenorhabditis elegans Mutants with Long (age–1) and Short (mev–1) Life Spans. *Journal of Gerontology: Biological Sciences* 53A(1998):B240–B244.

Agarwal, S., and R. S. Sohal. "Relationship Between Susceptibility to Protein Oxidation, Aging, and Maximum Life Span Potential of Different Species." *Experimental Gerontology* 31(1996): 365–372.

Larsen, P. L. "Aging and Resistance to Oxidative Damage in Caenorhabditis Elegans." *Proceedings of the National Academy of Sciences, USA* 90(1993):8905–8909.

Lass, A., S. Agarwal, and R. S. Sohal. "Mitochondrial Ubiquinone Homologues, Superoxide Radical Generation, and Longevity in Different Mammalian Species." *Journal of Biological Chemistry* 272(1997):19199–19204.

Martin, G. M., S. N. Austad, and T. E. Johnson. "Genetic Analysis of Aging: Role of Oxidative Damage and Environmental Stresses." *Nature Genetics* 13(1996):25.

Sohal, R. S., and B. H. Sohal. "Hydrogen Peroxide Release by Mitochondria Increases During Aging." *Mechanisms of Aging Development* 57(1991):187–202.

Sohal, R. S., S. Agarwal, A. Dubey, and W. C. Orr. "Protein Oxidative Damage is Associated with Life Expectancy of Houseflies." *Proceedings of the National Academy of Sciences, USA* 90(1993):7255–7259.

Sohal, R. S., S. Agarwal, M. Candas, M. J. Forster, and H. Lal. "Effect of Age and Caloric Restriction on DNA Oxidative Damage in Different Tissues of C57BL/6 Mice." *Mechanisms of Aging Development* 76(1994):215–224.

Stadtman, E. R., and C. N. Oliver. "Metal-catalyzed Oxidation of Proteins." *Journal of Biochemical Chemistry.* 266(1991):2005–2008.

Tanaka, M., J. S. Gong, J. Zhang, M. Yoneda, and K. Yagi. "Mitochondrial Genotype Associated with Longevity." *Lancet* 351(1998):185–186.

Wallace, D. C. "Mitochondrial Genetics: A Paradigm for Aging and Degenerative Diseases?" *Science* 256(1992):628–632.

_____. "Mitochondrial DNA in Aging and Disease." *Scientific American* 274(1997):40–47.

Yu, B. P. "Aging and Oxidative Stress: Modulation by Dietary Restriction." *Free Radical Biological Medicine* 21, no.5(1996): 651–668.

Telomere

Bodnar, A. G., M. Ouellette, M. Frolkis, S. E. Holt, C. P. Chiu, G. B. Morin, C. B. Harley, J. W. Shay, S. Lichtsteiner, and W. E. Wright. "Extension of Life-span by Introduction of Telomerase into Normal Human Cells." *Science* 279(1998):349–352.

Heat Shock Proteins

Curtsinger, J. W., H. H. Fukui, A. A. Khazaeli, A. Kirscher., S. D. Pletcher, D. E. Promislow, and M. Tatar. "Genetic Variation and Aging." *Annual Review of Genetics* 29(1995):553–575.

Genetics of Alzheimer's Disease

Corder, E. H., A. M. Saunders, W. J. Strittmatter, D. E. Schmechel, P. C. Gaskell, G. W. Small, A. D. Roses, J. L. Haines, and M. A. Pericak-Vance. "Gene Dose of Apolipoprotein E Type 4 Allele and the Risk of Alzheimer's Disease in Late Onset Families." *Science* 261(1993):921–923.

Rebeck, G. W., T. T. Perls, H. L. West, P. Sodhi, L. A. Lipsitz, and B. T. Hyman. "Reduced Apolipoprotein Epsilon 4 Allele Frequency in the Oldest Old. Alzheimer's Patients and Cognitively Normal Individuals." *Neurology* 44, no.8 (August 1994): 1513–1516.

Tanzi, R. E., P. H. St. George-Hyslop, J. L. Haines, R. J. Polinsky, L. Nee, J. F. Foncin, R. L. Neve, A. I. McClatchey, P. M. Conneally, and J. F. Gusella. "The Genetic Defect in Familial Alzheimer's Disease is Not Tightly Linked to the Amyloid Beta-protein Gene." *Nature* 329(1987):156–157.

Chapter 6
WHO WILL BE TOMORROW'S CENTENARIANS?

Myth: The Older You Get, The Sicker You Get

Olshansky, S. J., B. A. Carnes, and C. K. Cassel. "The Aging of the Human Species." *Scientific American* 268, no. 4(1993):46–52.

The Methuselah Gene

Lin, Y. J., L. Seroude, and S. Benzer. "Extended Life-span and Stress Resistance in the Drosophila Mutant Methuselah." *Science* 282(1998):943–945.

Costs of Care

Lubitz, J., J. Beebe, and C. Baker. "Longevity and Medicare Expenditures." *New England Journal of Medicine* 332(1995):999–1003.

Perls, T. T., and E. R. Wood. "Acute Care Costs of the Oldest Old: They Cost Less, Their Care Intensity Is Less and They Go to Non-Teaching Hospitals." *Archives of Internal Medicine* 156(1996): 754–760.

Compression of Morbidity

Fries, J. F. "Aging, Natural Death, and the Compression of Morbidity." *New England Journal of Medicine* 303, no. 3(1980):130–135.

Vita, A. J., R. B. Terry, H. B. Hubert, and J. F. Fries. "Aging, Health Risks, and Cumulative Disability." *New England Journal of Medicine* 338, no. 15(1998):1035–1041.

Twin Studies and Heritability of Longevity

Herskind, A. M., M. McGue, N. V. Holm, T. I. A. Soerensen, B. Harvald, and J. W. Vaupel. "The Heritability of Human Longevity." *Human Genetics* 97(1996):319–323.

McGue, M., J. W. Vaupel, N. Holm, and B. Harvald. "Longevity Is Moderately Heritable in a Sample of Danish Twins Born 1870–1880." *Journal of Gerontology* 48(1993):B237–B244.

Sibling Studies and Familiality of Longevity

Alpert, L., J. Vaupel, and T. T. Perls. "Extreme Longevity in a Family. A Report of Multiple Centenarians Within a Single Generation." In *Age Validation of the Extreme Old*, edited by B. Jeune and J. Vaupel. Odense Monographs on Population Aging 4, Odense, Denmark: Odense University Press, 1998.

Perls, T. T., L. Alpert, C. G. Wager, J. Vijg, and L. Kruglyak. "Siblings of Centenarians Live Longer." *Lancet* 351(1998):1560.

Chapter 7

YOU HAVE THE GENES, USE THEM!
WHAT TO TAKE AND WHAT TO DO

Strategies to Preserve Cognitive Health

Birren, J. E., and D. E. Deutchman. *Guiding Autobiography Groups for Older Adults: Exploring the Fabric of Life.* Baltimore: The Johns Hopkins University Press, 1991.

Birren, J. E., and L. Feldman. *Where to Go from Here: Discovering Your Own Life's Wisdom in the Second Half of Your Life.* New York: Simon & Schuster, 1997.

Gordon, B. *Remembering and Forgetting in Everyday Life.* New York: Mastermedia, 1995.

Kapur, N. *Managing Your Memory: A Self-help Memory Manual for Improving Everyday Memory Skills.* Gaylord, Mich.: National Rehabilitation Services, 1991.

Lapp, Danielle C. *Don't Forget! Easy Exercises for a Better Memory at any Age.* New York: McGraw-Hill Paperbacks, 1996).

Mark, V. with J. M. Mark. *Brain Power.* Boston: Houghton Mifflin, 1989.

Skinner, B. F., and M. E. Vaughn. *Enjoy Old Age: Living Fully in your Later Years.* New York: Warner Books, 1985.

Exercise

Fiatarone, M. A., E. C. Marks, N. D. Ryan, C. N. Meredith, L. A. Lipsitz, and W. J. Evans. "High-intensity Strength Training in Nonagenarians. Effects on Skeletal Muscle." *Journal of the American Medical Association* 263(22):3029–3034.

Nelson, M. E., M. A. Fiatarone, C. M. Morganti, I. Trice, R. A. Greenberg, and W. J. Evans. "Effects of High-intensity Strength Training on Multiple Risk Factors for Osteoporotic Fractures. A Randomized Controlled Trial." *Journal of the American Medical Association* 272, no. 24(1994):1909–1914.

Paffenbarger, R. S., Jr., R. T. Hyde, A. L. Wing, I. M. Lee, D. L. Jung, and J. B. Kampert. "The Association of Changes in Physical-activity Level and Other Lifestyle Characteristics with Mortality among Men." *New England Journal of Medicine* 328, no. 8(1993):538–545.

Treuth, M. S., G. R. Hunter, T. Kekes-Szabo, R. L. Weinsier, M. I. Goran, and L. Berland. "Reduction in Intra-abdominal Adipose Tissue after Strength Training in Older Women." *Journal of Applied Physiology* 78, no. 4(1995):1425–1431.

Cholesterol

Hebert, P. R., J. M. Gaziano, K. S. Chan, and C. H. Hennekens. "Cholesterol Lowering with Statin Drugs, Risk of Stroke, and Total Mortality. An Overview of Randomized Trials." *Journal of the American Medical Association* 278, no. 4(1997):313–321.

Dietary Fat

Mensink, R. P., and M. B. Katan. "Effect of a Diet Enriched with Monounsaturated or Polyunsaturated Fatty Acids on Levels of Low-density and High-density Lipoprotein Cholesterol in

Healthy Women and Men." *New England Journal of Medicine* 321, no. 7(1989):436–441.

_____. "Effect of Dietary Trans Fatty Acids on High-density and Low-density Lipoprotein Cholesterol Levels in Healthy Subjects." *New England Journal of Medicine* 323, no. 7(1990): 439–445.

Willett, W. C., M. J. Stampfer, J. E. Manson, G. A. Colditz, F. E. Speizer, B. A. Rosner, L. A. Sampson, and C. H. Hennekens. "Intake of Trans Fatty Acids and Risk of Coronary Heart Disease among Women." *Lancet* 341(1993):581–585.

Hypertension

Mulrow, C. D., J. A. Cornell, C. R. Herrera, A. Kadri, L. Farnett, and C. Aguilar. "Hypertension in the Elderly. Implications and Generalizability of Randomized Trials." *Journal of the American Medical Association* 272, no. 24(1994):1932–1938.

Cancer Prevention Overview

Harvard Report on Cancer Prevention, Volume 1: Causes of Human Cancer. *Cancer Causes and Control*, Vol. 7 Supplement, November 1996.

Obesity

Bal, D. G., and S. B. Foerster. "Changing the American Diet. Impact on Cancer Prevention Policy Recommendations and Program Implications for the American Cancer Society Cancer." 67, no. 10(1991):2671–2680.

Homocysteine

Boushey, C. J., A. A. Beresford, G. S. Omenn, and A. G. Motulsky. "A Quantitative Assessment of Plasma Homocysteine as a Risk Factor for Vascular Disease. Probable Benefits of Increasing Folate Intakes." *Journal of the American Medical Association* 274, no. 13(1995):1049–1057.

Omenn, G. S., A. A. Beresford, and A. G. Motulsky. :Preventing Coronary Heart Disease, B Vitamins and Homocysteine." *Circulation*(1998):421–424.

Vitamin E

Alpha-tocopherol, Beta Carotene Cancer Prevention Study Group. "The Effect of Vitamin E and Beta Carotene on the Incidence of Lung Cancer and Other Cancers in Male Smokers." *New England Journal of Medicine* 330(1994):1029–1035.

Diaz, M. N., B. Frei, J. A. Vita, and J. F. Keaney. "Antioxidants and Atherosclerotic Heart Disease." *New England Journal of Medicine* 337(1997):408–416.

Hodis, H. N., W. J. Mack, L. LaBree, L. Cashin-Hemphill, A. Sevanian, R. Johnson, and S. P. Azen. "Serial Coronary Angiographic Evidence That Antioxidant Vitamin Intake Reduces Progression of Coronary Artery Atherosclerosis." *Journal of the American Medical Association* 273, no. 23(1995):1849–1854.

Jessup, W., S. M. Rankin, C. V. De Whalley, J. R. Hoult, J. Scott, and D. S. Leake. "Alpha-tocopherol Consumption During Low-density-lipoprotein Oxidation." *Biochemistry Journal* 265(1990): 399–405.

Kushi, L. H., A. R. Folsom, R. J. Prineas, P. J. Mink, Y. Wu, and R. M. Bostick. "Dietary Antioxidant Vitamins and Death from Coronary Heart Disease in Postmenopausal Women." *New England Journal of Medicine* 334, no. 18(1996):1156–1162.

Meydani, S. N., M. Meydani, J. B. Blumberg, L. S. Leka, G. Siber, R. Loszewski, C. Thompson, M. C. Pedrosa, R. D. Diamond, and B. D. Stollar. "Vitamin E Supplementation and In Vivo Immune Response in Healthy Elderly Subjects. A Randomized Controlled Trial." *Journal of the American Medical Association* 277, no. 17(1997):1380–1386.

Perrig, W. J., P. Perrig, and H. B. Stahelin. "The Relation Between Antioxidants and Memory Performance in the Old and Very Old." *Journal of the American Geriatrics Society* 45(1997): 718–724.

Rapola, J. M., J. Virtamo, S. Ripatti, J. K. Huttunen, D. Albanes, P. R. Taylor, and O. P. Heinonen. "Randomised Trial of Alpha-tocopherol and Beta-carotene Supplements on Incidence of Major Coronary Events in Men with Previous Myocardial Infarction." *Lancet* 349(1995):1715–1720.

Rimm, E. B., M. J. Stampfer, A. Ascherio, E. Giovannucci, G. A. Colditz, and W. C. Willett. "Vitamin E Consumption and the Risk of Coronary Heart Disease in Men." *New England Journal of Medicine* 328, no. 20(1993):1450–1456.

Sano, M., C. Ernesto, R. G. Thomas, M. R. Klauber, K. Schafer, M. Grundman, P. Woodbury, J. Growdon, C. W. Cotman, E. Pfeiffer, L. S. Schneider, and L. J. Thal. "A Controlled Trial of Selegiline, Alpha-tocopherol, or Both as Treatment for Alzheimer's Disease. The Alzheimer's Disease Cooperative Study." *New England Journal of Medicine* 336, no. 17(1997):1216–1222.

Stampfer, M. J., C. H. Hennekens, J. E. Manson, G. A. Colditz, B. Rosner, and W. C. Willett. "Vitamin E Consumption and the Risk of Coronary Disease in Women." *New England Journal of Medicine* 328, no. 20(1993):1444–1449.

Tardif, J. C., G. Cote, J. Lesperance, M. Bourassa, J. Lambert, S. Doucet, L. Bilodeau, S. Nattel, and P. de Guise. "Probucol and Multivitamins in the Prevention of Restenosis after Coronary Angioplasty. Multivitamins and Probucol Study Group." *New England Journal of Medicine* 337, no. 6(1997):365–372.

Weber, P., A. Bendich, L. J. Machlin. "Vitamin E and Human Health: Rationale for Determining Recommended Intake Levels." *Nutrition*, no. 13(1997):450–460.

Selenium

Blot, W. J., J. Y. Li, P. R. Taylor, W. Guo, S. Dawsey, G. Q. Wang, C. S. Yang, S. F. Zheng, M. Gail, and G. Y. Li. "Nutrition Intervention Trials in Linxian, China: Supplementation with Specific Vitamin/Mineral Combinations, Cancer Incidence, and Disease-specific Mortality in the General Population." *Journal of the National Cancer Institute* 85(1993):1483–1492.

Clark, L. C., G. F. Combs, Jr., B. W. Turnbull, E. H. Slate, D. K. Chalker, J. Chow, L. S. Davis, R. A. Glover, G. F. Graham, E. G. Gross, A. Krongrad, J. L. Lesher, Jr., H. K. Park, B. B. Sanders, Jr., C. L. Smith, and J. R. Taylor. "Effects of Selenium Supplementation for Cancer Prevention in Patients with Carcinoma of the Skin. A Randomized Controlled Trial. Nutritional Prevention of Cancer Study Group." *Journal of the American Medical Association* 276, no. 24(1996):1957–1963.

Kok, F. J., A. M. de Bruijn, R. Vermeeren, A. Hofman, M. de Bruin, and R. J. Hermus. "Serum Selenium, Vitamin Antioxidants and Cardiovascular Mortality: A 9-year Follow-up Study in the Netherlands." *American Journal of Clinical Nutrition* 45(1987): 462–468.

Willett, W. C., B. F. Polk, J. S. Morris, M. J. Stampfer, S. Pressel, B. Rosner, J. O. Taylor, K. Schneider, and C. G. Hames. "Prediagnostic Serum Selenium and Risk of Cancer." *Lancet* 2(1983): 130–134.

Vitamin C

Knekt, P., A. Reunanen, R. Jarvinen, R. Seppanen, M. Heliovaara, and A. Aromaa. "Antioxidant Vitamin Intake and Coronary Mortality in a Longitudinal Population Study." *American Journal of Epidemiology* 139(1994):1180–1190.

Rimm, E. B., M. J. Stampfer, A. Ascherio, E. Giovannucci, G. A. Colditz, and W. C. Willett. "Vitamin E Consumption and the Risk of Coronary Heart Disease in Men." *New England Journal of Medicine* 328(1993):1450–1456.

Stampfer, M. J., C. H. Hennekens, J. E. Manson, G. A. Colditz, B. Rosner, and W. C. Willett. "Vitamin E Consumption and the Risk of Coronary Disease in Women." *New England Journal of Medicine* 328(1993):1444–1449.

Beta-Carotene

Gey, K. F., U. K. Moser, P. Jordan, H. B. Stahelin, M. Eichholzer, and E. Ludin. "Increased Risk of Cardiovascular Disease at Suboptimal Plasma Concentrations of Essential Antioxidants: An Epidemiological Update with Special Attention to Carotene and Vitamin C." *American Journal Clinical Nutrition* 57, no. 5 Supplement(1993):787S–797S.

Morris, D. L., S. B. Kritchevsky, and C. E. Davis. "Serum Carotenoids and Coronary Heart Disease. The Lipid Research Clinics Coronary Primary Prevention Trial and Follow-up Study." *Journal of the American Medical Association* 272(1994):1439–1441.

Rimm, E. B., M. J. Stampfer, A. Ascherio, E. Giovannucci, G. A. Colditz, and W. C. Willett. "Vitamin E Consumption and the Risk of Coronary Heart Disease in Men." *New England Journal of Medicine* 328(1993):1450–1456.

Stampfer, M. J., C. H. Hennekens, J. E. Manson, G. A. Colditz, B. Rosner, and W. C. Willett. "Vitamin E Consumption and the Risk of Coronary Heart Disease in Women." *New England Journal of Medicine* 328(1993):1444–1449.

Gotu Kola

Arpaia, M. R., R. Ferrone, M. Amitrano, C. Nappo, G. Leonardo, and R. Del Guercio. "Effects of Centella Asiatica on Mucopolysaccharide Metabolism in Subjects with Varicose Veins." *International Journal of Clinical Pharmacological Research* 10(1990):229–233.

Babu, T. D. "Cytotoxic and Anti-Tumor Properties of Certain Taxa of Umbelliferae with Special Reference to Centella Asiatica." *Journal of Ethnopharmacology* 48(1995):53.

Belcaro, G. "Efficacy of Centellase in the Treatment of Venous Hypertension Evaluated by a Combined Microcirculatory Model." *Current Therapeutic Research* 46(1989):1015.

Cesarone, M. R., G. Laurora, M. T. DeSanctis, and G. Belcaro. "Activity of Centella Asiatica in Venous Inssufficiency." *Minerva Cardioangiolia* 40(1992):137–143.

Maquart, F. X., G. Bellon, P. Gillery, Y. Wegrowski, and J. P. Borel. "Stimulation of Collagen Synthesis in Fibroblast Cultures by a Triterpene Extracted from Centella Asiatica." *Connective Tissue Research* 24(1990):107–120.

Pointel, J. P., H. Boccalon, M. Cloarec, C. Ledevehat, and M. Joubert. "Titrated Extract of Centella Asiatica (TECA) in the Treatment of Venous Insufficiency of the Lower Limbs." *Angiology* 38(1987): 46–50.

Green Tea

Chung, F. L., M. A. Morse, K. I. Eklind, and Y. Xu. "Inhibition of Tobacco-Specific Nitrosoamine Induced Lung Tumerigenesis By Compounds Derived from Cruciferous Vegetables and Green Tea." *Annals of the New York Academy of Sciences* 686(1993): 186–201.

Duke, J. A. *Handbook of Medicinal Herbs.* Boca Raton, Fla.: CRC Press, 1985.

Graham, N. H. "Green Tea Composition, Consumption, and Polyphenol Chemistry." *Preventive Medicine* 21(1992):334.

Kono, S. "Physical Activity, Dietary Habits and Adenomatous Polyps of the Sigmoid Colon: A Study of Self-Defense Officials in Japan." *Journal of Clinical Epidemiology* 44(1991):1255.

Sadakata, S. "Mortality Among Female Practitioners of Chanoyu (Japanese 'Tea-Ceremony')." *Tohoku Journal of Experimental Medicine* 166(1992):475.

Wang, H., and Y. Wu. "Inhibitory Effect of Chinese Tea on N-Nitrosation in Vitro and in Vivo." *IARC Scientific Publications* 105(1991):546.

Grape Seed

Bagchi, D., R. L. Krohn, A. Garg, M. Balmoori, D. J. Bagchi, M. X. Tran, and S. J. Stohs. "Comparative in Vitro and in Vivo Free Radical Scavenging Abilities of Grape Seed Proanthocyanidins and Selected Antioxidants." *FASEB Journal* 11(1997):3369.

Maffel, R. "Facino Free Radicals Scavenging Action and Antienzyme Activities of Procyanidines from Vitis Vinifera. A Mechanism for Their Capillary Protective Action." *Arzneimittel-Forschung* 44(1994):592.

Toukairin, T. "New Polyphenolic 5'-nucleotidase Inhibitors Isolated from the Wine Grape 'Koshu' and Their Biological Effects." *Chemical Pharmacological Bulletin* 39(1991):1480.

Estrogen

Brinton, L. A., and C. Schairer. "Estrogen and Progestin Compared with Simvastatin for Hypercholesterolemia in Postmenopausal Women." *New England Journal of Medicine* 336(1997):1773.

Cauley, J. A., D. G. Seeley, W. S. Browner, K. Ensrud, L. H. Kuller, R. C. Lipschutz, and S. B. Hulley. "Estrogen Replacement Therapy and Mortality among Older Women. The Study of Osteoporotic Fractures." *Archives of Internal Medicine* 157, no. 19(1997):2181–2187.

Darling, G. M., J. A. Johns, P. I. McCloud, and S. R. Davis. "Estrogen and Progestin Compared with Simvastatin for Hypercholesterolemia in Postmenopausal Women." *New England Journal of Medicine* 337, no. 9(1997):595–601.

Grodstein, F., M. J. Stampfer, J. E. Manson, G. A. Colditz, W. C. Willett, B. Rosner, F. E. Speizer, and C. H. Hennekens. "Postmenopausal Estrogen and Progestin Use and the Risk of Cardiovascular Disease." *New England Journal of Medicine* 335, no. 7(1996):453–461.

Vision

Cheraskin, E. "Antioxidants in Health and Disease." *Journal of the American Optometry Association* 67, no. 1(1996):50–57.

Leske, M. C., L. T. Chylack, Jr., Q. He, S. Y. Wu, E. Schoenfeld, J. Friend, and J. Wolfe. "Antioxidant Vitamins and Nuclear Opacities: The Longitudinal Study of Cataract." *Ophthalmology* 105, no. 5(1998):831–836.

Mares-Perlman, J. A., R. Klein, B. E. Klein, J. L. Greger, W. E. Brady, M. Palta, L. L. Ritter. "Association of Zinc and Antioxidant Nutrients with Age-related Maculopathy." *Archives of Ophthalmology* 114, no. 8(1996):991–997.

Prashar, S., S. S. Pandav, A. Gupta, and R. Nath. "Antioxidant Enzymes in RBCs as a Biological Index of Age Related Macular Degeneration." *Acta Ophthalmology* (Copenhagen) 71, no. 2(1993):214–218.

Seddon, J. M., U. A. Ajani, R. D. Sperduto, R. Hiller, N. Blair, T. C. Burton, M. D. Farber, E. S. Gragoudas, J. Haller, and D. T. Miller.

"Dietary Carotenoids, Vitamins A, C, and E, and Advanced Age-related Macular Degeneration. Eye Disease Case-Control Study Group." *Journal of the American Medical Association* 272, no. 18(1994):1413–1420.

West, S., S. Vitale, J. Hallfrisch, B. Munoz, D. Muller, S. Bressler, and N. M. Bressler. "Are Antioxidants or Supplements Protective for Age-related Macular Degeneration?" *Archives of Ophthalmology* 112, no. 2(1994):222–227.

Chapter 8
O PIONEERS! RECLAIMING THE FUTURE

Resource Utilization

Lubitz, J., J. Beebe, and C. Baker. "Longevity and Medicare Expenditures." *New England Journal of Medicine* 332(1995):999–1003.

Manton, K. G., L. Corder, and E. Stallard. "Chronic Disability Trends in Elderly United States Populations: 1982–1994." *Proceedings of the National Academy of Sciences, USA* 94, no. 6(1997):2593–2598.

Perls, T. T., and E. R. Wood. "Acute Care Costs of the Oldest Old: They Cost Less, Their Care Intensity Is Less and They Go to Non-Teaching Hospitals." *Archives of Internal Medicine* 156(1996): 754–760.

Compression of Morbidity

Vita, A. J., R. B. Terry, H. B. Hubert, and J. F. Fries. "Aging, Health Risks, and Cumulative Disability." *New England Journal of Medicine* 338, no. 15(1998):1035–1041.

DHEA

Casson, P., and J. Buster. "No Definite Benefits Yet Shown for Dehydroepiandrosterone." *Annals of Internal Medicine* 125(1996):218.

Durante, R., B. Mohr, J. Dusek, J. McKinlay. The Relation Between DHEAS, Testosterone and Cognitive Functioning in Older Men. Abstract. *The Gerontologist* 37, October 1997.

Horani, M., and J. Morley. "The Viability of the Use of DHEA." *Clinical Geriatrics* 5(1997):34–51.

Lane, M. A., D. K. Ingram, S. S. Ball, and G. S. Roth. "Dehydroepiandrosterone Sulfate: A Biomarker of Primate Aging Slowed by Calorie Restriction." *Journal of Clinical Endocrinology and Metabolism* 82, no. 7(1997):2093–2096.

Okie, S. "Can Hormones Stop Aging." *Washington Post* (Feb. 24, 1998).

Wolf, O. T., E. Naumann, D. H. Hellhammer, and C. Kirschbaum. "Effects of Dehydroepiandrosterone Replacement in Elderly Men on Event-related Potentials, Memory, and Well Being." *Journal of Gerontology: Medical Sciences* 53A(1998): M385–M390.

Human Growth Hormone

Ezzat, S., M. J. Forster, P. Berchtold, D. A. Redelmeier, V. Boerlin, and A. G. Harris. "Acromegaly. Clinical and Biochemical Features in 500 Patients." *Medicine* 73, no. 5(1994):233–240.

Ezzat, S. "Living with Acromegaly." *Endocrinology and Metabolism Clinics of North America* 21:753–760.

Colao, A., P. Marzullo, D. Ferone, S. Spiezia, G. Cerbone, V. Marino, A. Di Sarno, B. Merola, and G. Lombardi. "Prostatic Hyperplasia: An Unknown Feature of Acromegaly." *Journal of Clinical Endocrinology and Metabolism* 83(1998):775–779.

Jaffe, C. A., and A. L. Barkan. "Acromegaly. Recognition and Treatment." *Drugs* 47, no. 3(1994):425–445.

_____. "Treatment of Acromegaly with Dopamine Agonists." *Endocrinology and Metabolism Clinics of North America* 21(1992): 713–735.

Krishna, A. Y., and L. S. Phillips. "Management of Acromegaly: A Review." *American Journal of Medical Science* 308, no. 6(1994): 370–375.

Lamberts, S. W., A. W. van den Beld, and A. J. van der Lely. "The Endocrinology of Aging." *Science* 278(1997):419–424.

Melmed, S. "Acromegaly." *New England Journal of Medicine* 322(1990):966–977.

National Institute on Aging, National Institutes on Health. *Can Hormones Reverse Aging?* Washington, D. C.: Public Information Office, 1996.

Rudman, D., A. G. Feller, H. S. Nagraj, G. A. Gergans, P. Y. Lalitha, A. F. Goldberg, R. A. Schlenker, L. Cohn, I. W. Rudman, and D. E. Mattson. "Effects of Human Growth Hormone on Body Composition in Men over 60 Years Old." *New England Journal of Medicine* 323(1990):1–6.

Melatonin

Brzezinski, A. "Melatonin in Humans." *New England Journal of Medicine* 336(1997):186.

Thomas, J. N., and J. Smith-Sonneborn. "Supplemental Melatonin Increases Clonal Lifespan in the Protozoan Paramecium Tetraurelia." *Journal of Pineal Research* 23, no. 3(1997):123–130.

Testosterone

Bjorntorp, P. "Neuroendocrine Ageing." *Journal of Internal Medicine* 238, no. 5(1995):401–404.

Deutscher, S., M. W. Bates, M. J. Caines, R. E. LaPorte, A. Puntereri, and F. H. Taylor. "Determinants of Lipid and Lipoprotein Level in Elderly Men." *Atherosclerosis* 60, no. 3(1986):221–229.

Lin, M. F., T. C. Meng, P. S. Rao, C. Chang, A. H. Schonthal, and F. F. Lin. "Expression of Human Prostatic Acid Phosphatase Correlates with Androgen-stimulated Cell Proliferation in Prostate Cancer Cell Lines." *Journal of Biological Chemistry.* 273, no. 10(1998):5939–5947.

Sexuality

Starr, B., and S. Weiner. *The Starr–Weiner Report on Sex and Sexuality in the Mature Years.* Briarcliff Manor, N.Y.: Stein and Day, 1981.

Oxidative Damage

Adachi, H., Y. Fujiwara, and N. Ishii. "Effects of Oxygen on Protein Carbonyl and Aging in Caenorhabditis Elegans Mutants with

Long (age–1) and Short (mev–1) Life Spans." *Journal of Gerontology: Biological Sciences.* 53A(1998):B240.

Genetics of Aging

Alpert, L., J. Vaupel, and T. T. Perls. "Extreme Longevity in a Family. A Report of Multiple Centenarians Within a Single Generation." In *Age Validation of the Extreme Old,* edited by B. Jeune and J. Vaupel, 20–40. Odense Monographs on Population Aging 4. Odense, Denmark: Odense University Press, 1998.

Miller, R., C. Chrisp, A. U. Jackson, and D. Burke. "Marker Loci Associated with Life Span in Genetically Heterogeneous Mice." *Journal of Gerontology: Medical Sciences* 53A(1998):M257–M263.

Perls, T. T., L. Alpert, C. G. Wager, J. Vijg, and L. Kruglyak. "Siblings of Centenarians Live longer." *Lancet* 351(1998):1560.

Tanaka, M., J. S. Gong, J. Zhang, M. Yoneda, and K. Yagi. "Mitochondrial Genotype Associated with Longevity." *Lancet* 351(1998):185–186.

APPENDIX

INTERNET RESOURCES

How to Determine Quality of Online Health Information

Check each website's source and funding. Be cautious of sites with information that comes from a single source, that promote one product or position, or that tout "miracle cures" that sound too good to be true. Also be wary of anonymous information. Check how often the information is updated and who reviews it. Authors' affiliations and credentials should be provided. The sources of information and proper attributions should be provided.

Use of the terms "board-certified," "academy," or "college" may be used to convey a false sense of reputability. In the United States, there are 24 approved medical specialty boards, which are all overseen by the American Board of Medical Specialties (http:// www.abms.org).

The New England Centenarian Study
http://www.med.harvard.edu/programs/necs

PREVENTIVE HEALTH AND INTERVENTION

American Heart Association
http://www.americanheart.org

Your first step in visiting this information-rich site is to take the cardiovascular disease risk quiz. The quiz helps teach you what your specific risk factors are and which ones you can do something about. There is an easy-to-use reference guide as well as suggested nutrition and exercise programs. Log on to this site to get the most up-to-date research findings presented at the American Heart Association meeting. The AHA also performs a very important public advocacy role, which you can become involved in at various levels.

National Heart Foundation of Australia
http://www.heartfoundation.com.au

We found this site to be one of the most user-friendly sites available on the Internet. If you are looking for information about cardiovascular health and treatment of heart problems, this is a wonderful site to visit. School programs and health professionals will find website pages specifically tailored to their needs.

Ontario Heart and Stroke Foundation
http://www.hsf.ca

The Foundation supports two-thirds of heart and stroke research in the universities and teaching hospitals of Ontario, Canada. Its health promotion programs are outstanding. Descriptions of these programs, up-to-date assessments of current treatment options, and valuable links to other sites can be found here.

Shape Up America!
http://www.shapeup.org

Founded by C. Everett Koop M.D., the recent Surgeon General of the United States, Shape Up America! is a broad-based effort by industry, medical/health, nutrition, physical fitness, and related organizations and experts to promote healthy weight and increased physical activity. There are no sales pitches and the information and guidelines are based on proven, scientifically sound, and reasonable methods of maintaining a healthy weight and increasing physical activity. The site's content changes frequently with new fitness programs, new recipes, and, in general, fun ways to be healthy.

Longevityworld
http://www.longevityworld.com

The site is hosted by Dr. Bernard Starr, writer, producer, and host of *The Longevity Report*, a New York City–based radio show, and *Longevity Report* columnist for the Scripps Howard News Service. He provides a timely discussion of aging-related issues.

Third Age
http://www.ThirdAge.com

Third Age Media publishes an informative weekly health newsletter, *The Long Life Letter*, which provides updates on the latest research into health, longevity, diet, and exercise. It also provides valuable links to other Internet sites.

MEDICAL AND RESEARCH NEWS—JOURNALS

Harvard Medical School health publications
http://www.harvardhealthpubs.org

Harvard Medical School's Health Publications online provides current and archived articles from its five publications: the *Harvard Health Letter*, the *Harvard Heart Letter*, the *Harvard Mental Health Letter*, the *Harvard Women's Health Watch*, and the *Harvard Men's Health Watch*. These publications are timely and reliable health news and education for both the lay public and the health care professional.

Journal of the American Medical Association (JAMA)
http://www.ama-assn.org/public/journals/jama/jamahome.htm

JAMA's website is geared primarily towards the health professional, publishing articles, guidelines, and information about disease treatment and prevention and health policy.

The Lancet
http://www.thelancet.com

The Lancet is Britain's premier medical journal, covering a broad range of medical topics from basic laboratory research findings to important new clinical treatments.

Medscape
http://www.medscape.com

This is a very broad-based site that offers up-to-date information for health professionals from multiple specialties and subspecialties. The presentation is user-friendly to the point that many non–health professionals will find this a valuable resource for finding health information they need.

Nature
http://www.nature.com
and
Science
http://www.sciencemag.org/

Some of the science world's most exciting breakthroughs are published in these two journals. *Nature*'s website requires a subscription. Much of the *Science* website is accessible without a subscription, and interesting and well-balanced commentaries on the science reported in the journal is immediately available.

The New England Journal of Medicine
http://www.nejm.org

The New England Journal of Medicine is among the most prestigious journals in the medical field. Very high peer review standards make most reports appearing in this journal particularly trustworthy and germane. Editorial commentary helps the lay consumer and the health professional put various news items and articles into appropriate context.

Scientific American
http://www.sciam.com

Scientific American's website presents not only its current issue's articles but also has a very useful archive, which should contain an excellent review of your particular subject of interest in the scientific world.

RESEARCH NEWS— RESEARCH ORGANIZATIONS AND FOUNDATIONS

AARP Andrus Foundation
http://www.andrus.org

and

Alliance for Aging Research
http://www.agingresearch.com

and

American Federation for Aging Research
http://www.afar.org

These organizations support biomedical research that promotes healthier aging and furthers understanding of the aging process and its associated diseases and disorders. Its website provides information on funding opportunities, national and local meetings, and timely news items about aging issues.

National Institute on Aging
http://www.nih.gov/nia/

The NIA is America's leader in sponsoring and directing the aging research agenda. Its website not only provides information on research opportunities, it also gives important authoritative commentary about recent research findings and other age-related issues spanning the full spectrum of gerontology.

STATISTICS

National Center for Health Statistics (United States)
http://www.cdc.gov/nchswww/

Looking for the latest American health and social statistics? Here is a great place to start.

Volunteering

International Executive Service Corps
http://www.iesc-org
Address: Stamford Harbor Park
Ludlow Street
Stamford, CT 06902
Tel: (203) 967-6000

The International Executive Service Corps enables more than 13,000 American business executives, mostly retirees, to share their expertise with companies and individuals in developing nations.

InterAction, American Council for
Voluntary International Action
http://www.interaction.org/index.html
Address: 1717 Massachusetts Ave., N.W., Suite 801
Washington, DC 20036
Tel: (202) 667-8227

This site is wonderful for facilitating communication between volunteer organizations and those who wish to donate their time to a worthy cause while reaping many personal rewards in return.

Travel

Saga Holidays Roads Scholar Program
http://www.sagaholidays.com
Address: 222 Berkeley Street
Boston, MA 02116
Tel: 800-621-2151

Elderhostel
http://www.Elderhostel.org
Address: 75 Federal Street
Boston, MA 02110
Tel: 617-426-7788

GENERAL

American Association of Retired Persons (AARP)
http://www.aarp.org/
Address: 601 E Street, N.W.
Washington, DC 20049
Tel: (800) 424-3410

The AARP has one of the largest memberships in the country, representing the interests of older Americans. Their website is a wealth of information providing lists of carefully screened resources, information about healthy aging, and advice about aging-related concerns.

American Society on Aging
http://www.asaging.org
Address: 833 Market St., Suite 511
San Francisco, CA 94110

This site highlights news and activities from its informative forums and networks which include the Multicultural Coalition on Aging, Lesbian and Gay Aging Issues Network, Older Adult Education Network, Forum on Religion, Spirituality and Aging, Mental Health and Aging Network, Managed Care and Aging Network, Aging, and the Disability & Rehabilitation Network. The Business Forum on Aging focuses on the implications and opportunities of the older person market and an aging workforce.

The International Federation on Aging
http://www.ifa-fiv.org

The International Federation on Aging facilitates a world-wide forum on aging issues and concerns and fosters the development of associations and agencies that serve or represent older persons. Currently it links more than 100 associations representing or serving older persons at the grassroots level in fifty nations around the world. It also links individuals with interests in aging issues.

International Year of Older Persons
http://www.un.org/esa/socdev/iyop.htm

The United Nations General Assembly decided to observe the year 1999 as the International Year of Older Persons "in recognition of humanity's demographic coming of age" and the promise that holds for "maturing attitudes and capabilities in social, economic, cultural and spiritual undertakings." This website contains important documents and links.

INDEX

ABOUT THE AUTHORS

Thomas T. Perls, M.D., M.P.H., is Assistant Professor of Medicine, Harvard Medical School, and a geriatrician at Beth Israel Deaconess Medical Center. He is the founder and director of the New England Centenarian Study (NECS). His work has been published in major scientific journals, described in the popular press, and highlighted in television documentaries and national news shows.

Margery Hutter Silver, Ed.D., a neuropsychologist, is associate director of the NECS, a clinical instructor in psychology at the Harvard Medical School, and a staff member of the Department of Psychiatry at Beth Israel Deaconess Medical Center. She is co-editor of the *Journal of Geriatric Psychiatry*.

John F. Lauerman, a freelance writer in Brookline, Massachusetts, is health columnist for *Harvard Magazine* and an award-winning contributor to national magazines. He is the author, with David Nathan, M.D., of *Diabetes: Understand Your Condition, Make the Right Treatment Choices, and Cope Effectively*.